Essentially a Mother

Essentially a Mother

A FEMINIST APPROACH TO THE LAW OF
PREGNANCY AND MOTHERHOOD

Jennifer Hendricks

with thanks

UNIVERSITY OF CALIFORNIA PRESS

University of California Press
Oakland, California

© 2023 by Jennifer Hendricks

Cataloging-in-Publication Data is on file at the Library of Congress.

ISBN 978-0-520-38825-3 (cloth : alk. paper)
ISBN 978-0-520-38826-0 (pbk. : alk. paper)
ISBN 978-0-520-38827-7 (ebook)

Manufactured in the United States of America

32 31 30 29 28 27 26 25 24 23
10 9 8 7 6 5 4 3 2 1

for my mother, Susan

CONTENTS

Introduction

After a long struggle with infertility, Mina Kim at last had a successful course of in vitro fertilization and became pregnant with twins. But shortly after their birth, a court took them away and placed them in two separate homes—not because Mina had abused or neglected them but because the fertility clinic she used for her IVF had made a mistake. Instead of the embryos made from Mina's eggs and her husband's sperm, the clinic had given her embryos that came from two other couples. In the eyes of the law, she was not the boys' mother, only a surrogate, albeit an involuntary one.

Haley Thornton was one of the few: a fourteen-year-old girl who reported her rape, testified against her rapist, and saw him convicted of the crime. But after she gave birth to a child conceived from the rape, her rapist sued her for paternity rights. The courts held that because he was genetically the child's father, he had the same rights as any other father, including the right to seek full or partial custody of the child. Haley would thus be tethered to her rapist as her co-parent for the next eighteen years.

Tiana Baca agreed to serve as a surrogate mother for Christine and Peter Miller. She became pregnant through IVF using Peter's sperm and a donated egg. During the pregnancy, Christine told Tiana that the surrogacy contract entitled the Millers to control her life, and she was only allowed to say "yes, ma'am." Christine also called Tiana the N-word in an email, and Peter used racial slurs and profanity in talking about Tiana's husband on Facebook. Because of these incidents, Tiana decided late in her pregnancy that she would refuse to give the baby to the Millers. The courts, however, considered the Millers' behavior irrelevant to Tiana's contractual obligations and forced her to hand the baby over to them.

Each of these stories was a real legal case, although I've given the people fictional names because their real names were kept out of the public court records.[1] The thread that connects them is that the legal system doesn't think gestating a child matters much when it comes to parental rights. The United States Supreme Court has described pregnancy and childbirth as amounting to nothing more than being "present at the birth," and courts across the country equate a man's ejaculation with a woman's nine-month labor. Even more infuriatingly, they do so while claiming to act in the name of sex equality, and feminist lawyers and scholars have handed them the tools for this rationalization.

Lawyers, judges, and legislators have long debated how to treat women and men fairly in situations where biological sex differences, like the ability to become pregnant, seem important. All three of the cases above raised this problem of fairness for people who are biologically different because the cases required courts to weigh the rights of genetic parents against the rights of the women who gave birth. Today, either a mother or a father can be a parent by virtue of their genes alone, since both can contribute their genes to a child through IVF and the resulting embryo can be gestated by someone else. In the past, however, the genes-only parent was always the father. In a series of cases in the 1970s known as the Unwed Father Cases, the Supreme Court faced the question of how to fairly allocate parental rights when parents' roles in creating a child are so different. The Supreme Court gave a two-part answer. First, the court said the mother's role in gestating the child gave her automatic parental rights to her newborn child, but the father's genetic tie did not give him automatic rights. Second, the court held the father's disadvantage didn't have to be permanent. Like a mother, a father had a biological tie to the new baby. What he lacked, in the court's eyes, was the sort of caretaking relationship that the mother had established through gestation. The court decided to let the father make up the difference by taking care of the child after the birth. Once he did so, he would have parental rights equal to the mother's.

This holding—that the law had to award parental rights once the father made up his disadvantage—is unique among the Supreme Court's rulings in sex-equality cases. In most cases, pregnancy is a disadvantage rather than an advantage for women. For example, pregnancy is a disadvantage in the workplace, where women who want children usually need to take time off work for childbirth, whereas men can reproduce without missing a shift. According to the Supreme Court, that disparity is nature's fault, so it isn't the law's problem. The law doesn't have to make the rules of the workplace fit women's biology by giving women a right to maternity leave. But the Unwed Father Cases held the law *did* have to make the rules of parenthood fit men's biology by giving them a chance to make up the gap created by nature. With that holding, the Supreme Court created a double standard in sex-equality law. It gave men a leg up when their biology was a disadvantage in having children but left women to fend for themselves when their biology was a disadvantage at work.

Later cases made the double standard even worse. Courts gradually abandoned the idea from the Unwed Father Cases that gestation and childbirth create a mother-child relationship that the law should protect. Instead, the Supreme Court and other courts downgraded the role of pregnancy and defined parenthood in terms of genes alone. The law started giving men automatic rights to their genetic offspring. Rapists could thus claim parental rights to the children of their victims, and genetic fathers could claim rights to children who had already been adopted by other parents. Meanwhile, many fathers who formed caretaking relationships with their children—as the Unwed Father Cases told them to do in order to gain parental rights—found, especially if they were poor or minority fathers, that the law ignored their caretaking if they didn't file the right paperwork and pay child support. Later, with the advent of reproductive technology, courts again discounted the value of gestation to justify enforcing surrogacy contracts. Today, when clinics mix up embryos in the lab, the law turns women like Mina Kim into involuntary surrogate mothers who are forced to turn over the babies they have gestated and nurtured for nine months to the genetic parents who made a one-time contribution of egg and sperm.

Ironically, courts relied on feminist arguments and claimed the banner of sex equality as they gave more rights to men and devalued women's gestation. They were able to do so because many feminists were so concerned about stereotyping women as natural caregivers that they also devalued gestation and embraced the idea that if you contribute genes to a child, you're the parent. This idea appeals to some feminists because if genes are what matter to parenthood, then women and men are the same. And if they're the same, it's easy to win sex equality by asking courts to treat them the same—that is, asking courts to give equal rights to the female and male genetic parents. But this claim of equality is wrong because it ignores the physical and emotional tie of gestation and childbirth, which creates the child and also creates a relationship between the birth mother and child. Moreover, defining parenthood in terms of caretaking relationships, including the relationship created through gestation, doesn't depend on stereotypes about women's role in caregiving. The law can value pregnancy as a form of caretaking without stereotyping people of any gender.

This book is about the law of pregnancy, regardless of the gender identity of the pregnant person. I nonetheless use gender-specific words for parents, in part for clarity and in part because legal rules about sex equality are deeply rooted in a binary gender system tied to reproductive biology. As one example, I use *birth mother* in the biological sense to include anyone who gives birth: cisgender women, transgender men, and others. In general parlance, of course, the word *mother* also refers to any parent who identifies as a woman, though some writers use it to distinguish a more-involved parent (like a traditional mother) from a less-involved parent (like a traditional father), regardless of sex or gender.[2] *Mother* thus has a flexible relationship with gender identity. The word itself has feminine gender, but it can refer to a person who plays a particular role, regardless of that person's gender. I use *birth mother* rather than, say, *birth parent* or *gestational parent* because of the role that the connections among pregnancy, sex, and gender play in how judges and lawyers analyze and create the rules for pregnancy and parenthood.

Relatedly, I use the word *essentially* in the title of this book with tongue somewhat in cheek. The book doesn't argue or assume that women or birth mothers are essentially maternal in the sense of being inherently more nurturing or more loving toward children than other people are. All people have the capacity to love and nurture children, and performing the work of caring for a child helps to bring out this capacity. A woman who gives birth is essentially a mother because the work of caretaking is the essence of parenthood, and gestation is one way of performing that work.

PART ONE

Sex Difference and Accommodation

ONE

Mothers at Work

A LOT CAN TURN ON ONE word in a Supreme Court decision. In this passage from Justice Ruth Bader Ginsburg, writing for a majority of the Supreme Court in a case called *United States v. Virginia*, the key word is *artificial:*

> "Inherent differences" between men and women, we have come to appreciate, remain cause for celebration, but not for denigration of the members of either sex or for artificial constraints on an individual's opportunity.[1]

Artificial does a lot of work in that sentence. It implies its opposite: *natural.* The sentence condemns using inherent differences between the sexes to impose *artificial* constraints on individual opportunity, but it implies there exist other, *natural* constraints that are exempt from this condemnation. Perhaps, like the inherent differences themselves, these natural constraints are cause for celebration, or perhaps they are simply to be borne.

In *United States v. Virginia,* also known as the *VMI* case, the Supreme Court ordered the State of Virginia to let women attend the Virginia Military Institute, a public college with military-style education. Virginia had argued it could not admit women because of at least three "inherent differences" between the sexes: men are stronger, women need more privacy when they undress, and men are more likely to benefit from VMI's "adversative" style of education, while women thrive on cooperation and self-esteem. Whether all of those three differences are inherent is, to say the least, a matter of debate. The Supreme Court's skepticism on that point was a big part of why it ruled in favor of admitting women to VMI. There are other sex differences, however, that the Supreme Court has long accepted as inherent: differences that pertain directly to reproduction. Human reproduction requires a sperm, an egg, and gestation by a person who, regardless of gender identity, is biologically female to the extent of having a uterus. Technological advances are stretching some of these requirements, but they remain, as we say, the facts of life.

Sex-equality law has struggled to figure out what it means to treat people equally when these differences are in play. What is an artificial constraint, and what is a natural one? In cases like *VMI*, the Supreme Court has held that equality means treating women and men the same because the women and men in question were the same in their desire and qualifications for a VMI-style education. When people are the same, or pretty close to the same, equality means treating them the same. But what does equality require when people are different in some way that seems relevant to the situation at hand? For example, in employment law, we ask whether sex equality requires employers to make allowances for pregnancy, childbirth, and breastfeeding—biological processes that primarily constrain women. A pregnant woman might need a light-duty assignment during pregnancy, time off for childbirth, and a clean place to express milk afterwards. In recent years, schools, prisons, and even the US Congress have debated whether to stock their bathrooms with pads and tampons as they do with toilet paper. The drafters of building codes must decide whether "potty parity" means equal square footage, equal numbers of stalls, or equal waiting times.[2] And as the US lurches toward something like universal health care, politicians and pundits argue about what "universal" means when it comes to women's health. Coverage for contraception and abortion is always controversial, but a few have even argued that pregnancy and childbirth—even gynecological care of all kinds, from pap smears to mammograms—are special things that women need and ought to pay for separately, rather than just part of what it means to have health care. When should society provide the "extra" things that many women need, but most men don't, because of their reproductive biology?

In America, the first place we usually look for answers to that sort of question is our Constitution. The Fourteenth Amendment to the Constitution says that "no state shall . . . deny to any person . . . the equal protection of the laws," a passage known as the equal protection clause. This clause is the basis of equality law in the United States, from *Brown v. Board of Education* to the *VMI* case. In the 1970s, when the Supreme Court first started to think that sex discrimination might sometimes violate the equal protection clause, one of the first cases it heard involved pregnancy. The court thus faced early the question of what sex differences mean for sex equality. And in that case, the Supreme Court's answer was: nothing. Equality meant treating people the same when they were the same. When people were different, "equality," as a concept, just didn't apply. And officially, the court has mostly stuck to that answer ever since.

In chapter 2, I will argue that this official story is not quite true: the answer that sex differences mean "nothing" for sex equality has one major exception. When it is men who are different—men who are at a disadvantage because of sex differences—the Supreme Court has insisted that equality requires special accommodations to make up the gap. Men's main disadvantage is not being able to become pregnant. Chapter 2 will show how the Supreme Court required the law governing families and parenthood to make up for this disadvantage. The rest of this book is about the implications—for feminism, for society, and for children and parents—of this double standard, a standard that says women's reproductive burdens are to be borne individually but men's must be accommodated by law. When courts impose this double standard but stick to an official story that equality is only about being the same, the law becomes even more unequal and bound up with gender stereotypes.

PREGNANCY AND THE LAW OF EQUALITY

But first, the official story. In US constitutional law, the story about what reproductive biology means for sex equality started with that early pregnancy case, known as *Geduldig v. Aiello* and decided in 1974.[3]

In *Geduldig,* four women sued the State of California for denying their applications for disability-insurance benefits. As part of their jobs, all four women, like all other California workers, had to pay into an insurance program for temporary disabilities. If someone was physically unable to work for some weeks or months, the program replaced part of their income for that time. The four women in *Geduldig* were all temporarily disabled from their jobs because of pregnancy, so they applied for the insurance benefits. However, since its creation in 1946, the California program had refused to pay benefits for disabilities related to pregnancy. When the state denied the four women's claims, they sued under the equal protection clause.

Three of the women in *Geduldig* had pregnancies that ended in miscarriage or medically necessary abortion. The state denied their claims because the program excluded *all* disabilities arising out of pregnancy. But while they were litigating their case, a California court changed the rules for the program. Under the new rules, *complications* from pregnancy—problems like eclampsia or ectopic pregnancy—would be covered just like any other condition. The new rule applied retroactively, so the three women who had lost their pregnancies received their benefits. That left the fourth woman, Jackie Jaramillo, alone against the State of California when the case got to the Supreme Court. (The case is called *Geduldig v. Aiello* because Dwight Geduldig was the California official in charge of the program, and Carolyn Aiello was one of the other three women, whose name happened to be listed first. Her name stayed on the case even after California agreed to pay her benefits, but Jaramillo was the only plaintiff who was really still in the case.)

Jaramillo, who was supporting her family while her husband went to law school, had what the court described as a normal pregnancy, meaning she had no major complications. Of course, even the easiest childbirth makes other work physically impossible for some period of time, but California still refused to cover disability from a pregnancy it considered normal. Jaramillo argued there wasn't a meaningful difference between pregnancy and other temporary disabilities, except that pregnancy affected only women. Even though California's policy didn't say "women" or "on the basis of sex," it was still sex discrimination to single out pregnancy. The program covered nearly everything a man could need disability insurance for, including male-specific procedures like prostate surgery, mostly male disorders like gout, and even medically unnecessary procedures like circumcision, cosmetic surgery, sterilization, and orthodontic treatment. It covered all of these things "without regard to cost, voluntariness, uniqueness, predictability, or 'normalcy' of the disability."[4] Because men received comprehensive protection for a full spectrum of disabilities they might suffer, Jaramillo argued that equality required similarly comprehensive protection for women, including for normal pregnancy and childbirth.

But astonishingly, a majority of the Supreme Court concluded that the policy was not discriminatory because neither women nor men were covered for pregnancy. Rather than distinguishing between women and men, according to the court, the policy distinguished between pregnant and nonpregnant persons. As the court saw it, the strong *correlation* between pregnancy and a person's sex didn't turn a policy that targeted pregnancy into a policy that targeted women. In parsing the policy this way, the court was not accounting for transgender men or others who might be pregnant. To the contrary, the court that decided *Geduldig* considered the capacity for pregnancy to be women's defining trait, and the court has long been in the habit of using *gender* as merely a euphemism for *sex*. The holding in *Geduldig* was that *even though* pregnancy was the main characteristic that distinguished women from men, discriminating against pregnant people didn't count as discriminating against women.

To reach its holding that pregnancy discrimination was not sex discrimination, the court had to take a narrow view of what it means to treat people equally when they're different in some way. Under *Geduldig*, when nature imposes a burden on women, that's a problem for women, but it's not a problem for the law. Society doesn't have to make up for the difference; workplace rules don't need to be redesigned in light of women's natural burdens. After all, it wasn't California's fault that women got pregnant and men did not. In the words, both explicit and implicit, of the *VMI* decision, the inability to work due to pregnancy is a *natural* constraint on women, not an *artificial* one, which puts it outside the scope of equality law. Sex equality in *Geduldig* thus meant that women who could meet the demands of the workplace, on the workplace's own terms, could not be excluded or treated differently because of their sex. But the workplace need not adapt itself to women's needs.

A standard feminist criticism of *Geduldig* is that the court failed to consider how the arcs of women's and men's careers interact with family life.[5] Men, but not women, could have children without any disability, and the workplace had been designed with only men in mind. Indeed, the workplace was designed not just for any man but for the man who was what Professor Joan Williams has called the "ideal worker."[6] An ideal worker is not just a "non-pregnant person." He also has a wife at home who will handle the pregnancy and all the other homemaking that lets her husband focus on his career. Unlike Jaramillo, he can have children without interrupting his service to his employer. The workplace was designed for men like him. For many feminists, the discrimination was in that design. They believed that sex equality depended on restructuring the workplace, starting with some form of maternity leave. The flaw in *Geduldig* was that it ignored how California's insurance policy affected the careers of women and men over the long term. The court's parsing of pregnant and non-pregnant persons considered only a snapshot in time, ignoring the fact that the large majority of women would be pregnant at some point in their careers. An even larger majority were *at risk* of being pregnant at some point, and risk, after all, is what insurance is for.[7]

This feminist critique goes further than Jaramillo's argument in *Geduldig* itself. Jaramillo's lawsuit depended on the fact that California covered disabilities other than pregnancy. She asked only to be treated the same as a similarly disabled man. The feminist critique, however, suggests that pregnancy is in fact different from other disabilities, precisely because it is sex-specific. States and employers are generally free to offer their workers disability insurance or not. Jaramillo's argument was thus a modest one. She argued that once a state or employer *chose* to cover other disabilities, it had to cover pregnancy too. It could still choose not to cover anyone. But from a narrow sex-equality perspective, one could argue that there is a *greater* obligation to cover a sex-specific condition like pregnancy than to cover other, sex-neutral disabilities because the large majority of women will become pregnant at some point in their lives. Sex equality might require that the workplace be designed with both women's and men's reproductive patterns in mind, whether or not it also takes care of people with other, non-sex-specific disabilities.

Even though Jackie Jaramillo lost in the Supreme Court, her case spurred Congress to study the matter and come to a different conclusion. In 1978, Congress passed the Pregnancy Discrimination Act to outlaw pregnancy discrimination in employment. (Congress cannot overrule the Supreme Court's interpretation of the equal protection clause of the Constitution. It can, however, tinker with the meaning of "equality" for purposes of federal employment law.[8]) The PDA says employers must treat pregnant workers the same as other workers who are "similar in their ability or inability to work."[9] This was what Jaramillo had asked for.

Ironically, the State of California had by then come around to the view that pregnancy should be accommodated, at least a little, even if other disabilities are not. In 1978, it passed a new law giving pregnant women the right to four months of unpaid maternity leave. A new mother wasn't guaranteed her job when the four months were up, but her employer had to make a "good faith" effort to bring her back. One woman who tried to take advantage of the new law was Lillian Garland, a receptionist at the California Federal Savings & Loan Association.[10] While she was pregnant in 1982, she trained a new employee to cover for her during her maternity leave. But when she was ready to go back to work, CalFed told her they'd replaced her—with the person she had trained.[11] She complained to the state, which brought suit to enforce the maternity-leave law against CalFed. (Just like with Jackie Jaramillo in *Geduldig,* the name of the main character in the story is missing from the name of the case. When Lillian Garland's case got to the Supreme Court, it was called *CalFed v. Guerra* because Mark Guerra was the California official responsible for enforcing the maternity-leave law.)

CalFed v. Guerra was the mirror image of *Geduldig*. In *Geduldig*, California had singled out pregnancy to be excluded from a benefit that otherwise applied to all people and conditions. The Supreme Court said that was not sex discrimination. In *CalFed*, California singled out pregnancy for a special benefit that wasn't available for other conditions. CalFed argued it was discriminatory to require a benefit that was only for women. Under the logic of *Geduldig*, CalFed's argument would have failed because California was giving maternity leave to pregnant persons, not to women. But CalFed argued that the Pregnancy Discrimination Act had changed all that. Because the PDA said pregnant women had to be treated "the same as" other disabled workers, CalFed argued it was actually illegal to have maternity leave *except* as part of a larger disability program. Special rights for pregnant women were just as bad as a special exclusion.

Most feminists reject the notion that maternity leave and other accommodations for pregnancy constitute unfair "special rights" for women. Following the logic of the "ideal worker" argument, they believe the main reason workplaces *lack* accommodations for pregnancy is that workplaces were designed for men. In *CalFed*, however, many feminist lawyers had their own concerns about "special rights," and thus they disagreed with the California law—at least to a point. Perhaps surprisingly, the nation's largest feminist political organization, the National Organization for Women, filed a brief in the Supreme Court arguing *against* singling out pregnancy for benefits. NOW worried that benefits specifically for women would hurt the feminist cause.[12] Instead, women should prove themselves in the workplace on the same terms as men. Any special accommodations would only entrench stereotypes and help to justify discrimination.

The NOW feminists had reason to believe that family-friendly policies in the workplace could inadvertently encourage discrimination against women.[13] For example, when Neil Gorsuch was nominated to the Supreme Court, a minor scandal erupted about a class he had taught at my law school at the University of Colorado. According to some of the students in the class, then-Judge Gorsuch had argued that young women lawyers behave unethically if they take law firm jobs while planning to become pregnant and take maternity leave at the firm's expense.[14] Setting aside the mystery of how it could be unethical to accept a benefit designed and offered by your employer, this argument implied that it would be reasonable for law firms not to want to hire young women. For some feminists worried about this reaction by employers, sex equality should mean only that women be allowed their fair chance to compete on the same terms as men.[15] To the extent the workplace has problems—such as being hostile to family obligations of workers—maybe that should change, but it isn't a matter of sex equality. These feminists are wary of treating the conflict between work and family as a "women's issue," even when it comes to pregnancy. Not only in the workplace but in life generally, women are often defined by and reduced to the role of mothers. Surely breaking down that stereotype is a worthy feminist project.

Still, even feminists who were wary of "special treatment" for pregnancy recognized that women would have a tough time achieving equality at work without some sort of maternity leave. They therefore offered the Supreme Court a different solution to Lillian Garland's case against CalFed. CalFed's argument went like this:

- The PDA says pregnancy must be treated the same as other temporary disabilities.
- We don't allow temporary disability leave, so we don't allow pregnancy leave either. California is trying to make us offer pregnancy leave, but that would violate the PDA because pregnancy would be treated differently from other temporary disabilities.
- Therefore, the California law is invalid because when a state law (pregnancy leave) conflicts with a federal law (the PDA), the federal law always wins.

The NOW feminists responded:

- California law requires employers to provide pregnancy leave.
- The federal PDA requires employers to treat pregnancy the same as other temporary disabilities.
- Employers can obey both laws by allowing leave for all temporary disabilities, including pregnancy. Therefore, there is no conflict between the California law and the PDA.

Thus, these feminists argued that the Supreme Court should resolve the case not by eliminating maternity leave but by expanding it to other temporary disabilities.

This argument drew on ideas that contributed to what we know today as the reproductive justice movement. Centering the experiences of Black women like Lillian Garland, advocates for reproductive justice analyze race, class, disability, and other hierarchies simultaneously with gender. They argue that justice requires not merely time off work but also the comprehensive support that women and men need to bear and raise healthy children with dignity, in addition to access to contraception and abortion if they choose not to.[16] Many feminists today argue that justice requires society to meet the needs of all people, with pregnancy accommodations as one example.[17] After all, the "ideal worker" is not just a man with a wife at home but also one with no disabilities—essentially, a drone with an absolute minimum of human needs. Men, too, need the law to protect them from the dehumanizing impulses of capitalism. Congress has inched toward addressing that need with more comprehensive protection for workers. Following on the Pregnancy Discrimination Act, the Family and Medical Leave Act now requires some employers to give their workers unpaid leave for pregnancy, illness, or to care for family members. In these reforms, however, Congress has accepted the Supreme Court's basic view in *Geduldig* that equality is about sameness— that it means treating people the same when they are the same but not when they're different. Congress merely disagreed with the court about whether pregnancy-related disability was the "same as" other temporary disabilities. Unlike California, with its mandatory maternity-leave law, Congress has not singled out pregnancy for special accommodations.[18]

Although family-friendly policies for everyone should be part of the feminist platform, feminism still has a particular interest in maternity. That interest should include deep skepticism of the idea that a distinction between pregnant and non-pregnant persons is gender-neutral. If employers are going to discriminate against young women for fear they will take time off to have babies, it doesn't really matter if the policy that gives them the time off is called "maternity leave" or "disability leave." If Justice Gorsuch interviews a young woman and a young man for a clerkship, he will perceive them as equally likely to have a car accident or otherwise become temporarily disabled, except that he will correctly perceive the young woman as more likely to become pregnant. Bundling childbirth with other disabilities doesn't make women less likely to give birth or employers less likely to discriminate against them because of it. The feminist fear that family-friendly policies can encourage discrimination is well founded, but that discrimination already exists and can even be exacerbated when the law treats pregnancy as just another disability.[19]

Moreover, it's worth taking a moment to notice how small the stakes were in Supreme Court cases like *Geduldig* and *CalFed*. The average American woman gives birth to about two children in her lifetime. That's been true since the time of *Geduldig*. The maternity leave at issue in *Geduldig* was strictly time off for the roughly six weeks of physical disability due to childbirth—no extra weeks or months for bonding, breastfeeding, or other caretaking. That would mean, for example, that Justice Gorsuch was complaining about a woman lawyer being likely to take, say, twelve weeks of maternity leave over the course of a forty-year career.[20] The objection to hiring women because of those twelve weeks is all the more preposterous because, unlike with many other disability leaves, a worker's need for childbirth leave will typically be announced several months in advance, allowing plenty of time for planning, and the duration of the leave is more predictable. Our young lawyer will probably also take that leave relatively early in her career, when her work is less valuable (or at least less well paid). From her perspective, maternity leave is essential to combining work and family. But it is, in another sense, a trivial request. It is a stunning achievement of American capitalism that, for decades, employers had young women convinced that a family-friendly workplace was one that allowed you to take a few weeks off, unpaid, for actual childbirth. In reality, recovering from birth is the beginning, not the end, of work–family conflict.

Employers know that, and they didn't fight against maternity-leave laws because they imagined a world in which women scheduled childbirth outside working hours and took no time off. They fought giving women time off for birth because they wanted pregnant women to quit their jobs and not come back. A proper mother, they believed, relied on her ideal-worker husband for support. Employers like Justice Gorsuch's hypothetical law firm object not so much to the time women take to give birth as to the possibility that, afterwards, they will be less fully devoted to the job. The 1980s feminists like those at NOW who opposed stand-alone maternity leave were eager to prove those employers wrong by giving women the same opportunities as men to manifest their dedication to work, while hoping that men would eventually pick up some of the slack at home. Conversely, other feminists at the time argued for stand-alone maternity leave but knew it was only the first step toward a truly family-friendly system for organizing work.

For feminists whose long-term goal is workplaces that are fair for everyone, the question of whether maternity leave should stand on its own or be bundled with disability leave is partly a strategic one.[21] Should feminists work in the broader movement for humane working conditions, with the expectation that a rising tide for all workers will lift maternal boats? Or, as has sometimes been the case in the labor movement, should special benefits for mothers serve as the leading edge for protections that could eventually extend to everyone?[22] But beyond strategy, the split has its roots in two different understandings of the meaning of sex equality. Feminists who support the "sameness" view of sex equality hold that the same, sex-neutral rules should apply to everyone. They believe sex differences like pregnancy are relatively minor and can be smoothed over through universalizing strategies, like accommodating all physical conditions and disabilities. The competing view—the "difference" view—is that sex differences are substantial and important enough to require explicit recognition and accommodation in the law.

Feminists poured these debates and disagreements into two briefs they submitted to the Supreme Court in the *CalFed* case. One brief, filed by NOW and several other feminist organizations, argued for sameness equality and told the court pregnancy should be treated the same as any other condition. They asked the Supreme Court to require California to expand its maternity-leave law to cover all temporary disabilities. In the other brief, a different group of feminist organizations argued that achieving sex equality would require taking sex differences into account. They argued pregnancy was unique because it was specific to women, and therefore the court could uphold the maternity-leave law as it was. In the end, the second group prevailed, and the Supreme Court upheld California's maternity-leave law without expanding it to cover other disabilities. The court had to fudge a bit to do so, saying the Pregnancy Discrimination Act's demand that pregnancy be treated "the same as" other disabilities really meant "at least as well as." Favorable treatment for pregnancy was okay precisely because it helped level the playing field for women. The combination of *Geduldig* and *CalFed* meant that, as far as the Supreme Court was concerned, the *natural constraints* of pregnancy were irrelevant to sex equality. Even though *Geduldig* meant society was not required to change the workplace to make up for women's biology, *CalFed* said it was okay for California to choose to do so. The state could provide benefits for all disabilities, including pregnancy; provide benefits for pregnancy but *not* other disabilities; or provide benefits for all disabilities *except* pregnancy—all at the state's option.[23]

As for Lillian Garland, while her case worked its way through the courts, CalFed briefly hired her back but with a demotion to a job filing, typing, and cleaning storage rooms. Her bosses eventually forced her out after her case was featured on a national news show. Unemployed and sleeping on a friend's sofa, she lost custody of her daughter. When the Supreme Court finally ruled in her favor, she was able to settle with CalFed for a few thousand dollars.[24] *CalFed* was arguably a victory for the law of sex equality because it let California protect women's jobs while they gave birth. But the California law failed to give Garland the support she needed to bear and raise her child with dignity, and in that sense her case was a resounding failure for reproductive justice.

PREGNANCY AND STEREOTYPING

The range of feminist opinion on maternity leave reflects a tension between breaking down the stereotype that equates "woman" with "mother" (the goal of the sameness approach) and achieving equality for women who are mothers (the goal of the difference approach). It also reveals disagreement, even among feminists, about whether pregnancy is best thought of as a disability, a pervasive and necessary fact of life, or an individual choice, like having a hobby. We usually think of disability as arising from an illness or injury, something that occurs involuntarily. Pregnancy, on the other hand, is deemed a joyous event, presumptively chosen and often highly sought after. The presumed choice to get pregnant helps justify denying coverage under disability insurance. When we buy an insurance policy, the idea is usually that we are insuring *against* something. If the policyholder has control over whether to trigger coverage, and actively wants to do so, we worry she may take advantage of the policy, as Judge Gorsuch feared. We may also ask why society should subsidize one person's desire for a child.

This idea about choice was implicit in California's shift during the *Geduldig* litigation, when it decided to provide benefits for complications of pregnancy (which weren't chosen) but not for normal pregnancy (which was chosen, or so the courts assumed). Even in other health-care contexts, people sometimes question whether socially provided insurance ought to cover conditions that a person brought on herself. For example, if a person voluntarily engages in the risky sport of cave-diving, should the rest of us be responsible for the costs of her injuries? Similarly, when my mother was dying from lung cancer, I learned that lung cancer carries a stigma and its victims don't get the institutional support given to victims of other kinds of cancer because lung-cancer victims are seen as culpable for having smoked. And indeed, insurers often impose conditions on their coverage: life and health insurance policies might be contingent on not smoking or carry exclusions for high-risk hobbies. Nonetheless, most of the time, society sees lung cancer and cave-diving injuries as legitimate medical claims, which arise by accident even if the underlying cause was a risky choice. The person may have voluntarily smoked or gone underwater spelunking, but she didn't intentionally develop lung cancer or nearly drown. An employee isn't necessarily entitled to extra time off for cave diving or smoking breaks during the work day, but if she does those things on her own time and gets injured, insurance will kick in. The revised California policy in *Geduldig* treated pregnancy in a similar way. If the pregnancy went badly, it was covered because that was an accident, but normal pregnancy and childbirth were the woman's individual scheduling problem, just like a cave-diving hobby.

The California policy, however, can't be justified by the claim that normal pregnancy is voluntarily chosen. About half of pregnancies in the United States are unplanned, and some portion of those result from rape or other abuse.[25] Access to abortion is spotty, no longer constitutionally protected, and morally unacceptable to some women, which means that only a portion of the unplanned pregnancies that result in births are chosen in any meaningful way. Indeed, Jackie Jaramillo was pregnant only because of a medical failure—her IUD had malfunctioned—and she was religiously opposed to having an abortion.[26] Yet the Supreme Court's decision that her pregnancy didn't count as a disability didn't even mention that it was involuntary. Pregnancy, it seems, is women's problem regardless of how it occurs.

If choice doesn't explain *Geduldig*, what does? The answer is given in the California court decision that changed the policy to cover complications of pregnancy. In that decision, the California court explained that the purpose of excluding pregnancy from the policy was to exclude "maternity benefits."[27] In short, pregnant women were excluded from coverage because the legislature's purpose was to exclude pregnant women. There was no broader principle at work, just that the legislature didn't think women should keep their jobs after having babies. Even in 1974, the state couldn't openly defend the law on that basis in court, but the legitimacy of that bare desire to exclude mothers from the workplace was nonetheless what was at stake in *Geduldig*. The real issue in *Geduldig* was whether the desire to exclude pregnancy, which was clearly based on sexist assumptions about gender roles, was discriminatory. Focusing on a hyper-literal distinction between pregnant and non-pregnant persons was the Supreme Court's way of ignoring that context. The court could admit that California's policy harmed people who happened to be pregnant without acknowledging that the harm had anything to do with gender stereotypes.

Despite *Geduldig,* most people and nations—even the US Congress—have decided that sex equality requires some kind of accommodation for pregnancy at work. Current debates focus on the extent of the accommodations. One question that arises is whether it makes sense to keep likening pregnancy to a disability. Pregnancy, one sometimes hears, is not a disability because it is "normal" and is in fact an *ability.*[28] But feminists have learned from disability activists and scholars that disability is *with respect to* a particular task in a particular context.[29] For example, a person using a wheelchair may be disabled from entering a building (the task) because it has only stairs (the context); add a ramp, and the disability disappears. Similarly, pregnancy becomes a disability *with respect to* most jobs, not because at a particular stage of pregnancy a woman becomes "disabled," writ large, but because of the relationship between her pregnancy and her job.

That relationship affects how long pregnancy and childbirth disable a woman from work. In *Geduldig,* the American College of Obstetricians and Gynecologists weighed in that the period required to prepare for and recover from normal childbirth is about six to eight weeks. But the period of disability with respect to employment depends, of course, on the job. There are few jobs a woman can perform effectively while in active labor. Unless the birth is an actual part of the job—as for a surrogate mother or a royal princess—the woman is almost certainly disabled with respect to her job while she is giving birth. How long she is disabled before and after the birth depends not only on her health but also on her job description. For example, during pregnancy, a doctor might advise a woman not to lift more than twenty pounds. That restriction will pose no serious professional obstacle to a judge but could be disabling to a postal worker. For a preschool teacher, the effect might depend on whether she works at the sort of school where teachers hug and carry the children or the sort where they aren't allowed to touch. Similarly, the time needed to recover from childbirth depends not only on the woman's physical condition but also on what "recovery" requires. For a princess whose job description includes looking composed and beautiful in public, recovery might be as short as a few hours, as it was for Kate Middleton after her third childbirth.[30] The postal worker, the teacher, and even the judge will need a bit longer.

Even within a particular job description, there's room for debate about when a postpartum woman is ready to return to work, with a range of opinions about what "ready" should include. At a minimum, "ready" means physically able to perform the job, but what about emotionally? And what about the baby? Can the mother be "ready" if the baby hasn't yet learned to take a bottle? Is the mother "ready" if she can return to work but wants (needs?) extra breaks to express milk because she heeds advice (pressure?) from public-health officials to breastfeed?

In the United States, employers with maternity-leave policies for well-paid workers often offer much longer leaves than many of these definitions of "ready" would require. The same is true in many wealthy countries, where new mothers may be entitled to a year or more of paid time off. Such policies are meant to support families and to promote women's equality, but it's unclear how those goals should mix. Giving women long parental leaves, while giving men little or none, reinforces stereotypes that make women primary caretakers. Instead, the law of sex equality requires distinguishing between a mother's physical recovery from child*birth* and parents' early efforts at child*care*. The idea is to draw a line between time off that the birthing woman physically needs and time off for new-baby care, which should be available to all new parents.

The effort to draw that line is doomed to fail. Consider, for example, the case of Patti Tomasson. She and her husband were adopting a baby.[31] They lived in Canada, where new mothers received fifty weeks of parental leave (paid through a government insurance program), while fathers received thirty-five weeks. Because the Tomassons were adopting, however, Patti was told she would get only thirty-five weeks. The logic was that she was analogous to a father: she was having a baby, but not giving birth. She claimed that treating her this way discriminated against her for not being able to carry a baby herself. She was, after all, a *mother*, and to deny her a mother's share of leave was to deny her status as a mother. To treat her like a father was to treat her as something less than a mother. Most US feminists consider that a dangerous argument because it suggests that women inherently have a superior caretaking role for children.[32] We might say that Canada has decided it takes about fifteen weeks to prepare for and recover from the physical process of childbirth, so fifteen weeks is the allowance for inherent sex differences. The additional thirty-five weeks for mothers and the thirty-five weeks for fathers are a family-support policy. The right amount of leave is thus thirty-five weeks for each of the adoptive parents, with the extra fifteen weeks going to the birth mother. The Canadian courts agreed and denied Tomasson's claim in 2008.

Infancy, however, cannot be so neatly carved. Postpartum women do not go off by themselves to recover for fifteen weeks and then start parenting for the next thirty-five. For most women, those first weeks of recovery include a lot of baby time. If the law accommodates childbirth by giving more time off work to the women who do it, it is necessarily also giving them more time to bond with and care for the child.

There's also the matter of what's fair to the babies. Why should most Canadian babies get eighty-five weeks of full-time parental attention, while babies adopted by Canadian couples get only seventy weeks and babies with single parents even less? In an American example, a woman in Massachusetts, Kara Krill, brought a case similar to Patti Tomasson's.[33] Because it was the US rather than Canada, birth mothers got just thirteen weeks of leave, while fathers and adoptive mothers got a mere week. So babies could get fourteen weeks, two weeks, or one week of full-time care, depending on their parental demographics.[34] (Krill's case settled confidentially before trial.)

Equality law's imperative to separate the biological constraints of pregnancy from the caretaking demands of parenthood are further frustrated by the realities of breastfeeding. Breastfeeding has clear, proven benefits, even if its promotion too often shames parents who use formula. Here again, the biological process of pregnancy is inextricably intertwined with caretaking.[35] Full accommodation of breastfeeding and paid work would require either giving mothers extended leaves or incorporating the presence of babies at work. In the early twentieth century—before the advent of formula— teachers who agitated for maternity leave in New York explicitly demanded time off for "pregnancy and lactation."[36] Then formula arrived, changing expectations for new mothers at work and seeming to divide the biology of birth from social arrangements for caretaking. Now that breast is best again, electric breast pumps and breast milk for sale play the role of formula in cleaving biology from caretaking.[37] Breastfeeding is a problem for the sameness-equality approach, which lumps childbirth leave with other kinds of disability leave and uses gender-neutral rules for parents taking care of children. The sameness approach requires a neat distinction between the physical process of pregnancy and the social practice of caretaking. It has "no place for the inherent physicality of gestation and lactation," which are simultaneously biological functions and part of a parental, caretaking relationship.[38]

And finally, the social reality is that women *are* more likely than men to be primary caretakers for their children. It's hard to blame Patti Tomasson and Kara Krill, already likely feeling some stigma as adoptive mothers, for wanting full recognition of the social role of "mother." Even if we could sharply separate the biological and social functions of motherhood, social norms would still shape how parental leave affected families. Stereotypes and pressure from employers make it notoriously difficult for men to take paternity leave. And when they do, the result may not be what was expected. For example, universities have found that female faculty spend their parental-leave time taking care of their children, but many male faculty spend it on their academic research while their wives take care of the babies.[39] "Equality" in parental leave has not only failed to move men into caretaking roles but also ratcheted up the standards for research productivity, making it even more difficult to win tenure if you take parental leave for its intended purpose, or take none at all. Even if the long-term goal is fully equal parenting, turning a blind eye to entrenched practices may not be the best way to get there.

In *Geduldig*, when Jackie Jaramillo asked for disability benefits for her pregnancy as a matter of sex equality, she made a number of decisions about where to draw the line between, on the one hand, stereotyping women as primary caretakers and, on the other hand, accommodating the biology of pregnancy so women could be equal at work. She implicitly assumed that having children was an ordinary part of life, something workers of both sexes should be able to do without derailing their careers. She also assumed the key distinction between mothers and fathers was pregnancy and childbirth, not any special role in child-rearing. She didn't claim that her role as a *mother* required extended leave for childcare. Nor did she ask for any support for breastfeeding. The accommodation she sought was only for birth and recovery, and even then only to the extent that disabled men were similarly accommodated.

Although Congress disagreed with *Geduldig* on whether pregnancy discrimination was sex discrimination, the courts still control how the Pregnancy Discrimination Act is enforced in individual cases, and they tend to construe it as narrowly as possible.[40] For example, for years women brought claims under the PDA asking for accommodations for breastfeeding— usually they asked for time and space to express milk at work. In one case, Josephine Puente sued after her boss refused to let her take breaks to express milk, even though other employees were allowed to take longer and more frequent breaks to go outside and smoke.[41] She argued that lactation was a medical condition related to pregnancy, which meant it was covered by the PDA, and that her needs made her similar, in her "ability or inability to work," to the employees who were addicted to cigarettes. She lost. The federal court, echoing *Geduldig*'s declaration that pregnancy had little to do with sex, held in 2005 that lactation was "not a medical condition related to pregnancy" but rather a childcare choice. Over the years—and with prodding from Congress, the Equal Employment Opportunity Commission, and state agencies—the federal courts have for the most part reversed this position and grudgingly recognized lactation as related to pregnancy. Nonetheless, they still seem eager to interpret the PDA as narrowly as possible. For example, Peggy Young was a UPS delivery driver whose doctor advised her not to lift more than twenty pounds during the first half of her pregnancy.[42] She asked UPS to assign her to light duty and was denied. UPS argued that its policy was to provide light-duty accommodations to some temporarily disabled employees but not others and that it wasn't discriminatory to class pregnant women with the "no light duty" group. Ruling for UPS in a 2015 opinion by Justice Stephen Breyer, the Supreme Court derisively accused Young of seeking "most-favored-nation status." This decision further entrenched cases like Josephine Puente's. Even though the courts have admitted that lactation is related to pregnancy, an employer who allows smoking breaks but not, say, dog-walking breaks, could point to *Young* to justify classing milk breaks with the dogs.

In the wake of these hostile judicial interpretations of the PDA, the political world is again picking up the mantle of accommodation. Although it hasn't done anything about *Young,* Congress made some provisions for breastfeeding in the Affordable Care Act of 2010.[43] As always, Congress has been less enthusiastic about the other side of the coin of women's reproductive biology. The ACA required coverage of "preventive care" for women, but it was left to the Department of Health and Human Services to determine what that meant for contraception.[44] In debates over these provisions, the nation is working out what we think is natural, necessary, or normal, and what is optional, extra, or even self-indulgent.

That debate extends to the ultimate question of pregnancy: whether and when to have children. Are children our most precious resource? Or are they vanity projects that consume resources and hasten our civilizational collapse from climate change? Some disagreements over how much to accommodate childrearing are rooted in disagreements about whether society ought to encourage reproduction at all. After all, cave divers are also a valuable resource for society—as in 2018 when cave divers from around the globe rushed to Thailand to rescue twelve young boys and their soccer coach from a deep and watery cave[45]—but even if insurance covers their injuries, society doesn't subsidize their vacations. Perhaps a pregnancy with complications is like an injury but a normal pregnancy is like a vacation or a hobby. Here too we find implicit assumptions about what is reasonable. Judges and politicians alike lean strongly toward the "precious resource" view of children, at least in theory, so in *Geduldig,* the justices didn't even think it was relevant that Jaramillo was involuntarily pregnant. Even if they had, few people would have thought it reasonable to tell her to just have an abortion, nor do we give that advice to women with wanted pregnancies. Similarly, few people have argued that women don't really *need* maternity leave since they could instead adopt a child or negotiate a surrogacy contract. The pursuit of one's own biological children is widely accepted as normal and reasonable.

The bounds of what is normal can change over time. They include rules for what a good mother should do herself and what she may pay others to do. The demand to accommodate breastfeeding arose because of such a change. In the 1950s and 1960s, infant formula was normal and even preferred. Scientific hubris led many doctors to believe industrially produced formula had to be better than what women could make on their own.[46] As the norm shifted in the 1970s and 1980s to favor breastfeeding, more people thought the new norm should be accommodated. Similarly, American norms today allow professional women to hire someone else to perform many childcare tasks, but they don't yet allow a woman to hire a wet nurse, even though that practice has a long history. Those same norms approve of an aspiring mother who uses a surrogacy contract because she is *unable* to carry a pregnancy to term but condemn her if she merely prefers not to.

When these norms develop, they are not only gendered but also raced and classed. The tasks that one woman is socially allowed to outsource usually end up being performed by other, underpaid women. Professor Dorothy Roberts has described this organization of tasks as a distinction between "spiritual motherhood" and "menial motherhood."[47] The spiritual tasks are those that even the most privileged women must perform themselves in order for society to see them as good mothers. Menial tasks can be passed down the social ladder. The line between the spiritual and the menial shifts according to the demands of technology and the market. For example, Roberts argued in 1997 that the surrogacy industry was in the process of transforming pregnancy from a spiritual to a menial task. Even though the line shifts, the distinction between the valuable, spiritual tasks and the less valuable, menial ones remains.

Another shifting norm concerns the timing of childbirth. A long-standing feminist complaint about high-paying, professional careers has been that they demand intense commitment and long hours during women's peak childbearing years.[48] The biological clock competes with the tenure clock for professors, residency for doctors, and making partner for lawyers. Feminists have argued that the time demands that make these professions inconsistent with a joyous family life are arbitrary and should change. But a different, more neoliberal solution is on the horizon: egg freezing. Sometimes marketed to aspiring grandparents—"If your daughter isn't in a serious relationship, give her egg freezing for her 30th birthday! Or better yet, for college graduation!"—egg freezing is increasingly being offered as an employee benefit to women perceived as high-value employees.[49] "Don't take time off," employers are saying to their workers. "Freeze your eggs instead!" When such a practice becomes accepted and widespread, it can become a new norm. Just as most women are expected to hire childcare and return to work as soon as they are physically able—and to use formula or electric pumps instead of breastfeeding—these employers are using egg-freezing technology to create a new expectation for devotion to the workplace.

Debates over accommodation proceed from a baseline of norms that are themselves changeable and derived from a mix of biological reality, social structures, and cultural traditions. The motives for accommodations and the rhetoric used to justify them arise from the same mix of biology, society, and culture: some feminists focus on women's equality, at home and at work; others are concerned with protecting family life from the expanding demands of the neoliberal market; and anti-feminists see opportunities to push women into traditional roles. One thing almost all of these debates have in common is that they're phrased in terms of the need to respond to women's problematic biology—women's special needs, women's *difference,* which is encapsulated by pregnancy but can expand to include general caretaking responsibilities. If women are different, it is because men are not: men are normal, normative. In the law's eyes, because of women's differences—their deficiencies, their limitations, their natural constraints—they need special rules to compete and succeed like men. Even some feminists have despaired that reproductive biology means women can never be equal. Radical feminist Shulamith Firestone predicted that women would not be equal until technology freed us from female biology by inventing artificial wombs.[50] For Firestone, sex equality was incompatible with sexual reproduction. Her view implied that women would need special allowances until the mechanical wombs took over. That's different from saying women are just as well suited to having productive careers but the workplace has been unjustly structured to put them at a disadvantage. Firestone's pessimism is warranted only if we accept the sameness approach to equality. Sameness equality says that when people are the same, they should be treated the same, but it ignores the possibility that the inverse may also be true: when people are different, equality requires treating them differently. Instead, the sameness vision of equality is satisfied as long as both women and men work under the same rules for pregnancy in the workplace.

As we'll see in the next chapter, however, that vision of equality goes out the window when it is men rather than women who need an accommodation.

TWO

Fathers at Home

QUESTIONS ABOUT PREGNANCY AND equality have come before the Supreme Court in two ways. First, the court has heard claims of discrimination against pregnant women in the workplace, as in *Geduldig, CalFed,* and *Young v. UPS.* In those cases, the court used its superficial theory of sameness equality—that there's no sex discrimination in discriminating between pregnant and non-pregnant persons—to hold that women's biology need not be accommodated. Second, the court has considered men's rights as parents, especially when they are not married. When an unmarried woman gives birth, the child's connection to her is more obvious than its connection to the man courts call the "putative father." Cases about those fathers' rights started coming to the Supreme Court in the 1970s, around the same time as *Geduldig.* In *Geduldig,* women's reproductive biology was the disadvantage: being pregnant gets in the way of doing other kinds of work. In the parent-child cases, though, it was men whom the court perceived as disadvantaged because of their inability to become pregnant and give birth. Not being able to become pregnant was a disadvantage because the court refused to base parental rights on genes alone, which would have given both the mother and the father equal parental rights as soon as the baby was born. Instead, the court said parental rights spring from "relationships more enduring" than a mere genetic tie.[1] A biological father, by contributing genes, does not automatically get parental rights guaranteed by the Constitution. But when a woman becomes a biological mother by giving birth, the court saw her as having done more than just pass on her genes—she had physically nurtured and formed a meaningful relationship with the child. In other words, pregnancy is not just a disability. It's also an ability, and when it comes to gaining parental rights, it's an advantage.

When it came to parental rights, however, the Supreme Court decided the law would have to make up for men's biological disadvantage. Unlike in *Geduldig*, the court didn't say that the concept of equality applies only when people are the same and requires nothing when women and men are biologically different. Instead, it insisted there be a way for men to acquire the same parental rights as women. To provide that way, the court created a legal test for recognizing when men have established "relationships more enduring." The court held that once a man had satisfied the test, his parental rights were equal to the mother's. To give more rights to the parent who had given birth than to the parent who had not—to give different rights to formerly pregnant and non–formerly pregnant persons—was not merely unfair; it was sex discrimination against men.

The test the court came up with is known as the biology-plus-relationship test.[2] To create it, the court needed to find something men could do that would count as much as pregnancy and birth. It came up with the idea that the reason birth matters, beyond genes, is because pregnancy is a caretaking relationship: it is nurturing and establishing a bond with the child. When the father has done similar things, like playing with the child, changing diapers, and being present each day for the child—just like a mother, as the court saw it—he too should have parental rights. Even though he got there by a different path, it's still a matter of sex equality to treat his path as equivalent to the mother's. In short, when men's biology was seen as a disadvantage, instead of shrugging its shoulders and saying, "it's nature, our hands are tied," the Supreme Court used the law to work around nature and make things fair for men. The result was a novel version of equality doctrine for men only. Despite having held in *Geduldig* that the state had no duty to make up for the ways women fall short of male-oriented expectations at work, the court crafted a standard for men that entitled them to be treated, for family law purposes, as if they had gestated and given birth to a child.

MEN'S DISADVANTAGE

Traditionally, the law defined parental rights in terms of marriage, for both women and men. Under the law that the American colonies inherited from England, a child born outside marriage was legally *filius nullius*—"the child of no one."[3] Not even the mother was a legal parent of the child, who could be given to other parents at the state's option. Early on, American states modified this rule so the child of an enslaved woman would inherit the mother's status as a slave, even though she had no other rights as a parent.[4] By the nineteenth century, the states recognized free unmarried mothers as legal parents. Fatherhood remained a function of marriage: a man was the father of his wife's children.[5]

That system stayed in place until the 1970s, when the Supreme Court began to insist that men were entitled to direct relationships with children, even outside marriage. The court started with a 1972 case called *Stanley v. Illinois*.[6] *Stanley* was the first Supreme Court case to declare that an unmarried, biological father could have a constitutional right to be recognized as a legal parent. At the same time, the decision emphasized that genetic paternity, standing alone, did not confer constitutionally protected parental rights.

Illinois law at that time defined "parents" as "the father and mother of a legitimate child, or the survivor of them, or the natural mother of an illegitimate child." The biological father of an "illegitimate" child was excluded. One father to whom Illinois tried to apply this law was Peter Stanley, who had three children with the woman he lived with, Joan Stanley. The fact that they used the same last name suggests they considered themselves married; some states would have considered them common-law married. But Illinois had abolished common-law marriage, so when Joan died, the state saw her three children as orphans and Peter as a legal stranger to them. (The parties in family law cases often have the same last names, so I'll mostly follow the custom of referring to family members in case law by their first names.)

In reality, state officials knew Peter was the father, but they deemed him an inadequate one—neglectful, possibly alcoholic and abusive.[7] With Joan dead, if Peter had been legally the father, the state could have charged him with abuse and asked a judge to terminate his parental rights. The state would have had to prove him an unfit parent, which is supposed to be a high standard with a heavy burden of proof.[8] Based on what we know about Peter, the state might have succeeded in proving him unfit, but Peter would have had a chance to fight the charges and convince a judge he should keep his children.

Instead, the state took a shortcut. It argued that Peter was not a "parent" in the eyes of the law. Because he hadn't married Joan or formally "legitimated" the children by going to court and having himself declared their father, he had no rights to them at all. When Peter claimed custody of the children and challenged the state to prove him an unfit parent, Illinois responded that it need do no such thing: he was not a "parent" but a legal stranger. Thus, the state need not prove him unfit before taking the children away. Peter argued that this rule violated the equal protection clause: the law discriminated on the basis of sex and unfairly treated him, as an unwed father, differently from an unwed mother.

The Supreme Court disagreed with Peter's suggestion that biological mothers and fathers were the same when it came to parental rights. To the contrary, the court implicitly agreed with Illinois's claim that unwed mothers and fathers were fundamentally different. The dissenting justices articulated this point most clearly, but the majority did not disagree:

> On the basis of common human experience, . . . the biological role of the mother in carrying and nursing an infant creates stronger bonds between her and the child than the bonds resulting from the male's often casual encounter. . . . Centuries of human experience buttress this view of the realities of human conditions, and suggest that unwed mothers of illegitimate children are generally more dependable protectors of their children than are unwed fathers.[9]

Because of this difference between mothers and fathers, the court rejected Peter's argument, under the equal protection clause, that biological mothers and fathers are the same and therefore must be treated the same. Just two years later, in *Geduldig,* the Supreme Court would hold that "sameness" is needed to win an equal-protection claim. Women workers lost in *Geduldig* because the court didn't think pregnancy was the same as other disabilities, so the state didn't have to treat it the same. Under that logic, biological fathers' not being the same as biological mothers should have ended Peter's case.

But the Supreme Court was unwilling to rule against Peter Stanley. Conceding the possibility that "most unmarried fathers are unsuitable and neglectful parents," the court still refused to let the state apply this generalization to Peter without proof he deserved it. Because Peter had not only "sired" but also raised the children, the court thought he had at some point along the way acquired the same parental rights a mother has at the time of a child's birth.

Because the court didn't think mothers and fathers were the same, it didn't base its ruling solely on the equal protection clause. That is, the justices rejected Peter's claim that unwed fathers were always the same as unwed mothers and therefore had to have the same rights. Instead, the court turned to a neighboring clause of the Constitution, the due process clause, to supplement Peter's argument. The two clauses are part of the same sentence in the Fourteenth Amendment:

No state shall ... deprive any person of life, liberty, or property, without due process of law; nor deny to any person within its jurisdiction the equal protection of the laws.

The due process clause is also known as the liberty clause, because it protects our fundamental liberties. (Life and property have other, more specific protections in other parts of the Constitution.) The Fourteenth Amendment is what keeps your state and local authorities from punishing you for criticizing them, searching your house without a warrant, forcing you to attend the church of their choice, or locking you up without a trial. These rights are also parts of the Bill of Rights in the first ten amendments, but the Supreme Court has held that the Bill of Rights applies only to the federal government. Almost all the constitutional rights you have against your state and local governments come from the liberty and equal protection clauses of the Fourteenth Amendment. Of course, we know the government can sometimes take away our liberties, such as by putting us in jail. When it does so, however, it has to follow appropriate procedures—it has to give us "due process." Due process means a chance to tell your side of the facts ("I've raised these children since they were born") and argue your side of the law ("so the Constitution should protect my relationship with them"). Judges are responsible for asking "what process is due?" to protect liberty in any particular situation.

To know what process is due, the judge has to know what's at stake. If the government wants to send you to prison, the process due is a jury trial. But if you're a high-school student and the government (your principal) wants to send you to detention for swearing at the librarian, the process due is at most a few moments to tell your side of the story to the principal. In *Stanley,* the liberty at stake was Peter's custody of the children. If he was their parent in the eyes of the Constitution, then this liberty was a fundamental one, requiring lots of process. Parental rights can be taken away only by proving the parent unfit at a hearing in front of a judge. But if Peter was not a parent, there was no special liberty at stake at all, so no process would be due.[10] Because Peter had raised his children since birth, the court felt he should be considered a "parent." That meant he was entitled to a hearing before losing the children. Having used the liberty clause to get that far, the court circled back around to the equal protection clause and said, more specifically, that Peter was entitled to the same hearing (the same procedures and the same legal standards) that an unwed mother would receive if the state tried to take her children.

From the court's decision, it wasn't very clear when or how Peter qualified as a parent, for purposes of the Constitution, and it also wasn't clear how the liberty clause and the equal protection clause worked together to get Peter his parental rights. The opinion was probably so unclear because the justices in the majority agreed that Peter should have parental rights but didn't agree on why, so their opinion ended up a Frankenstein's monster of legal reasoning, jumping between the liberty clause and the equal protection clause while gesturing toward several explanations for the holding without really committing to one.[11]

In a later case, *Quilloin v. Wolcott* in 1978, the justices even suggested that maybe *Stanley* wasn't a sex-equality case at all. [12] In *Quilloin,* the mother wanted her new husband to adopt her child, which required cutting off the genetic father's rights. That meant the custody fight was between the two parents, whereas in *Stanley* it was between the father and the state. It's one thing to vindicate the father's rights when the state is trying to put the kids in foster care, but it would be another, thought some of the justices, to let an unwed father prevail over the mother. In *Quilloin,* the court implied that even a father who had an established relationship with his child could be cast aside if the state thought the remarried mother and her new husband would be the better parents.[13]

But the court shifted course again by the time it squarely faced that question. In *Caban v. Mohammed* in 1979, the court decided that mothers and fathers are equal once they both have caretaking relationships with the child.[14] In that case, Abdiel Caban and Maria Mohammed had two children and raised them together for several years, but then they broke up and married other people. Both of the new stepparents—Maria's husband and Abdiel's wife—wanted to adopt the children. At the time, courts weren't willing to let a child have more than two legal parents. The New York family court followed the traditional rule that unwed fathers were legal strangers to their children. It also believed that children were better off with married parents, so it granted the adoption to Maria's husband. The Supreme Court, more focused than it had been in *Stanley* on the question of sex equality, reversed that ruling. It said the state's preference for married parents was "not in itself sufficient to justify the gender-based distinction" between Maria's rights and Abdiel's. Because Abdiel had established a caretaking relationship with his children, he was entitled to parental rights equally with the mother. That meant he could block the children from being adopted by someone else.

Caban solidified the biology-plus-relationship test that had begun to form in *Stanley.* The court never abandoned its belief that pregnancy and birth uniquely established the mother's rights. For the birth mother, gestation counted for both the biology prong and the relationship prong in the "biology-plus-relationship" test for parenthood. But men who did not give birth could also have their caretaking relationships with children protected. The (stereo)typical unwed father, who, according to some on the court, was not a "dependable protector" of the child, could not claim rights based on biology alone.[15] But a biological father who also "established a substantial relationship" with the child was an equal parent with the mother.[16]

The biology-plus-relationship test drew on aspects of both the liberty clause and the equal protection clause. Parenthood can be an important, even central, part of both women's and men's lives, which is why it counts as fundamental under the liberty clause. So it seems only fair that the path to parenthood be open to both women and men on comparable terms. In order to give men a path (despite having decided that the bare fact of biological fatherhood didn't establish parenthood in the way that giving birth did) the court used the equal protection clause to fashion a non-gestational definition of parenthood "in terms the male can fulfill."[17]

Stanley, Quilloin, and *Caban* were key decisions in a line of cases known collectively as the Unwed Father Cases. Although they established "biology-plus-relationship" as the test for unwed fathers' rights, important questions remained:

1. How important is the "biology" prong of the test? What about step-parents, same-sex partners, or "duped dads" who raise a child under the mistaken belief that they're the biological father?

2. What, exactly, does a biological father have to do to meet the "relationship" prong of the test? How long does it take before he has rights?

3. What rights, if any, does he have if he wants to meet the "relationship" prong but doesn't get a chance? What if the mother won't let him see the child?

1. How Important Is Biology?

None of the parties in the Unwed Father Cases disputed who the biological father was, and the Supreme Court didn't pay much attention to the biology prong when it created the biology-plus-relationship test. In taking biological paternity for granted as an element of the test, the court rushed past how the law had historically defined fatherhood. Before blood testing and the Unwed

Father Cases, fatherhood was more a matter of being married to a mother than of strict biology. The "marital presumption of paternity," by which the law presumed that a woman's husband was the father of any child she bore, was impressively resistant to biological fact. For example, it is said that in old England the husband's paternity was presumed so long as he had not been *extra quatouor maria*—beyond the four seas of England—for the duration of the pregnancy.[18] If Ulysses had stepped ashore at Land's End the day before Penelope went into labor in John o'Groats, the law, more interested in orderly succession than in ferreting out biological truth, may have said, "Good enough." (We might wonder how Ulysses would react in this scenario, but we can say, at least, that the law was trying very hard to tie paternity to marriage.) As with the *filius nullius* rule, which said that in general a child born outside marriage had no legal parents, in America the marital presumption had an exception for race. The law might ask a White husband to accept a child whose conception within the marriage bed was logistically impossible because he was a thousand miles away at the time of conception, but it didn't expect him to accept a child of the wrong color.[19] The advent of blood tests further weakened the marital presumption in many states. It's harder to maintain a legal fiction like the marital presumption when a blood test can prove it wrong. But as we will see, the presumption still has teeth for opposite-sex couples, and some states have extended it to lesbian couples, so the wife of the birth mother can automatically become a legal parent just as a husband can.[20] Despite this historic and continuing disregard for biology when the birth mother is married, the Supreme Court latched onto biology in the Unwed Father Cases as a sort of substitute for marriage, creating the possibility of connection between man and child.

There are good reasons for genetic connections to matter in the legal definition of parenthood, including that most people feel those connections to be meaningful. In addition, as Professor Gary Spitko has pointed out, a man's paternity, like marriage, is evidence of at least some sort of relationship with the mother, implying a reasonable probability that they expect to co-parent.[21] Still, it's worth remembering that the Supreme Court didn't give much thought to the biology prong of "biology-plus-relationship." Therefore, we don't really know if the outcome of *Stanley* or *Caban* would have been different if it were discovered, after years of parenting, that Peter Stanley and Abdiel Caban were mistaken about their paternity, or even if they had known all along they weren't biological fathers but chose to be parents anyway. Many would say the outcome should be the same, with parental rights based solely on the relationship prong. Someday the Supreme Court may agree that the Constitution protects parental rights based on caretaking relationships alone, even with no biological tie.[22]

2. What Kind of Relationship Is Required?

If that were to happen—if an adult with no biological connection to a child could leverage a caretaking relationship into constitutionally protected parental rights—we would expect the standard for that relationship to be pretty high. Courts won't want friends or neighbors to acquire parental rights to other people's children casually. And indeed, while state family law occasionally recognizes "de facto" parents based on caretaking, the burden of proof is high. A de facto parent has to prove they have a strong, parent-like relationship with the child. In addition, to gain rights, the de facto parent must show that the child's existing parent consented to their becoming like a parent to the child. You can't become a de facto parent by bonding with the child secretly behind the original parent's back. In the recent past, this caretaking path to parenthood held special importance for same-sex couples who could not legally marry, because it gave the law a non-biological, non-marital way to recognize a family. States have also sometimes allowed stepparents to become de facto parents, with a right to continue their connection to the kids even if their marriage with the original parent breaks up. And rules for de facto parents protect grandparents and other relatives who step in after the death or incapacity of a legal parent. If the Supreme Court were ever to decide that the Constitution protects de facto parents, then perhaps the biology-plus-relationship test would become a sliding scale, in which a stronger relationship could make up for the lack of biology. At one end of the scale, if the child had no other parent and would otherwise go to foster care, as in *Stanley,* the relationship requirement could be lenient. At the other end, it could be especially demanding for a latecomer without a biological connection. In the middle might be cases like *Caban* and *Quilloin,* in which the father had biology on his side but was competing with the mother rather than foster care.

The mothers in *Caban* and *Quilloin* both wanted their new husbands to adopt their children. But unlike Abdiel Caban, who had lived with and raised his children for years, Leon Quilloin had only a sporadic relationship with his eleven-year-old son. According to the Supreme Court, he provided irregular financial support, visited on many occasions, and brought gifts from time to time. He had never lived in the same home with the child, so he had not "shouldered any significant responsibility with respect to the daily supervision, education, protection, or care of the child." Leon himself believed his son's rightful place was with his mother, but he wanted to continue visiting.[23] The court concluded that Leon had never been a functional member of the child's family. It therefore allowed the stepfather's adoption, which made Leon a legal stranger to his son.

In my opinion, the Supreme Court's decision in *Quilloin* was wrong because the standard it set was too high. Although it was fair to say Leon had never been responsible for daily childcare, he had been a continuous presence in the boy's life since birth. It seems to me that eleven years as a visiting father could count for as much as some shorter amount of time as a live-in father. Moreover, when the family court asked the boy his wishes, he said he wanted to be adopted by his stepfather *and* continue visiting with his biological father. While it was not then legally possible to grant this wish, the court could have achieved nearly the same effect by denying the adoption. That way, at least as long as the mother and stepfather stayed married, the child would have had all three parents in his life. Today, many scholars and even some courts argue the law should sometimes recognize more than two parents.[24] Alternatively, some argue for a middle status between "parent" and "stranger," which would allow for visits but not full parental rights. That would limit the number of full legal parents to one or two while still protecting other important relationships. Any of those options might have been better for the boy in *Quilloin*.

Quilloin is unusual in that the court's opinion let us hear the child's voice even as it dismissed his request. Testing the father-child bond from the child's perspective would be one way to evaluate whether their relationship is solid enough to secure parental rights. Many scholars today believe parental rights can only be justified in the first place if they benefit the child. But a purely child-centered approach would give little weight to the father's involvement during the pregnancy or even early infancy. As the Supreme Court suggested when it gave the father equal rights to older children in *Caban*, mothers might have exclusive say over newborns, with the father's rights ripening later as he joined in rearing the child. But parental rights don't exist solely for the sake of children. Adult heartbreak should matter too.[25] A man who goes through pregnancy with his partner might not yet be said to have a two-way relationship with the newborn, but he is likely to have made an attachment in his own heart, and in many cases the mother has encouraged him to do so. Perhaps we should "count" pre-birth conduct for the sake of protecting the father's emotional attachment to the developing child.[26] After all, the biology-plus-relationship test is based on the mother's similar attachment to the newborn.

Later developments in family law reduced the pressure on courts to specify the details of the relationship requirement, like whether the relationship can be established during pregnancy. Unmarried couples can now declare themselves the legal parents of a newborn by filling out a form at the hospital right after the birth. A large portion of unmarried couples are still together when their baby is born, and they often agree that both should be recognized as legal parents. In those cases, the mother and father can sign a "voluntary acknowledgement of parentage," or VAP, which has a similar effect—making both of them legal parents—as if they were married.[27] Once the VAP is signed, there's no need for the biology-plus-relationship test. Instead, the test is needed only in cases where the mother declines to sign a VAP because she doesn't want the biological father to acquire parental rights. Either she wants to raise the child herself, without the biological father, or she wants to place the child for adoption. In those cases, the key question is what rights the father does or doesn't have when he admittedly has not yet met the relationship requirement. That is, what rights, if any, arise from his genetic parenthood alone?

3. Who Decides?

The Supreme Court faced that question most clearly in a 1983 case called *Lehr v. Robertson.*[28] Jonathan Lehr was the biological father of a baby whose mother, Lorraine Robertson, disappeared from the hospital with the child shortly after giving birth. She married another man when the baby was eight months old. More than a year later, she and her husband asked a court to allow the husband to adopt her daughter. In the meantime, Jonathan had been searching for them. He had hired private investigators and filed a petition to obtain a declaration of paternity and visiting rights.[29] Lorraine, her husband, and the judge all knew about Jonathan's petition, but they went ahead and finalized the adoption without telling Jonathan about it first. Despite Jonathan's efforts, he lost his claim that he, like Peter Stanley and Abdiel Caban, was entitled to parental rights under the Constitution.

Once again, however, the Supreme Court wasn't clear about how it reached its decision. The key question was this: Did Jonathan lose because he failed to establish a relationship with the child, or because, in the court's eyes, he didn't try hard enough? In other words, if a biological father fails to satisfy the relationship prong of biology-plus-relationship, is his failure excused—and parental rights awarded based on genes alone—if the mother denied him access to the child? This question goes to the heart of what the Constitution protects when it protects parental rights. Does the Constitution protect only a father's *existing* relationship that has blossomed into full-fledged parenthood of the child? Or does it also protect a genetic father's *opportunity* to form such a relationship with the child? This question is important for the dynamic between the mother and father. In one interpretation, the birth mother controls access to the child and decides whether a protected relationship with the father ever comes into existence. In the other interpretation, the state is constitutionally required to force the mother to make the child available to the father.[30]

The first interpretation—that the birth mother decides—finds support in the Supreme Court's clear focus, in *Lehr* and other cases, on the presence or absence of a caretaking relationship between father and child. That focus is consistent with modern, child-centered ideas about parental rights. If the purpose of parental rights is to protect children's bonds with their caretakers, then what matters is whether the bond exists, not the reason why it doesn't. And because it's hard to fault Jonathan Lehr for not having a relationship with his genetic daughter, *Lehr* seems to mean the genetic father's rights depend solely on whether he has formed a sufficient relationship with the child, regardless of the reason. That would mean the mother isn't obliged to give him access to the child (or even tell him of the child's existence) if she would prefer to parent without him.

On the other hand, some parts of the court's opinion in *Lehr* focused on the father's personal responsibility for not establishing a relationship with his child, and the court managed to find fault even with Jonathan Lehr. Despite his other efforts, Jonathan failed to do the one thing that would have gained him at least some rights under state law: send a postcard to the state's "putative-father registry" to claim his paternity. It isn't clear why Jonathan never sent that postcard. Most fathers, of course, have never heard of such a thing as a putative-father registry, but Jonathan had a lawyer who seems to have known about it and chosen not to register. Whatever the reason was, by harping on Jonathan's failure to send the postcard, the Supreme Court lent support to the view that a father's rights turn not on the existence or nonexistence of a relationship with the child but on whether the father is *at fault* for the lack of relationship. If he did all he could to try to form a relationship, perhaps he has parental rights even if he failed. *Lehr* thus gives some support to a more expansive interpretation of genetic fathers' rights. In this view, the genetic tie, even with no caretaking relationship at all, creates an entitlement to the child.

This broader reading of *Lehr*, however, overlooks two important considerations. First, even if Jonathan had mailed in his postcard, the state wouldn't automatically have given him parental rights. Instead, the state court would have notified him of the date of the adoption hearing. Jonathan then could have attended the hearing and *argued* that it would best for the little girl if the court recognized him as the father, while Lorraine would have argued that adoption by her new husband would be better. In *Lehr*, the Supreme Court implicitly approved this entire process for choosing the legal father, which implied it approved of merely giving the genetic father the chance to be heard in court (and even that only if he followed the procedures the state had laid out for registering), not an automatic right to demand access to the child.

Second, interpreting *Lehr* broadly to give fathers automatic parental rights (again, as long as they follow the prescribed procedures), overlooks that the mother's claim to the child is already established, with full constitutional protection, at the time of birth. The birth mother is, in Professor Jessica Feinberg's coinage, "Parent Zero."[31] The Supreme Court was clear in the Unwed Father Cases that a father with only a genetic connection is not equivalent to a birth mother. Under the usual rules of parental rights, the state cannot force an existing parent to accept another parent into her family against her will. For example, when a stepparent claims rights as a de facto parent, they must prove their spouse welcomed them as a co-parent. Part of being a parent, then, is being the gatekeeper for who else can become a potential parent to your child. The birth mother's existing rights thus support the first interpretation of *Lehr*, that the Constitution protects only *existing* relationships that have blossomed into full-fledged parenthood. Fathers should prevail in cases like *Stanley*, where the mother had died and so the alternative to giving parental rights to Peter was to put the children in state custody. Fathers should also prevail in cases like *Caban*, where the children were old enough to have fully established relationships with both parents and there was no longer a reason, as there might be with a newborn, to give the mother's rights priority. But in a case like *Lehr*, the unwed mother would have a chance during pregnancy or immediately after birth to veto the genetic father's ability to establish parental rights.

If the mother has this veto power, it might be absolute, or it might be subject to judicial oversight. She might, for example, be required to explain why she doesn't want the biological father to be a legal father, and to convince a judge that her decision won't harm the child. That's essentially the system the state had in place in *Lehr*. If Jonathan had mailed his postcard to the putative-father registry, there would have been a hearing to decide whether the adoption was best for the child, and both Jonathan and Lorraine would have presented their arguments. In its decision in *Lehr*, the Supreme Court showed remarkably little curiosity about what those arguments would have been. The court didn't even seem to wonder why Lorraine had disappeared a few days after giving birth. For many feminists, the sparse facts in the Supreme Court opinion bring one possibility strongly to mind: domestic violence. Pregnancy is a common trigger for violence by a male partner, and a hospital birth may provide an opportunity for escape. Of course, there are many other possible explanations for what happened in *Lehr*. In some of the proceedings, Jonathan's lawyer alleged that Lorraine had a "history of emotional instability"—apparently a bout of post-partum depression after a prior birth.[32] Regardless of the true story, the mystery of Lorraine's disappearance suggests a third possible answer to the question of what rights the genetic father has if the birth mother won't let him see the child. As we've seen, the first possible answer is that the father has no rights until he establishes a relationship with the child, which he can't do without the mother's cooperation. The second possible answer is that he has an absolute right of access to the child so he can establish a relationship if he wants to. The third, in-between answer is that a judge could decide whether the father gets that chance against the mother's wishes, based on the reasons she gives for wanting to exclude him. In short, the person who decides whether the genetic father should become part of a new baby's family is either the birth mother, the genetic father, or a judge. In chapter 5, I'll argue that it's unfair to the birth mother to give this decision to the genetic father. The courts should either let the birth mother choose the baby's family or, at least, give great weight to her preference.

THE ROLE OF MARRIAGE

The Supreme Court has never answered any of these questions about how to apply the biology-plus-relationship test. But no matter how you interpret *Lehr*, the Unwed Father Cases accommodated men's biological disadvantage in a way the Supreme Court refused to do for pregnant women in *Geduldig*. Although the court indulged in some unpleasant stereotypes about unwed fathers, the court ultimately claimed it was trying to promote sex equality by protecting their relationships with children to the same degree the mothers' relationships were protected. If we take the court at its word, it gave us a remarkably flexible and accommodating theory of equality, in contrast to the rigid, hyper-literal approach of *Geduldig*. However, an alternative reading of the Unwed Father Cases has been put forth by conservatives and feminists alike that does not take the court at its word. Some scholars from both camps have argued the Unwed Father Cases are not about promoting sex equality but rather about entrenching the traditional nuclear and patriarchal family (a cause for praise from conservatives and condemnation from feminists).[33] Professor Janet Dolgin, for example, argues the court's requirement of a relationship with the child is just "code" for requiring a marriage-like relationship with the mother.[34] Peter Stanley and Abdiel Caban won their cases because they had lived in marriage-mimicking nuclear families, while Leon Quilloin lost because he had never been more than a visitor to his son's home (and Jonathan Lehr was completely absent). Challenging the court's claim that it was championing sex equality, Professor Serena Mayeri similarly concludes that "marital supremacy" was the real winner of the Unwed Father Cases.[35]

Lehr, however, is at least a partial counterexample to this critique. While Jonathan never lived "as a family" with Lorraine and the baby after the birth, he did live with Lorraine in what seems to have been a long-term relationship right up until she went into labor. If what matters is the marriage-like relationship between the adults, then Jonathan's claim should have been just as strong as Abdiel Caban's. The difference between them is that Abdiel also lived "as a family" with the children. The fact that their mother lived in the same household isn't surprising, but neither was it the key to Abdiel's acquiring parental rights. Most involved fathers are likely to look at least a little "traditional" in having lived with the child at some point. Isolated visits, as in *Quilloin*, weren't enough for parental rights. Abdiel did live with Maria, the children's mother, at the same time he lived with the children, but that doesn't mean his rights were protected only because he had lived in a way that mimicked marriage. Indeed, it's hard to imagine the court would deny the claim of a father who had lived with and cared for the children separately from the mother rather than with her as a nuclear family. A father's living with and raising the children on his own would also have secured him parental rights.

Describing these outcomes as marital supremacy depends on looking at them from the father's point of view rather than the mother's. In each case, if the unwed father had married the mother, he would have had automatic parental rights through the marital presumption of paternity, which presumes the birth mother's husband is the father. Traditionally, courts and society saw marriage as something entirely under the man's control. The question was whether he, having impregnated her, would "step up" and "offer" to marry her. She, desperate to salvage what she could of her reputation, not to mention the hope of financial support, would of course accept. According to the feminist critics of the Unwed Father Cases, the court was willing to forgo the actual wedding as long as the man offered a similar deal by establishing a marriage-like household with the mother and child. His parental rights rose or fell on how well he conformed to the expectations of traditional marriage. In the name of combating this marital supremacy, feminist critics advocate stronger rights for unwed fathers who avoid not only marriage itself but also the marriage mimicry they see the court rewarding. That is, a man should be able to secure parental rights based on his genes alone, regardless of whether he has acted like a traditional husband.

From the mother's perspective, however, giving stronger rights to the father is a form of marital supremacy because it means forcing the terms of marriage on her even if she has avoided wedlock. Consistent with the marital presumption, most couples—married or not—understand marriage as a commitment to co-parent whatever children they may produce or acquire together. Indeed, the Supreme Court has said it's safe to assume that married fathers automatically satisfy the biology-plus-relationship test.[36] That seems fair. Spouses will usually understand children as a joint undertaking. Their joint commitment is enforced at divorce, when courts strongly favor shared custody regardless of who took care of the kids during the marriage. Today, courts stand ready to impose this same scheme on unmarried parents, whether or not they have ever lived together.[37] Requiring the father either to marry the mother or establish a marriage-like household with her can thus be read as a requirement to gain her consent to having him as a co-parent. Expanding fathers' rights based on genes alone would turn the mother's consent to sex into consent to a lifetime of shared parenting—in other words, the terms of the marital presumption.

In granting rights to unwed fathers, the Supreme Court made a point of rejecting arguments for equality between married fathers and unmarried fathers. Instead it relied on equality between mothers and fathers. Mothers, not married fathers, were the model for the biology-plus-relationship test. The court didn't hold that unwed fathers were protected when and because they were similar to married fathers. They were protected when and because they were similar to mothers, which supports the court's claim that it was pursuing sex equality rather than marital supremacy. Nor did the court's criteria for fatherhood endorse traditional gender roles. Although the court praised the putative fathers for paying child support or condemned them for not paying it, it didn't define fatherhood solely in financial terms. It focused instead on "the daily supervision, education, protection, [and] care of the child"—activities that are, on the whole, stereotypically maternal.[38] The court's descriptions of what counts as a parental relationship track remarkably well with those of feminist and child-centered scholars who argue family law should promote and reward "fathering" in the sense of caretaking, not merely begetting.

This definition of "fathering" is not only more traditionally feminine but also more accessible to men who are less able to prove their worth with their wallets. In its concern for the rights of unwed fathers, the Supreme Court may have been especially motivated by the desire to protect nonmarital families in marginalized communities, especially African American communities. Professor Josh Gupta-Kagan suggests the justices may have believed, incorrectly, that Peter Stanley was Black.[39] And at least two justices, William Brennan and Thurgood Marshall, were likely attuned to how Illinois's exclusion of unwed fathers from its definition of "parent" disproportionately affected Black men. By accommodating men based on caretaking rather than marriage, the court not only made up for men's sex-based disadvantage in reproduction but did so in a way available to men with less traditional patriarchal privilege.

Doctrinally, too, sex equality was the official rationale for the outcome of *Caban,* the case in which the biology-plus-relationship test emerged as the test for parenthood. By holding that the parents had equal rights, so either could block the other's spouse from adopting, *Caban* prevented Abdiel and Maria's children from becoming "legitimate"—that is, it prevented them from becoming the children of married parents. In doing so, the court repudiated the state's desire for marital legitimacy as a reason for giving mothers more rights than fathers. Moreover, the majority that decided *Caban* included Justices Brennan and Marshall, liberal lions who, among their other support for women's rights, dissented from *Geduldig's* holding that pregnancy discrimination was not sex discrimination. In other words, they supported using law to make up for sex differences in both cases. On the other side, the justices who dissented in *Caban* and would have denied unwed fathers nearly all parental rights were in the majority in *Geduldig*. They were, at least, consistent in refusing to make up for biological differences, regardless of which sex had the advantage. By contrast, the deciding swing votes in the two cases—Justices Potter Stewart, Warren Burger, and William Rehnquist—were those who refused to accommodate women in *Geduldig* but accommodated men in *Caban*. It's plausible to suppose these swing justices were more sympathetic when men's rights were at stake. It's less plausible that Justices Brennan and Marshall, after siding with women in *Geduldig* and many other cases, fell back in *Caban* to defend the patriarchal family against the likes of the much more conservative Justices Burger, Stewart, Rehnquist, and John Paul Stevens.[40]

Of course, one need not agree with Justices Brennan and Marshall that their approach was best for sex equality. Perhaps in their concern for disadvantaged fathers who were shut out of marriage by poor job prospects, they rushed in to compensate men by restoring them to their place in the patriarchal family. In support of her argument that the Unwed Father Cases perpetuated marital supremacy, Professor Mayeri points out, "Even those who embraced African-American civil rights often believed a patriarchal family structure essential to racial progress."[41] One way men of color in the United States are subordinated to White men is by being denied the privileges of masculinity, and perhaps that is what the justices were trying to fix. Activist Anita Sarkeesian has summarized this dynamic with the maxim, "In the game of patriarchy, women are not the opposing team. They are the ball."[42] In other words, the oppression of women is how men compete with and measure their status relative to each other, so hierarchies based on gender are always interwoven with hierarchies based on race and other systems of subordination. Gaining rights for minority men can mean giving them power over women, just as gaining rights for White women sometimes means shoring up their racial privilege. It's possible the justices fell into this trap and were unconsciously motivated not by sex equality but by a desire to shore up men's patriarchal privilege, which women were evading by avoiding marriage. Despite the feminist credentials of a few of the justices, as Mayeri points out, there is little evidence the justices collectively "regarded paternal involvement as part of a larger feminist agenda of upending traditional gender roles."[43]

While the question of the justices' motives and biases is an interesting one, the law is what they wrote in their opinions. When lawyers invoke precedent, they always choose which aspects of the old cases to emphasize and try to extend. In my view, if the court claims to be promoting sex equality and the cases will bear that reading, feminists should run with it. In the Unwed Father Cases, the Supreme Court refused to base its rulings on equality between married and unmarried men, instead judging men's rights by a more feminine standard. And when Justice Antonin Scalia sought to explicitly enshrine a preference for nuclear families in an opinion of the court in 1989, he marshaled only four votes—not a majority on a court of nine. His attempt came in *Michael H. v. Gerald D.*[44] Michael had had an affair with Carole, who was married to Gerald. Carole's daughter, Victoria, was born from the affair but was initially treated as a child of the marriage, hence Gerald's daughter under California's marital presumption of paternity. When Carole left Gerald to live with Michael, blood tests showed Victoria was Michael's child. Carole took a few years to choose between the two men, going back and forth with Victoria in tow. In the end, she chose Gerald, and Michael sued for the right to visit Victoria. He challenged the marital presumption, which gave Gerald, as the husband, automatic parental rights to his wife's child. Justice Scalia wrote an opinion that said California's law should be upheld because there was no reason to allow an adulterer like Michael to benefit from the biology-plus-relationship test and disrupt a nuclear family, no matter how close the relationship between Michael and Victoria had been. But Justice Scalia and the three justices who joined his opinion ended up in a tie with four justices (including Brennan and Marshall) who thought Michael should have parental rights. After all, he satisfied the biology-plus-relationship test. In the middle was Justice Stevens, who often had his own idiosyncratic way of deciding a case.[45] Justice Stevens agreed with denying Michael full parental rights, mostly because he wanted to defer to Carole. But he also wanted Michael to be able to visit with Victoria.[46] In other words, Justice Stevens wanted to give Michael that middle status between "parent" and "stranger," allowing for visits but not full custody. He voted with the majority to uphold the marital presumption and declare Gerald the father, but he refused to join Justice Scalia's opinion and instead suggested that Michael should refile his case and ask for visitation with Victoria, not full parental rights. Justice Stevens's vote splintered the Supreme Court and left Michael in an odd position. California was extremely unlikely to give him visitation, and he had only one vote from the Supreme Court suggesting he should get it. Importantly, however, Justice Scalia's attempt to officially establish marital supremacy fell one vote short of becoming law.

All of the Unwed Father Cases assumed a mother's rights are established by the birth of the child. The title of this book, *Essentially a Mother,* refers to that assumption. I don't mean that women, or even pregnant women, are essentially "maternal" in the sense of being inherently more nurturing or loving toward children than men or anyone else. Rather, my claim is that the Supreme Court was correct to assume the mother's rights are established by the fact of birth. A woman who gives birth is essentially a mother because she has, by the act of birth, satisfied the biology-plus-relationship test. For the moment, however, set aside the rightness or wrongness of this claim that childbirth should give rise to parental rights, and consider how the court used that premise to confer rights on fathers.

The court held that the father is different from the mother at the time of birth and that he remains different unless and until he establishes a caretaking relationship with the child. But if that relationship is established, his right to be recognized as a parent is protected as a matter of sex equality under the equal protection clause. Although *Lehr* shows this test is rigorous, the standard is not as high as it might have been. The court did not require the father to show he had put his physical health at risk for the child in a manner comparable to the birth mother's risk: he need not have rescued the child from a burning house or donated a kidney. Instead, the test is satisfied by ordinary parental caretaking of the sort that is compatible with men's biology. This approach to equality realizes that when women and men are not quite the same, fairness requires some accommodations. A person can acquire parental rights through giving birth to her child, or by caring for his child. The criteria are roughly comparable but tailored to the biological conditions of the sexes. Even better, the criteria are also adaptable to the biological conditions of individuals, regardless of gender identity. For example, a transgender man who gives birth is just as much a "birth mother" as any other formerly pregnant person, and a woman can contribute an egg for her wife or partner to gestate and become a parent in the "male" way, by caring for her genetic child.

When women workers asked for accommodations in the workplace in *Geduldig,* the Supreme Court treated the disadvantages of pregnancy as natural and thus beyond legal redress. It let the state define rights by taking men's biology (that is, men's inability to become pregnant) as the norm. If the court had used the same approach in *Stanley* and *Caban* as it did in *Geduldig,* it would have let the state define parenthood so only birth mothers could qualify as parents. The court would have said that being the genetic father of a child didn't make a man the same as their mother, who grew them in her body at risk to life and health. Therefore, because the equal protection clause doesn't require equal rights for people who aren't the same, the court would have concluded that states weren't required to give full parental rights to fathers.

But that isn't how the Unwed Father Cases ended. The court didn't stop its analysis (as it did in *Geduldig*) with the observation that women and men aren't the same and therefore needn't be treated the same. Instead, having identified a relevant biological difference, the court took another step. It insisted the law make up the difference for those who lack the ability to become pregnant. To make up for that lack, the court used motherhood as the model for crafting the biology-plus-relationship test to accommodate fathers' physical disadvantage. As the court later explained, it made sense to allow a man to acquire parental rights comparable to a mother's by creating a test "in terms the male can fulfill."[47] There's a lot for feminists to like about the Unwed Father Cases. They recognize the importance of gestation and birth while valuing and praising caregiving by men. Accordingly, my complaint is not that the Unwed Father Cases should have been decided differently. It is that the court should have done the same thing in *Geduldig*. Women, too, should have received the benefit of a flexible, accommodating theory of equality.

The Unwed Father Cases arose from a natural sex inequality, a difference that gives one sex an advantage in making a baby and becoming a parent. However, the cases are also relevant to other equalities and inequalities. As we've seen, some members of the Supreme Court were probably worried about inequalities of race and class. Justices Brennan and Marshall may have believed the state wanted to take Peter Stanley's children not only because of his sex but also because of his race (or what they thought was his race) and his class. As I'll discuss in more detail later, protecting the rights of unwed fathers can sometimes help protect families from race and class prejudice in the child-welfare system. For some other families, however, the implications of the Unwed Father Cases are more mixed. The suggestion that pregnancy is the model form of parenthood could be an obstacle for many people and couples. Does it mean, as Patti Tomasson and Kara Krill feared, that adoptive parents are second class? It shouldn't. Pregnancy, biology-plus-relationship, and adoption are each a path to parenthood, but the Unwed Father Cases say all parents are equal once they arrive at the destination. A more difficult problem is posed by the path of surrogacy. Does justice for all aspiring parents—such as gay male couples or others unable to gestate—require that surrogacy contracts be legal and enforceable? Surrogacy also brings us back to questions of class: which paths to parenthood will be open only to those who can pay a hefty toll?

To the extent the legal system has begun to formulate answers to some of these questions, it has, frustratingly, done so without much regard for the caretaking relationships at the heart of the Unwed Father Cases. Instead, courts have taken the Unwed Father Cases in a very different direction. Rather than defining fatherhood as a caretaking relationship, courts have recast men's rights to fatherhood in terms of genetic rights and ownership of children. Men like Peter Stanley—threatened with state removal of their children due to the mother's absence—have been explicitly excluded from parental rights. The next two chapters explain why the Supreme Court's relationship-focused approach in the Unwed Father Cases was probably doomed from the start. The rest of the book chronicles the collapse of the biology-plus-relationship test, draws lessons from that collapse, and shows how to bring caretaking back to the center of the law of parenthood.

THREE

What the Law Protects . . .

THE UNWED FATHER CASES WERE unusual in two ways. First, they were unusual as sex-equality cases because they made up for biological sex differences by creating the biology-plus-relationship test, rather than holding that men's inability to become pregnant meant a father could never be equal to a birth mother. Second, they were unusual as parental rights cases. In constitutional law, parental rights were founded on traditions about a father's right to control his child, similar to a person's right to control property. A father's rights came from owning his children, not from taking care of them or establishing a meaningful relationship with them. The Unwed Father Cases and the biology-plus-relationship test were thus unusual because they treated the father's caretaking as the key to parental rights. They offered a new way of thinking about constitutional parental rights in terms of relationships rather than ownership. This new approach, however, was up against a long, tenacious tradition of treating children as property.

WHAT IT MEANS TO BE A LEGAL PARENT

Parental rights are set out in the law of each state, which means the states take the initiative to write the rules of parenthood, as Illinois had done in *Stanley*. In that case, Illinois had defined "parents" as "the father and mother of a legitimate child, or the survivor of them, or the natural mother of an illegitimate child." But parental rights are also protected by the Fourteenth Amendment, which the Supreme Court is in charge of interpreting. In the Unwed Father Cases, the Supreme Court interpreted the Fourteenth Amendment—both the liberty clause and the equal protection clause—to tell the states when they had to recognize an unwed father as a parent. Fathers like Peter Stanley and Abdiel Caban, who lived with and cared for their children from birth, were entitled to be recognized as parents, but fathers like Leon Quilloin and Jonathan Lehr, who weren't intimately involved in their children's lives, were not. However, a state can be more generous with "parent" status than the Supreme Court demands. As I mentioned in chapter 2, I think Leon's case should have gone the other way. Leon may have been only a visitor in his son's life, but the relationship was important to the child. If a state agreed with me, it could adopt its own standard, more generous than the Supreme Court requires, and choose to recognize men like Leon as fathers.

This flexibility, however, has limits. A state cannot be so generous with parental rights that they become meaningless. For example, a state can't give automatic parental rights to kindergarten teachers, or even grandparents. That would violate the constitutional rights of the actual parents. Just as my right to swing my fist ends where your nose begins, a teacher's or grandparent's right to form relationships with her students or grandchildren ends where it would interfere with the rights of the parents. The Constitution thus tells states not only when they *must* recognize parental rights but also when they *may not* do so. The state can't give parental rights to one person when doing so would infringe on the parental rights of another. That was the basis for my suggestion, in chapter 2, that the existing rights of the birth mother limit the state's ability to give rights to a father based on genes alone. But there is some room, between *must* and *may not,* for the state to decide how to define "parent." Some states may recognize men like Leon as parents, while others may not.

The Supreme Court has also interpreted the Fourteenth Amendment to set rules for the rights that come with being a parent. The general rule is that parents have the "right to the care, custody and companionship of [the] child as well as the right to make decisions affecting the welfare of the child free from government interference, except in compelling circumstances."[1] The Supreme Court started staking out this broad set of rights for parents in the 1920s, in a pair of cases about education. In the first case, *Meyer v. Nebraska,* Nebraska had passed a law making it illegal to teach a foreign language to schoolchildren under fourteen years old.[2] The Supreme Court struck down that law in 1923. Two years later, in *Pierce v. Society of Sisters,* it struck down an Oregon law that required all children to attend public schools rather than religious or other private schools.[3] In both cases, the Supreme Court spoke of parental rights as part of a broad spectrum of individual liberty:

While this Court has not attempted to define with exactness the liberty thus guaranteed [by the Fourteenth Amendment's liberty clause], the term has received much consideration and some of the included things have been definitely stated. Without doubt, it denotes not merely freedom from bodily restraint, but also the right of the individual to contract, to engage in any of the common occupations of life, to acquire useful knowledge, to marry, establish a home and bring up children, to worship God according to the dictates of his own conscience, and generally to enjoy those privileges long recognized at common law as essential to the orderly pursuit of happiness by free men.[4]

This general liberty to choose one's path through life included the right of parents "to direct the upbringing and education of children under their control."[5] The court's sweeping statements in these cases established that states must grant parents a great deal of authority over their children.

Although the Constitution limits states by telling them that they *must* recognize parental rights for people like Peter Stanley and also that they *may not* define parenthood so broadly as to render it meaningless, the situation is different when it comes to the rights parents have over their children. On the one hand, the sweeping language of *Meyer, Pierce,* and other cases means parental rights *must* be broad and include control over many aspects of the child's life. On the other hand, there is almost no amount of authority that states *may not* give parents over their children. That is, the state is almost never obliged to limit the parent's rights, even to protect the child from the parent. For example, even though *Meyer* and *Pierce* ensured parents some control over their children's education, there is no constitutional right to homeschool your children. Yet many states have given parents this right, sometimes with virtually no oversight of the content or quality of the homeschooling.[6] Homeschooling makes it easier for parents to hide physical or sexual abuse, it can leave children unprepared for adulthood, and parents who homeschool may discriminate between girls and boys in what they are allowed to learn.[7] If state officials aren't bothered by these risks, there's nothing in the Constitution (as so far interpreted by the Supreme Court) to make states do anything to mitigate them.

The state may even let parents severely beat their children. In the case of *DeShaney v. Winnebego County,* four-year-old Joshua DeShaney's father beat him into a coma.[8] The child-protection agency had known of the ongoing abuse and had a thick file on Joshua's case. His social worker later said, "I just knew the phone would ring some day and Joshua would be dead."[9] Yet the state did nothing but continue to honor Joshua's father's right to custody, and that was just fine with the Supreme Court. The court said the state had no duty to protect Joshua from "the dangers that Joshua faced in the free world." This "free world" is one in which parents have nearly unlimited legal power over children, power that the state enforces. If Joshua had run away, police would have forced him back to his father's house. If someone else had tried to help him, the law would have called that person a kidnapper and returned him again to his father. Joshua's father's freedom put Joshua in an institution for the severely disabled for eight years, until he was adopted by parents who took care of him until he died in 2015, aged thirty-six.

Of course, all states try to reduce child abuse, even though the Supreme Court has told them they don't have to. At least the court has said states *may* protect children from their parents. In the 1944 case of *Prince v. Massachusetts,* Sarah Prince was a Jehovah's Witness who was raising her niece, Betty.[10] To fulfill their religious duty to evangelize, Sarah and Betty sold religious pamphlets on the streets of Boston, which violated the state's laws against child labor. Because Sarah had custody of Betty, the Supreme Court treated her as having parental rights to her niece, but it still upheld her conviction for endangering a child. The court explained—rather hyperbolically under the circumstances—that constitutional parental rights do not extend so far as to allow parents "to make martyrs of their children."

Yet parents continue to make martyrs of their children. Even though *Prince* gave states permission to act when a child is in danger, state agencies can be shockingly reluctant to intervene when, for example, religious parents risk their children's lives or force them to suffer needless pain by denying them medical care.[11] Although *Prince* authorizes states to protect children, state officials often choose to look away. By absolving the state of responsibility for looking away while Joshua DeShaney was beaten, the Supreme Court made clear it would not impose a constitutional limit on the power states give parents over their children.

WHY PARENTS HAVE THE RIGHT TO CONTROL THEIR CHILDREN

Why are parents allowed such sweeping power? Courts and scholars have come up with four main justifications for parents' rights over children:

1. parents own their children in a way that is analogous to, if not quite the same as, owning property (the property rationale);

2. parental rights protect minority cultures, because each group is allowed to raise its children according to its own beliefs (the pluralism rationale);

3. children owe their parents obedience because the parents feed, house, and educate them (the contract rationale); and

4. parents naturally know and do what's best for their children and so can be trusted with enormous power (the best-for-the-child rationale).

The first two justifications treat the child as a vehicle for the parent's desires. Under the property rationale the child is entirely a creature of the parent, while under the pluralism rationale the child is a creature of the parent's cultural traditions. The third and fourth rationales treat the child as a person in her own right but one who is not yet able to make her own decisions. Under the contract rationale, parental rights are considered fair to the child because of what the child gets in return. The last rationale—parental rights are best for the child—erases the parent's own interests from the equation and claims parents should have rights because children's welfare is paramount and parents are the ones most likely to protect it.

Each rationale has implications for what rights parents should have, when the state should be able to intervene between parents and their children, and even how "parent" should be defined. For example, the contract rationale implies that the person entitled to parental rights is the person who pays for the child's food and shelter, but the best-for-the-child rationale would favor the person who spends the most time caring for the child. Understanding these rationales will help explain why the relationship prong of the biology-plus-relationship test, which required "relationships more enduring" to establish parental rights, has itself proved unenduring.

1. Property

The oldest and most persistent justifications for parental rights say that children are property or property-like. One version of this rationale says children are their parents' literal property because the parents created them out of their bodies.[12] You own your body and its parts, so you also own your child. Another version points out that the child exists because the parents exerted an effort to make the child, and working to make something is a traditional, philosophical basis for property rights.[13] If parents own their children in one of these senses, the theory goes, they should have the right to control them. Taken to extremes, treating children as property could imply that parents' rights are unlimited. For example, William Blackstone, who despite being an eighteenth-century English judge is one the most important jurists in American legal history, believed that in ancient Rome, fathers held the power of life and death over their children.[14] He was probably wrong, but for our purposes, what's important is that Blackstone *thought* this was the law in ancient Rome, from which both he and America's founding fathers traced their legal heritage. While the rights of parents today are more restricted by comparison, the fact that there are limits doesn't necessarily mean the law has stopped treating children as property. Many property rights come with limits. Animals are property but are legally protected from a few kinds of extreme cruelty. We own our body parts, but we may not be allowed to sell them, just as we're not allowed to sell our children. The idea of children as property can thus coexist with limits that protect children from abuse.

There is, however, a more glaring flaw in the logic of calling children property because they're their parents' body parts or the products of their parents' labor. Traditionally, it was the father, not the mother, whose rights were supposed to be justified by these arguments. Clearly, if ownership derives either from body-part-ness or from labor performed, the mother's claim would be superior to the father's. Traditional justifications glossed over this inconvenient fact either by treating wives, too, as the property of their husbands (and if you own the cow, you own the calf) or by adopting fanciful theories of reproduction in which the father's "seed" was all that mattered, the mother serving only as fertile ground.[15] But mostly the disparity between mothers and fathers on either measure of property rights was swept under the rug.

2. Pluralism

The Supreme Court's cases about parental rights typically treat children like property. But the Supreme Court has also offered another explanation for parental rights that may feel less intuitive. According to this explanation, parental rights are tools for making the United States a diverse, pluralist democracy. The idea is, if parents have control over their children, the children will continue the parents' culture, especially their religion. Catholic parents can raise Catholic children, Amish parents can raise Amish children, and so on. In *Meyer*, when it struck down Nebraska's ban on foreign languages, the Supreme Court explained this theory by contrasting America's cultural diversity with the uniformity of ancient Sparta:

In order to submerge the individual and develop ideal citizens, Sparta assembled the males at seven into barracks and intrusted [sic] their subsequent education and training to official guardians. Although such measures have been deliberately approved by men of great genius [including Plato, whom the court quotes], their ideas touching the relation between individual and state were wholly different from those upon which our institutions rest.

Our institutions rest instead on a "fundamental theory of liberty [that] excludes any general power of the state to standardize its children."[16] The family is a bulwark against this dangerous standardization. It serves as a microculture that must control the rearing of its own children in order to survive and reproduce itself. Child-rearing gives not only parents but also the groups to which they belong, such as religions, the chance to propagate themselves.

The prospect of Spartan boarding schools in this country may seem an idle threat, but one irony of the court's early pronouncements about parental rights is they were written at a time when the US government was sending American Indian children to exactly those kinds of schools. From the 1860s to the 1980s, the US removed tens of thousands of Native children from their homes and sent them to government-controlled boarding schools for the stated purpose of eliminating their culture.[17] The Fourteenth Amendment was supposed to outlaw such horrors. As one of the Civil War Amendments, the Fourteenth was part of a program not just to abolish slavery (that was the job of the Thirteenth) but to dismantle white supremacy. Protecting parental rights was part of this goal. Forced separation of children from their parents was one of American slavery's most brutal practices, one frequently highlighted in abolitionist campaigns.[18] Interpreting the Fourteenth Amendment to protect parental rights was thus a step toward the unrealized goal of abolishing not just slavery but also racial subordination.

Meyer and *Pierce* themselves were less extreme examples of how a law that curbs parents' rights might actually be aimed at a minority community. In *Meyer,* Nebraska had outlawed teaching foreign languages to young children in school. Why would a state do that? It wasn't because lawmakers thought children's brains would be overtaxed by learning another language. Children were still allowed to learn dead languages like Latin. In fact, Nebraska's hostility was not directed equally at all foreign languages. The ban was enacted in 1919, shortly after World War I, a time of fierce anti-German sentiment in a place with a large German immigrant community. The purpose and main effect of banning foreign languages was to ban German from the schools.

Similarly, the Oregon law struck down in *Pierce* banned all private schools but was largely aimed at Catholic schools. Although then, as now, there were good and sincere reasons to call for universal public schooling, there was also a significant element of anti-Catholicism, and the ban on private schools passed with the support of the Ku Klux Klan.[19] From the Indian boarding schools to *Meyer* and *Pierce* to family separation under slavery or at the border, attacks on parental rights are often part and parcel of attacks on minority groups. The parental rights protected by the liberty clause are thus intertwined with the aspirations of the equal protection clause. When the government restricts parental rights, it's worth asking whether equality is also under attack.

In siding with the parents in *Meyer* and *Pierce,* the Supreme Court may have protected minority German and Catholic communities, but the court's empathy for minority parents has its limits too. In *Prince,* for example, the over-the-top suggestion that religious leafletting was tantamount to martyrdom suggests some judicial hostility toward Jehovah's Witnesses. And below the surface, *Meyer* and *Pierce* had their own strains of judicial bias. Although it's true that prejudice against Germans and Catholics contributed to the Nebraska and Oregon laws, Professor Barbara Bennett Woodhouse has shown that there was also a strong current of egalitarianism. Advocates for universal public schooling subscribed to the "melting pot" vision of America and wanted all children to be educated together. They knew the rich wouldn't care about the quality of public schools if they could send their children to private ones, and they feared the private schools would teach aristocratic rather than democratic values. As Governor Walter Pierce of Oregon argued, before lending his name to the case in which the Supreme Court struck down the ban on private schools,

> Every one of [my] six children was educated in the public schools from the primary to the college and university.... I believe we would have a better generation of Americans free from snobbery and bigotry if all children ... were educated in the free public schools of America.[20]

There's good reason to believe it was the threat to elite enclaves, not concern for persecuted minorities, that propelled the Supreme Court to strike down the Nebraska and Oregon laws. Woodhouse points out that the author of the court's opinions in both cases was James McReynolds, "the most bigoted, vitriolic, and intolerant individual ever to have sat on the Supreme Court."[21] He was a "legendary" anti-Semite who refused to shake hands or attend dinners with the Jewish members of the court. He often walked off the bench if a woman lawyer appeared in a case.[22] In their brief in *Pierce,* the lawyers trying to persuade him to strike down the Oregon law emphasized the threat to elite institutions, not the threat to downtrodden minorities:

> If the state can thus destroy the [private] primary school, it can destroy the [private] secondary school, the college, and the university. Harvard, Yale, Columbia, Princeton . . . All could be swept away.[23]

God forbid. In short, if there was any minority Justice McReynolds was trying to protect in *Meyer* and *Pierce,* it was probably the minority we now call the One Percent.

Although Justice McReynolds is an unsavory standard-bearer, he wasn't wrong that parental rights can protect minorities and foster cultural diversity.[24] But the pluralism rationale for parental rights, like the property rationale, treats children as vehicles for their parents' values and aspirations.[25] In *Pierce,* the Supreme Court condemned the notion that the child was a "mere creature of the state" but treated him nonetheless as a mere creature of his parents, "who nurture him and direct his destiny." Under either approach—property or pluralism—the child exists to fulfill the desires of the parents.

3. Contract

In contrast to the property and pluralism rationales, the contract theory of parental rights treats the child as her own person. To justify giving one person the power to control another, contract theory says the parent's control over the child is part of an implicit contract. The child trades her obedience for life, food, shelter, and education.[26] Of course, we know the child never had a choice about the terms of this contract. Parental rights are like the Terms and Conditions of your cell phone contract, but for your life. Or, more loftily, they are like the Constitution and other laws that were enacted by earlier generations but to which we are all bound. The terms of the parent-child contract—how much support parents must provide (minimal) and how much obedience they can expect in return (total)—are similarly set by law.

If you were in a legal dispute with your cell phone company, would you be bound by the Terms and Conditions? Unlike a newborn child, you did, at some point, check a box agreeing to them. You may even have affirmed (probably falsely) that you had read them. Even so, a court wouldn't necessarily enforce them against you. First, it would consider the circumstances under which you agreed. Suppose you had agreed to the terms when you were trying to call 911, and the phone company would only put your call through if you agreed to pay an extra $1,000. A court wouldn't hold you to this ransom. Second, the court would consider the reasonableness of the terms. Even when there's no emergency, no one actually expects you to read all those Terms and Conditions. If the company tried to sneak in a grossly unreasonable term, like permission to use your nude photos in their ads, no decent judge would enforce it.

How does the parent-child contract stand up to these inquiries about circumstances and reasonableness? First, the newborn baby is like you trying to call 911—not in a great bargaining position. Just as you might have no choice but to agree to a $1,000 price tag for calling an ambulance, a baby, if we could ask her, would likely accept her parents' dominance over her life in exchange for the means to survive. A desperate buyer will agree to any price. (We call that price gouging.) And even if our little newborn could refuse to sign the parent-child contract with her birth parents, her only other option would be the same terms with different parents.

The United States, unlike many other wealthy countries, recognizes no universal human right to life's necessities. Babies, like other people who can't earn their keep in the free market, are expected to rely on family members to provide for them. Feminist scholars, following the lead of Professor Martha Fineman, call this system "the privatization of dependency."[27] All of us are inevitably dependent on others for some part of our lives, when we are young, sick, or old. Our society expects our needs during those times to be dealt with privately, within the family, rather than socially. Professors Clare Huntington and Elizabeth Scott explain how the privatization of dependency in the United States leads to a rule of strong parental rights:

> In a country in which family-state relations are governed by libertarian principles, parents are burdened with the weighty responsibility of raising the next generation of citizens. . . . Strong protection of parental rights shows respect for and deference to parents for the important job they undertake. . . . Society then benefits when parents perform their duties satisfactorily and children mature to healthy adulthood; otherwise the state itself must assume responsibility at substantial cost.[28]

This description suggests that the important "contract" is not the one between the parent and the child but a similarly implicit contract between the parent and the state. *Society,* not the child, gives parents their enormous power, and society then benefits when the parents turn out acceptable adult citizens. The child is the object of this contract, not one of the parties. Society gives the parent extraordinary power and thereby washes its hands of responsibility for the child's welfare.

Even if we imagine the child as a party to the contract, we must still ask the second question: are the terms of the deal reasonable? Under the contract theory, the legitimacy of parental rights depends on whether the child is getting a fair trade. As is often so when one party to the contract has no say in writing its terms, that's a tough case to make. The contract theory credits the parents with bringing the child into existence. Existence, however, is a mixed blessing. Although once we exist, nearly all of us choose to continue to exist, entire spiritual worldviews are premised on the observation that existence is suffering. Philosophers routinely assume there is no value in existence—no one has a stake in her own existence, since if she didn't exist, she wouldn't care. There is a wide range of opinion about whether parents give their children "the gift of life" or, rather, inflict it upon them for their own selfish reasons. As the world comes to grips with the climate apocalypse that today's older generations have prepared for the young, opinion may shift more strongly toward the latter view.

Once a child exists, it can cost a lot to reach adulthood in today's America, and the unpaid labor of nursing, cooking, teaching, bathing, and all the other tasks of caregiving is even more substantial. But how much money would it take for you to agree to live for eighteen years under the control of another person, even if that person loved you? Parents themselves often link their right to control their child's behavior to the food and shelter they provide, especially with teenagers. "As long as you live under my roof," they say, "you'll follow my rules." Or, "I'm paying for your phone, so I can read your texts." But in other relationships, financial support is not necessarily linked to control. Spouses don't legally control each other but are obliged to support each other, sometimes even after divorce. In some states, adult children can be legally responsible for supporting their parents even if they exert no control over their lives.[29] Providing financial support doesn't necessarily give the provider the right to invade the other person's privacy or regulate the minutiae of their daily life. It is unsurprising that the terms of the parent-child contract were written by people (adult judges and legislators) who knew they would never again find themselves on the child's side of the deal.

The truth about the "contract" justification is that it's an after-the-fact attempt by scholars to justify the law as it is. Historically, parents had broad rights over their children because adults had power and children did not. The adults justified their power by describing the children as property or by pointing to the food, shelter, and education they provided. But no one ever sat down and tried to write the rules for parental rights based on what would be a fair trade for that support. Parents' power over children came first, and the attempt at justification came later. Unlike the property and pluralism rationales, the idea of an exchange between parent and child recognizes the child as a separate person from the parent. If the law were sincere about this justification, however, it would have to scale back the degree of control parents have over children's lives in order to make the contract a fair trade.

4. Best for the Child

The fourth and final major justification for parental rights is also the most popular one today: the idea that parents, more than anyone else, will naturally do what's best for their children.[30] This rationale has two related parts. First, it claims the parent *wants* to do what's best for the child, and second, it claims the parent *knows* better than anyone else what's best for her particular child. The desire to do what's best comes from "natural bonds of affection," which the Supreme Court believes flow from parenthood.[31] Knowledge of the particular child's needs comes from being the child's caretaker.[32] The caretaking parent is the most knowledgeable expert about what's best for her child and will naturally want to act on that knowledge.

As an example, consider a parent's power to force a child to take music lessons. In my family, my mother required my brothers and me to take piano lessons starting in elementary school. I was allowed to quit in my junior year of high school. My younger brother was allowed to quit earlier, in middle school, on the condition that he switch to another instrument. (He chose guitar.) But my other brother, the middle child, was never allowed to quit. Why not? Because my mother saw and heard joy in his playing that had disappeared from mine and the younger brother's, while the elder brother's protestations about wanting to quit had become noticeably pro forma. That brother went on to study music in college and continues to play. Decades later, the youngest and I have both taken piano lessons as adults, but I think my mom made the right call for us at the time. The best-for-the-child rationale recognizes the expertise of caretakers like my mom.

But even the best-for-the-child rationale can lead to the pitfall of treating the child as something less than a full person. Proponents of this rationale often define what's good for children according to measurable outcomes. For example, Professors Huntington and Scott use outcomes to defend America's tolerance for corporal punishment. All US states allow spanking and other violence against children, limited only by vague standards of reasonableness. They allow it mainly because a great many adults believe parents are entitled to hit their children and that hitting is a necessary form of discipline. However, even people who reject those archaic, disproven beliefs don't necessarily think the state should try to eliminate corporal punishment. The state has a dismal track record when it comes to doing what's best for children, and its strategies—putting children in foster care or parents in prison—are often worse than leaving a child in an imperfect home. The state's interventions are also strongly biased by race and class. The best-for-the-child approach doesn't argue that parents always know what's best for their children or that, even when they know, they'll always do it. Rather, the idea is that most of the time parents know and do well enough, so deferring to parents is better than handing things over to the state. Even "reasonable" spanking may be bad, but not as bad as breaking up the family and putting the child in foster care.

Huntington and Scott go further, however, defending spanking on its merits. In the process, they demonstrate the risk of treating the child as an adult-in-progress rather than a full person in the here and now. They assert, "There is not clear evidence that spanking is harmful to children."[33] What can this mean? The whole point of spanking is that it harms: it *hurts*. To say that it isn't harmful requires a very specific definition of "harm." Huntington and Scott acknowledge that some researchers have found spanking to be "associated with a greater likelihood of detrimental child outcomes," but they rely on other researchers who criticize those findings "for failing to distinguish between instances of extreme and excessive punishment and normative spanking that did not cause injury beyond mild pain."[34] The assumption implicit in this defense of spanking is that spanking does not "harm" a child unless it causes "detrimental child *outcomes*" like PTSD or acting out. The immediate pain of being hit doesn't count. (Try telling an adult who has been assaulted that they weren't really "harmed" because the attack wasn't extreme and excessive, caused only mild pain, and left only transient marks on their body—all common standards for acceptable violence against children.) To claim an absence of "clear evidence that spanking is harmful" in this sense is to demand proof while also excluding the most relevant evidence: the child's tears.

Admitting the child's evidence, including her view on whether she was harmed when spanked, would not require abandoning parental rights, but it would require trimming them, especially for teenagers. Professors Anne Dailey and Laura Rosenbury reject the assumption, implicit in analyses like Huntington and Scott's, that children are "unformed beings or adults-in-waiting" whose interests should be measured by outcomes.[35] That starting point leads Dailey and Rosenbury to propose a different system, less deferential to parents, than the one we have. They argue the law's priority should be to protect the child's relationships with caregivers rather than to protect the parent's right to control the child. Their work shows that, like the contract rationale, the best-for-the-child rationale suffers from a mismatch between the justification (that parental rights serve children's interests) and the sweeping power the law gives to parents. As Professor Samantha Godwin points out, the law "effectively enable[s] parents to use the threat of violence or confinement to force their children to do whatever the parent desires, so long as it falls outside of narrowly-defined abuse statutes."[36] That level of control, and especially the use of violence to enforce it, is hard to justify based on the child's interests alone.

In addition, once a person is deemed a legal parent, they acquire the full panoply of parental rights regardless of whether they actually *have* the knowledge and expertise about the child that comes from intimate caretaking. Outside of the Unwed Father Cases, family law mostly doesn't require the parent to do any caretaking in order to have parental rights. A parent can cede the actual work of caring for the child—like taking him to piano lessons and supervising his practice—to their spouse, to another relative, or to a paid nanny and still have full parental rights, including the right to decide whether the child must keep playing the piano.

This disconnect between caretaking and parental rights is explicit when parents divorce. When divvying up a child between two parents, courts distinguish between "parental functions" and "caretaking functions."[37] "Caretaking functions" means the physical, day-to-day care of the child, the sort of intimacy that, according to the best-for-the-child rationale, should give rise to parental rights. "Parental functions" means making decisions. The distinction between the two comes from the old property-based system, in which fathers were like owners who made decisions, and mothers provided caretaking. Rather than basing parental rights on caretaking, the law deliberately separated them in order to protect the rights of traditional fathers, who did little caretaking, over the traditional mothers who did. At divorce, parents frequently receive joint "parental" rights regardless of who does the caretaking, just as they each receive half of the marital property. In short, the system today, like the old property system, treats parental authority more like ownership than like expertise derived from caretaking. Like the contract rationale, the best-for-the-child rationale is an attempt to justify legal rules that developed for other reasons in a way that will be more appealing to people with modern values who balk at describing children as property. But also like the contract rationale, the best-for-the-child rationale fails to justify the law as it actually is. As Godwin remarks, "If it just so happened that families based on parental domination over children were in fact [best] for children, it would be a coincidence."[38]

HOW THE LAW RESISTS CHANGE

The history and sweeping nature of parental rights show they are rooted in seeing the child as property, but we aspire to justify those rights under more palatable standards like what's best for the child.[39] At the same time, the older, more selfish explanations for parental rights still resonate for many parents, not necessarily because the parents want to dominate and control their children in selfish ways but because parents have positive feelings of connection and protectiveness toward their children. One reason the idea of children as property is persistent is that property rights are highly valued and respected in the law.[40] Legal culture channels positive feelings about children into the language of property because, as we'll see in chapter 4, the law lacks respect for human relationships. Treating children as property simultaneously elevates them to the category most valued by law and creates the conditions for domination by their "owners."

Consider, for example, the evolution of the parenting trend known as the free-range–kids movement. Proponents of free-range parenting argue kids' lives today are stifled by overprotective parents, teachers, and others whose constant meddling stops children from having fun and learning to solve problems on their own. The movement is a reaction against the "intensive parenting" that predominates in upper-middle-class America.[41] Its most prominent advocate, Lenore Skenazy, became famous for letting her nine-year-old son ride the New York subway by himself, which is pretty small potatoes compared to what nine-year-olds are capable of but shocking by the standards of our time.[42] Free rangers argue it's better for children to have more independence than they typically do today. Children, they say, vary widely in when they are ready for new levels of independence, and parents are the ones who know best when a particular child is ready. Thus there shouldn't be a blanket rule about how old you have to be to ride the subway. Each parent should decide when their child is ready to try it.

So far, that all sounds rooted in the fourth justification for parental rights. A child should have as much independence as that particular child is ready for, as judged by the person in the best position to know. But over time, free rangers increasingly butted heads with authorities who wanted to impose blanket rules. In my home state of Colorado, for example, the state child-welfare agency once declared that children were incapable of being left unsupervised "even for brief periods" until they were at least fourteen years old.[43] This sort of absurdly overbroad rule is never meant to be, and never will be, enforced against all parents. It's the kind of rule the state can use when it wants to pile up accusations against someone it has already decided to target—and the targets are overwhelmingly poor parents and parents of color. To their credit, the self-styled free-range parents of the upper middle class have helped publicize the persecution of poor parents charged with neglect for violating such dictates.[44] But when parents run afoul of overzealous state agencies, their strongest legal defense is grounded in cases like *Meyer* and *Pierce,* which speak in terms of the parent's rights rather than what's best for children. As the free-range movement fought back against state overreach, its advocates got in the habit of speaking the language of parents' rights. This rhetoric at times distorted the mission. For example, Skenazy once reflexively expressed support for the anti-vaccination movement as a matter of parents' rights. But as she later acknowledged, denying your child a life-saving vaccine has nothing to do with the free-range philosophy that it's better for kids to make their own mistakes and develop their independence. Decisions about vaccines are different in kind from decisions about practicing the piano or riding the subway. They require scientific expertise about the human body in general more than parental expertise about a particular child. Parents' power to deny basic medical care to their children is, rather, an example of a parental right that can only be justified if children are like property. Even a movement that started out squarely in child-focused territory gradually shifted its rhetoric, and then its substance, as it engaged with a legal system in which parents' rights are a more winning argument than children's interests.

Something similar happened with the biology-plus-relationship test. When the Supreme Court first developed it in the Unwed Father Cases, the relationship prong of the test offered an alternative to property as an explanation for the parent's feeling of connection to the child. The caretaking relationship explains why we expect a parent to do what's best for the child—why the parent wants to do so and also why the parent knows better than other people. By adopting the biology-plus-relationship test, the Unwed Father Cases opened a door to defining parenthood in terms of that caretaking relationship and its value to the child. Like the free-range–kids movement, however, the biology-plus-relationship test ran up against a legal system that was in the habit of thinking about parental rights as property rights. As we'll see in chapters 5, 6, and 7, the existing legal system transformed the test rather than vice versa.

One might have expected a test created by the Supreme Court to fare better in a legal system that is supposed to follow that court's lead. But the biology-plus-relationship test was up against more than just a long tradition of treating children as property. It conflicted with other deep-seated commitments in the law—commitments to protecting men's rights over women's and to placing little value on caretaking relationships. Chapters 5 through 7 will show how the legal system thwarted the biology-plus-relationship test. But first, chapter 4 will show that feminist theory explains why it did so.

———

... and Why

LEGAL RIGHTS ARE DESIGNED to preserve individual autonomy, not caretaking relationships. It's a design that tends to favor powerful people over those with less power and thus also, on balance, to favor men over women. Many feminists have for this reason called autonomy a "masculine" value, and some have argued that women are inherently more focused on relationships. But you needn't accept claims about inherent sex differences to see how the law favors autonomy over relationships. Family law, including the law of parenthood, follows this pattern, such as by emphasizing property-like control over children rather than caretaking relationships with them. The Unwed Father Cases were an opportunity to move in a different direction. With the biology-plus-relationship test, those cases made caretaking relationships central to the definition of parenthood. Feminist analysis explains, however, that this shift toward focusing on relationships was destined to be fleeting because the law places a higher value on autonomy. Like the free-range–kids movement, the biology-plus-relationship test transformed to reflect the law's favored values. Later chapters will describe how the courts altered the biology-plus-relationship test to avoid protecting relationships. This chapter sets out a feminist theory for understanding why.

LIBERAL AND CULTURAL FEMINISM

You'll recall from chapter 1 that feminists have differing views on how to deal with pregnancy in the workplace. Some feminists argue for pregnancy-specific policies like maternity leave to help reconcile women's reproductive lives with their working lives. Others, concerned about reinforcing traditional roles, prefer gender-neutral policies, like disability insurance for all conditions (including pregnancy) or family leave that supports parenthood in general rather than motherhood in particular. The latter preference for sex-neutral policies is associated with "liberal feminism," so called because of its roots in liberal political theory. Here, the word *liberal* is not the opposite of *conservative* in the way those words are used in US politics. Rather, *liberal* refers to a set of beliefs once held in common by the Democratic and Republican parties. It encompasses commitments to democratic government, individual rights, and (usually) the free market. Liberal feminists generally believe in the soundness of liberal political theory, but they criticize its past incarnations from women's perspectives.[1] Liberal feminists want to ensure women's access to opportunities traditionally reserved for men. They emphasize the ways women can, like men, embody supposedly masculine qualities like competitiveness and ambition. Liberal feminism thus focuses on how women can achieve the same things as men if given the chance.

Another group of feminists take sex differences as their starting point. These are known as "difference feminists" or "cultural feminists"—terms that suggest women and men are different in ways that produce "female" and "male" cultures. The key alleged differences are pregnancy and mothering. Many cultural feminists claim those experiences lead to broad differences between women's and men's outlooks on life.[2] You can see the influence of cultural feminism in political groups like Mothers Against Drunk Drivers, Moms Demand Action, and Lawyer Moms of America, in which women claim special moral authority *as mothers* to object to drunk driving, gun violence, and kidnapping children at the border. Although there are extremes in both groups, especially in popular culture—liberal feminists who exhort women to "lean in" to capitalism, and purported cultural feminists who would confine both women and men to their separate spheres—most of the time the differences between liberal and cultural feminists are matters of emphasis.[3] Nonetheless, they do have different starting points in how they think about sex differences.

Starting with the premise that women are different leads to particular ways of analyzing legal problems of sex equality. For example, consider again the *VMI* case, about whether the Virginia Military Institute should be forced to admit women. Justice Ruth Bader Ginsburg, herself a liberal feminist, wrote the majority opinion giving women the chance to prove they could be just as militaristic as the men for whom VMI was designed. A cultural feminist would have mixed feelings about this result. While acknowledging that women who wanted to go to VMI should have an equal chance with men, a cultural feminist would be more concerned about Virginia's decision to sponsor a locally prestigious, expensive school that plays to "male" preferences but not a comparable, yet different, "female" institution.

Virginia used this idea after a lower court found that the men-only policy at VMI was unconstitutional. Rather than admit women to VMI, Virginia offered to create a separate "women's leadership program" at a local private college, and the court agreed that if Virginia sponsored that program, it wouldn't have to admit women to VMI. Specially tailored for women, the program emphasized cooperation and self-esteem, in contrast to VMI's emphasis on competition and humiliation. Virginia argued this solution would work better than admitting women to VMI because it would give the typical woman the supportive environment that she, unlike a man, needs to succeed. The Supreme Court rejected this plan because Virginia's typical woman was a *stereo*typical woman. It might be true that more men than women want a VMI-style education, but that doesn't mean *all* men want to attend pseudo-military academies or *all* women want the opposite. The court thought the unusual, militarily inclined woman who wanted to go to VMI should have a fair shot at applying. A cultural feminist would want to know why typical women were left out in the cold.[4]

Perhaps the most famous text of cultural feminism is Professor Carol Gilligan's 1992 book, *In a Different Voice,* which is about moral reasoning and developmental psychology. The centerpiece of *In a Different Voice* is a study Gilligan performed of how women made decisions about abortion in the immediate aftermath of *Roe v. Wade,* the 1973 case that made abortion a constitutional right until it was overruled in 2022.[5] Gilligan argued that women tended to reason about moral problems differently—in a "different voice"— than men did. Women, she found, were more likely to emphasize their connections to others and the importance of relationships, while men emphasized individual rights and principles of justice. In another study reported in the book, Gilligan found this sex difference appearing even in preteen girls and boys. That study used a tool called the Heinz dilemma, a philosopher's tale that is supposed to test a person's moral reasoning. It goes like this:

> In Europe, a woman was near death from a special kind of cancer. There was one drug that the doctors thought might save her. It was a form of radium that a druggist in the same town had recently discovered. The drug was expensive to make, but the druggist was charging 5 times what it cost him to make the drug. He paid $400 for the radium, and charged $2,000 for a small

dose of the drug. The sick woman's husband, Heintz [*sic*], went to everyone he knew to borrow the money, but he could only get together about $1,000, half of what it cost. He told the druggist that his wife was dying, and asked him to sell it cheaper or let him pay later. But the druggist said, "No, I discovered the drug, and I'm going to make money from it, so I won't let you have it unless you give me $2,000 now." So Heintz got desperate and broke into the man's store to steal the drug for his wife.

Should Heintz have done that? Why?[6]

In asking this question, the psychologist is less interested in whether someone answers "yes" or "no" than in the reasons given for the choice. The psychologist evaluates those reasons according to a scale for judging the maturity of the person's moral reasoning. An immature response might focus narrowly on Heinz's own interest: he shouldn't steal the drug, because he will be miserable in prison; or he should steal the drug, because he will be happy if his wife survives. A mature response invokes principles of justice: he should steal the drug, because a life is worth more than property; or he shouldn't steal the drug, because there may be others who need it just as much. Girls and women typically score lower than boys and men on this test, indicating to traditional researchers that even as adults, women's moral reasoning is less "mature" than men's.

Gilligan, however, had a different explanation for how women and girls reasoned about Heinz's dilemma. First consider how Jake, an eleven-year-old boy, responded. He thought Heinz should steal the drug:

> For one thing, a human life is worth more than money, and if the druggist only makes $1,000, he is still going to live, but if Heinz doesn't steal the drug, his wife is going to die. [*Interviewer: Why is life worth more than money?*] Because the druggist can get a thousand dollars later from rich people with cancer, but Heinz can't get his wife again. [*Why not?*] Because people are all different and so you couldn't get Heinz's wife again.[7]

Jake goes on to explain that if Heinz is prosecuted for the theft, the judge will agree with Jake's reasoning and thus, presumably, impose a lenient sentence. On the standard scale, this is an age-appropriate response demonstrating an intermediate level of maturity. Jake has moved beyond entirely selfish forms of reasoning ("Do I like my wife enough to go to jail for her?") and instead appeals to principles he believes are widely shared in society.

Amy, despite being matched with Jake by age, intelligence, education, and social class, scores a full level below Jake on the standard scale, on the basis of this response:

[*Should Heinz have stolen the drug? Why?*] Well, I don't think so. I think there might be other ways besides stealing it, like if he could borrow the money or make a loan or something, but he really shouldn't steal the drug— but his wife shouldn't die either. . . . If he stole the drug, he might save his wife then, but if he did, he might have to go to jail, and then his wife might get sicker again, and he couldn't get more of the drug, and it might not be good. So, they should really just talk it out and find some other way to make the money.[8]

Throughout her interview, Amy continues to insist that "if Heinz and the druggist had talked it out long enough, they could reach something besides stealing." In law school, we call this behavior fighting the hypo. The hypothetical question in the Heinz dilemma asks for a choice between two options: steal the drug or let your wife die. Amy refuses to choose, insisting there must be another way. As Gilligan explains, hypothetical questions like Heinz's dilemma inherently "divest moral actors from the history and psychology of their individual lives and separate the moral problem from the social contingencies of its possible occurrence."[9] Amy is fighting the hypo because she rejects this stripped-down scenario, demanding more context in search of a better answer than the two on offer. On the standard scale, Amy's refusal to face up to Heinz's stark choice is scored as immaturity. In Gilligan's analysis, however, Amy has a point when she refuses "to see the dilemma as a self-contained problem in moral logic." Amy instead sees the dilemma as embedded in "a narrative of relationships that extends over time. . . . Jake [sees] a conflict between life and property that can be resolved by logical deduction, Amy a fracture of human relationship that must be mended with its own thread."[10]

Observations like this one led Gilligan to formulate her theory of women's different voice, which she described as an "ethic of care," as opposed to the more typically male "ethic of justice." She argued it was wrong to score Amy as less mature in her moral reasoning. Rather, Amy was on a different track. After all, the standard scale was developed using male test subjects. When it was applied to women, researchers had simply pronounced the women defective rather than wondering if there might be something wrong with their scale.[11]

In *In a Different Voice,* Gilligan took no formal position on whether the different voice she heard was hardwired into female brains or arose through socialization. She did make sure to point out that the association between sex and a person's style of moral reasoning was merely an association in her test subjects—not an absolute dichotomy and not necessarily applicable to everyone. She hinted at a complex explanation for the differences when she observed, "Clearly, these differences arise in a social context where factors of social status and power combine with reproductive biology to shape the experiences of males and females and the relations between the sexes."[12] Her goal, however, was not to explain the origin of the difference she observed but to rectify the omission of women's different voice from the psychological literature. Regardless of whether women's different voice was inherent or learned, Gilligan wanted it recognized as valid.

Gilligan's research and that of those who followed in her footsteps was part of Virginia's defense in the *VMI* case. To justify offering a competitive, adversarial education only to men (while belatedly ginning up a cooperative, supportive one for women), the state relied on alleged experts in women's education, including at least one who considered herself a feminist.[13] These witnesses testified that sex differences in personality meant most women would thrive not in VMI's competitive environment but at its cooperative, feminine counterpart. Gilligan herself submitted a brief in the *VMI* case, in which she and other researchers rejected Virginia's interpretation of their work. They explained that the different voices she had documented were associated with gender but not caused by inherent sex differences. They also said there was too much variation within each sex for the statistical association to justify excluding women from an opportunity like VMI.[14] The point of Gilligan's research was that psychologists ought to recognize Amy's style of reasoning, like Jake's, as mature and valuable, not that society should pigeonhole every girl as an Amy and every boy a Jake. But that's what VMI did when it claimed that all girls were Amys who needed cooperative environments to learn in, while boys were Jakes who needed competition.

That dichotomy between cooperation and competition is just one of a long string of opposites that our culture labels "feminine" and "masculine":

cooperation/competition
relationships/autonomy
home/work
passive/active
body/mind
nature/technology
emotion/intellect

Cultural feminists have extensively documented how Western culture valorizes the "male" list and denigrates the "female," such as by celebrating the conquest of Mother Nature by technology.[15] The cultural feminist project is to elevate the "female" list, on the belief that emotions, relationships, and nature are as good and important as intellect, autonomy, and technology (or, for some feminists, better and more important). Cultural feminists agree that women have a *right* to attend VMI, but they are more concerned with the fact that Virginia exalted competitive, "masculine" values at the expense of cooperative, "feminine" ones—to the detriment of women, who disproportionately adhere to the feminine values (for whatever reasons).

CULTURAL FEMINISM AND THE LAW

The most comprehensive effort to apply cultural feminism to the law was a 1988 article by Professor Robin West called "Jurisprudence and Gender." In that article, West described a clash between liberalism and feminism, rooted in two different understandings of the human condition. American law, of course, is based on liberalism's version of what a person is, not feminism's. Liberalism assumes the most important thing about the human condition is that we are separate from each other. We were once "noble savages" who lived independently, at least in principle, before entering into the social contract in which we agreed to cooperate for shared benefits.[16] Our greatest values are autonomy and freedom. The law's job is to let us exercise our freedom while also protecting us from each other. (My freedom to swing my fist ends where your nose begins.) Law does this job with rules about property and contracts, which draw boundaries around each person's domain (property law) and enforce their bargains, which are reached through arm's-length negotiations in which each person pursues his own interests (contract law). American law takes this job so seriously that, West has argued, the law's notion of a "person" is "at best a sociopathic caricature of the 'individual' celebrated by classical liberals" like Adam Smith and John Stuart Mill.[17] (An example of this caricature is the soulless drone we met as the "ideal worker" in chapter 1.) Because the legal system focuses on policing the boundaries of each person's separateness, it emphasizes competition over cooperation, autonomy over relationships, and so on down the "male" side of the list.

Cultural feminism, according to West, offers a different account of the human condition. Cultural feminism posits that the most important thing about the human condition is that we're connected to each other through relationships.[18] The most important interactions aren't contests or negotiations between equals but the nurturing of the weak by the strong—paradigmatically, the nurturing of a child by its mother. Infantile dependence, not noble savagery, is our true original condition. If so, then the most important values are intimacy and Gilligan's ethic of care: morality based on relationships and responsibilities rather than autonomy and freedom.

It isn't hard to find examples showing the law prizes autonomy and freedom over relationships and caretaking. Indeed, the Supreme Court has expressly held the former are more important than the latter. Ever since the Supreme Court decided *Gideon v. Wainwright* in 1963, anyone charged with a crime and facing jail time has been entitled to a lawyer. If you can't afford a lawyer, the state has to give you one for free. However, you only have a right to a free lawyer in a case that could end with you going to jail, because in that case your freedom is at stake. You don't get a free lawyer in a private, noncriminal case like a divorce or a dispute with your landlord. Two decades after *Gideon,* a woman named Abby Gail Lassiter asked the Supreme Court to hold that a parent accused of child abuse or neglect should get a free lawyer, just as Clarence Earl Gideon did when he was accused of theft. Child abuse is a crime, and if the state prosecutes you and tries to send you to jail for it, you're entitled to a lawyer under *Gideon.* But the state doesn't always try to send parents to jail. Instead, it may ask a court to terminate parental rights, making the parent a legal stranger to the child.[19] Lassiter had become a legal stranger to her four-year-old son, William, in a confusing, disorganized hearing at which she did not have a lawyer. The state accused her of not following doctors' instructions when William was sick and, after the state took him away for that reason, not trying hard enough to stay in touch with him. The family court therefore "terminated Ms. Lassiter's status as William's parent."[20] On appeal, she asked the Supreme Court to hold that, since she couldn't afford a lawyer, the state should have given her a free one, as it would have done in a criminal trial.

In its decision in *Lassiter v. Department of Social Services,* the Supreme Court rejected her request and drew a sharp line. Although the court admitted that losing a child is a "unique kind of deprivation," that deprivation simply didn't compare to the loss of liberty suffered by a person who goes to prison. The court thus held that a person accused of a crime is entitled to a lawyer "even where the crime is petty and the prison term brief," but a parent facing permanent loss of her child is not. Only a legal system firmly committed to prioritizing autonomy over relationships could arrive at this flint-hearted ordering of harms.

The holdings of *Gideon* and *Lassiter* would strike a liberal feminist, as opposed to a cultural feminist, as having little to do with sex equality. *Gideon* assures all criminal defendants, female or male, the right to a lawyer. And whether you agree with *Lassiter* or not, it applies equally to all parents, regardless of sex. But to a cultural feminist, the disparate holdings of *Gideon* and *Lassiter* have everything to do with sex equality. Clarence Earl Gideon got a free lawyer but Abby Gail Lassiter did not because the court thought Gideon's freedom was more important than Lassiter's relationship with her son. In the same way that Gilligan argued women's different moral voice was just as mature as men's, cultural feminists argue Lassiter's loss was at least as weighty as Gideon's.

THE DEBATE OVER INHERENT DIFFERENCES

Why should it matter to feminists that the law prioritizes autonomy over relationships? That depends on what we make of the two competing accounts of the human condition. One version of cultural feminism accepts the traditional liberal account (the noble savage who enters a social contract but remains fundamentally separate) as an account of *men's* basic human condition. The autonomous individual of liberal theory is who boys like Jake, who solve moral dilemmas with logical deduction, grow up to become. The cultural feminist account (the nurtured infant who grows up to nurture in turn, existing always in a web of relationships) is an alternate account that describes *women's* fundamental condition. It describes who girls like Amy, who want to talk and work things out, grow up to become. If so, the Supreme Court was correct that, for men, jail is worse than losing parental rights. The reverse, however, would be true for women. Sex equality would mean giving equal solicitude to each kind of person, men who are fundamentally separate and women who are fundamentally tied to relationships.

That, anyway, is how cultural feminism has often been understood (some would say misunderstood), but it's a view that has failed the test of time and scrutiny. As Gilligan herself argued in her *VMI* brief, the evidence doesn't support claims that the species is made up of two such distinct, sex-based personality types. People aren't that simple. Law, on the other hand, is that simple—or at least that simple-minded. The law's idea of a person is based on liberalism's ideal of the autonomous man. It turns out the "autonomous man" and the "relational woman," too stylized to stand in for actual people, are nonetheless useful for analyzing the law because the law is built on promoting the interests of its ideal character, the autonomous man.

When the law decides autonomy (staying out of jail) is more important than relationships (keeping your child), it applies that rule to all comers, regardless of sex. But the impact falls more heavily on women because so many more women are custodial parents and thus more likely to face the loss of a child. It falls especially heavily on poor women of color, who are overwhelmingly the targets of cases terminating parental rights.[21] Few people would claim that parents of a particular race or economic class feel the loss of a child more or less acutely than any other group. But cultural feminists sometimes imply that women feel this loss more acutely than men, not just because they are more often the child's main caretaker but because women, inherently, place higher value on relationships and are thus more sensitive to their loss. Some cultural feminists argue that the facts of reproductive biology affect how women and girls develop these values. Pregnancy—or even the capacity for pregnancy and the anticipation of it—generalizes into a fundamentally feminine way of looking at the world. This outlook reveals itself in Amy's ethic of care. Similarly, belonging to a gender known primarily for not getting pregnant produces a different outlook, which leads to Jake's ethic of justice.

Cultural feminists can be difficult to pin down about how, exactly, this happens. Different writers have different takes on that question, and as Gilligan explained, the cause is likely a complex mix of social status and power combined with reproductive biology and other life experiences. West, for example, at times emphasizes the role of sex differences in reproductive biology as a strong influence on women's and men's development, but she also argues that the goal should be for all people to have a balance of both the ethic of care and the ethic of justice.[22] She even wrote a book, *Caring for Justice*, on how to achieve that. Gilligan's work became a bestseller and a cultural phenomenon because it was "widely understood as showing that women are [inherently] different from men," whether she meant it that way or not.[23] As you might imagine, many feminists are appalled to find claims about inherent personality differences labeled "feminist." Women's allegedly different voice can sound a lot like a good-old sexist stereotype of an emotional, not-so-logical woman. Cultural feminism may put an empowering spin on the notion that women have special moral authority as mothers, but the notion itself is also a Victorian stereotype, long used to justify protecting women from such morally compromising endeavors as the practice of law, medicine, and politics.[24] When Virginia called a purportedly feminist scholar to testify about how VMI's combative, competitive approach to education was inappropriate for women, she was widely seen as betraying the side.

Later research has confirmed the more nuanced and complex explanations for the sex differences identified in Gilligan's work and highlighted by cultural feminists. Despite valiant efforts, science has yet to find convincing evidence to support grand generalizations about Mars, Venus, or any other theory of innate, "hardwired" personality differences on a scale that would preordain either patriarchal gender ideologies or the different voice of cultural feminism.[25] In addition, there have been at least two major theoretical critiques of cultural feminism and its claims about women's basic nature. These critiques point out that research like Gilligan's doesn't happen in a vacuum but in a world already shaped by sexism and other systems of subordination, especially racism.

In the first of these critiques, a landmark article called "Race and Essentialism in Feminist Legal Theory," Professor Angela Harris argued that cultural feminism's description of "women" is actually based on White women. The *essentialism* of Harris's title is the practice of treating certain qualities, such as concern for relationships over rights, as characteristic of women and thus necessarily shared by all women. By ignoring race in its theories about the fundamental natures of both women and men, cultural feminism made gender difference the organizing principle of selfhood. Gilligan, like almost all developmental psychologists before her, studied a privileged, White population; she simply added gender to the mix. Limiting research this way means ignoring how race and gender interact, as well as ignoring that race is just as much in play when studying White women as when studying women of color. For example, White feminists often identify rape as a quintessential harm that women suffer under patriarchy. But the rape scenario they envision is more often "the strange black man in the bushes" than "the white employer in the kitchen or bedroom."[26] Moreover, for Black women, rape accusations signify "the terrorism of black men by white men, . . . aided and abetted by white women."[27] By treating rape as the ultimate gender crime, White feminists made the racialized fear of rape part of their definition of womanhood. They wrongly assumed that all women experienced sexism and patriarchy in the same ways.

In the second major critique of cultural feminism and its claims about women's basic nature, Professor Catharine MacKinnon criticized the idea that Gilligan's "different voice" is women's true voice, or even White women's true voice. She argued, "Women value care because men have valued us according to the care we give them." In response to the claim that women have a different voice, she commented, "Take your foot off our necks; then we will see in what tongue women speak."[28] Consider again Jake and Amy's answers to the Heinz dilemma. Gilligan used the Heinz story because it was a standard tool in psychology, but the standard story is quite gendered. The main character, Heinz, is male. The druggist is male. Heinz's wife is sick and helpless, seemingly without a role to play in the moral dilemma. She doesn't even have a name. It seems safe to assume Jake identifies with Heinz. He is primed to play the hero for his damsel in distress. It is less clear, however, with whom Amy should identify. Perhaps she identifies with the wife. She doesn't want to die, but the story doesn't offer her a chance to be the hero, only to be selfish by expecting her husband to risk prison to save her. She fears what could happen to her when he's gone. ("If he stole the drug, he might save his wife then, but . . . he might have to go to jail, and then his wife might get sicker again, and he couldn't get more of the drug.") Her gender disempowered by the story itself, she seeks to negotiate with the powerful druggist. Amy and Jake's responses could reflect the gendered power dynamics of the story as much as any sex-driven difference in moral reasoning.

Follow-up research after *In a Different Voice* tended to confirm the existence of a different voice—that is, the existence of two, distinctive styles of moral reasoning—but failed to establish a strong link to sex.[29] Researchers found girls and boys using both styles, under various circumstances. One thread that emerged was that traits Gilligan considered "masculine" are associated with people with power, while "feminine" traits characterize people who are disempowered.[30] For example, minority children of both sexes, like White girls, score poorly on the traditional "male"-centric scales. This finding bears out both Harris's and MacKinnon's critiques. MacKinnon's critique implied Amy's different voice was a product of subordination, not sex, as this later research has suggested. Harris's critique implied that neither Amy's nor Jake's voice could be attributed solely to gender because race and many other factors are always also at play. Although cultural feminism claimed Amy and the value she placed on relationships as typical of female culture, Black feminist scholars from Patricia Hill Collins in 1990 to Lua Kamál Yuille in 2020 have identified similar values as central to African American culture.[31] Professor Cornel West, a Black scholar of race and class, is known for saying "justice is what love looks like in public," a vision that resonates with Robin

West's call to reform the law around "caring for justice."[32] Jake was White *and* male *and* economically privileged. Perhaps it was only comparing him to Amy that made the difference between their approaches to the Heinz dilemma look like a gender difference.[33] This explanation suggests that the dichotomy between the "male" ethic of justice and the "female" ethic of care—between focusing on the rights of autonomous individuals and focusing on the relationships between them—is not a description of men and women but a function of the dynamics of power and subordination, which we often experience through gender but also along other lines.

The fact that women's different voices—or more likely, the different voices of a variety of intersecting, subordinated groups of people—may be a function of subordination doesn't mean those voices are lesser or we should go back to deeming Amy less mature than Jake. If Amy's moral reasoning is shaped by her disempowerment, then so is Jake's shaped by his relative power. If the foot on someone's neck affects her moral voice, then surely the possessor of the foot is also affected. For example, Amy's strategy of talking things out with the druggist is a strategy for someone without power. If you don't have the power to take what you want, talk and negotiation are your only options. But Amy's faith in human relationships may also be naïve. Most of us know that "just talk it out long enough" is an unlikely strategy for persuading pharmaceutical manufacturers to forego profits. Talking it out doesn't shift the power dynamics of the situation, and caring too much about preserving a personal relationship in the midst of a power struggle can be a weakness.

Conversely, Jake's response to the Heinz dilemma assumes that others (including the sentencing judge) will see Heinz's dilemma the same way he does, which suggests he too has a blind spot: an inability to perceive that others may view the world differently from him. Consider the concept of "double consciousness," which W. E. B. Du Bois introduced in 1897.[34] Du Bois explained double consciousness as an inward sense of doubleness that Black people experience because of the necessity of "always looking at one's self through [White] eyes."[35] This concept has been applied to various kinds of subordination, including gender. When a person lacks power, they are more likely, out of necessity, to be highly attuned to the feelings and perceptions of those around them who have more power. For example, abused children are highly sensitive to shifting moods and emotional dynamics in their homes, and they often retain that sensitivity as adults. Double consciousness is a form of empathy, but it is also a survival strategy that gives subordinated people greater insight into their "superiors" than vice versa. Jake may have a harder time developing this skill. We should expect that men's voices, too, would change if gender subordination were a thing of the past. The same would be true of subordination across racial and other lines. Perhaps a truly human voice is a mixture of the ethic of care and the ethic of justice, or perhaps it is something else entirely.[36]

RELATIONAL FEMINISM

In the legal world, cultural feminism eventually came to be called *relational feminism*. This term emphasizes the value that cultural feminists place on relationships while downplaying any claims about inherent sex differences or separate female and male cultures. Instead, in Professor Mary Becker's telling, relational feminism offered an alternative to patriarchy's value system—an alternative set of values that would help achieve "human happiness and fulfillment for women (and men)."[37] This shift, focusing on the value system rather than on the characteristics of individual women and men, foreshadowed ambitious efforts to respond to critiques like Harris's and MacKinnon's. Relational feminists recognized that real, actual people value both their autonomy and their relationships. Rather than categorize people as adhering to one or the other, relational feminists set out to analyze how the law's skewed value system thwarted hopes of happiness and fulfillment for so many.

Relational feminists acknowledge that, despite the uniqueness of pregnancy, there is no simple dichotomy between women's and men's experiences. For example, even if only some of us experience pregnancy as adults, we all start out on the baby's side of that relationship. (We may not remember it, but neither does the autonomous man, exalted in law, remember being a noble savage before the social contract, although in his case that's because it never happened.) As Robin West puts it, "we have all had the experience of being cared *for*."[38] The shared experience of needing to be cared for is the core of vulnerability theory, which Professor Martha Fineman created as an alternative to liberalism. Starting out as a relational feminist, Fineman found that "what I had been analyzing as a gender problem was actually a societal problem that extends well beyond a gender equality frame."[39] Similarly, Professor Jennifer Nedelsky has developed an alternative to liberalism based on the concept of a relational self who still values autonomy but who exists in an ever-shifting web of relationships, not in isolation. Nedelsky, too, describes her work as "extending beyond feminism, even though I could not have written it without my feminism and feminist scholarship."[40]

Both Fineman and Nedelsky retain the key insights of relational feminism (such as the priority the law places on autonomy over relationships, as in *Gideon* and *Lassiter*) but avoid the trap of essentialism by focusing on power rather than treating women's orientation toward relationships as an innate characteristic. Fineman, for example, discusses the law's typical, theoretical man (the ideal worker, the man who fears prison more than losing his child). She attributes this man's value system not to reproductive biology but to American history. The "person" imagined by American law was originally "white, male, property-owning or tax-paying, of a certain age and/or religion and free." Although protest movements and a civil war have peeled away some of those qualifiers, the law's idea of a person has nonetheless continued to reflect "the needs and political sensibilities of an eighteenth-century male citizen sheltered by institutions such as the patriarchal family and the privileges of a master–servant mentality."[41] By instead incorporating a full vision of human nature, feminist theory can strive for universality not by making essentialist claims about all women or all men but by moving away from classifications and instead attacking the skewed values of the legal system. As Harris wrote, "We need not wait for a unified theory of oppression; that theory can be feminism."[42]

Relational feminists criticize how the law values preserving autonomy over protecting relationships, which is why it is no contradiction to relational-feminist theory when individual men suffer under patriarchy.[43] The legal system's preference for autonomy over relationships can favor certain men or certain women, depending on the situation. That brings us back to the Unwed Father Cases. In those cases, it was men rather than women who needed protection for their relationships, not for their autonomy. Peter Stanley and Abdiel Caban were in a situation like Abby Lassiter's, all of them seeking to maintain their relationships with their children. Peter's and Abdiel's individual gender didn't "match" the theoretical gender of their claim, while Abby's did. Also unlike Abby, Peter and Abdiel won their cases. The court recognized the value of their relationships. The Supreme Court was perhaps more able to sympathize with the need to protect relationships when the claimants were men. We should nonetheless classify the Unwed Father Cases as "feminist," at least from a relational-feminist perspective, because they placed value on caretaking relationships.

Before we can make that ruling, however, we need to examine some additional nuances of this feminist theory of the law's priorities. The system West described in her article "Jurisprudence and Gender" has four parts. The first two make up the dichotomy between the "masculine" ideal of living autonomously and the "feminine" ideal of living in a web of relationships. Complementing each of these primary values is a hidden vulnerability. We must consider all four, the two primary values and their corresponding vulnerabilities, before we can classify the Unwed Father Cases and explain why the legal system rejected the biology-plus-relationship test those cases created.

THE UNDERSIDES OF AUTONOMY
AND RELATIONSHIP

The hidden vulnerability of autonomy is loneliness. Consider the archetypal man, whose fundamental nature lies in his separateness from all other men. He values his freedom and autonomy above all else, but like Adam in the Garden, he is lonely. He craves connection but is embarrassed to admit it. He longs to reach across the gaping void around him and touch another human soul. It turns out family law meets his need for connection. Family law is organized around marriage, its key legal institution for fostering intimacy. Marriage has the trappings of autonomy: it is a contract, and today it is understood to be a voluntary one between equals. Yet within it, lonely souls are said to be united as one. In *Obergefell v. Hodges,* the case that made same-sex marriage a constitutional right, the Supreme Court described marriage like this:

> From their beginning to their most recent page, the annals of human history reveal the transcendent importance of marriage. The lifelong union of a man and a woman always has promised nobility and dignity to all persons, without regard to their station in life. Marriage is sacred to those who live by their religions and offers unique fulfillment to those who find meaning in the secular realm. Its dynamic allows two people to find a life that could not be found alone, for a marriage becomes greater than just the two persons. Rising from the most basic human needs, marriage is essential to our most profound hopes and aspirations.[44]

This passage, written by Justice Anthony Kennedy, has been the target of some derision—from Justice Scalia, who dissented from the decision,[45] but also from supporters of same-sex marriage for whom the sentimentality was a bit much. Many people who objected, on principle, to discriminatory laws that banned same-sex marriage were nonetheless skeptical about the institution of marriage itself. But for Justice Kennedy, marriage was a solution to the existential loneliness of man. He went on: "Marriage responds to the universal fear that a lonely person might call out only to find no one there." This isolated, lonely individual of Justice Kennedy's (and the law's) imagination needs the institution of marriage to fulfill his need for connection. While the autonomous man pursues his self-interest in a free market governed by freedom-enhancing laws about property and contracts, marriage gives him a haven in a heartless world.[46]

The institution of marriage allows this lonely soul to form relationships with a spouse and children. The Constitution doesn't guarantee any of us will find love through marriage or parenthood, but the Declaration of Independence promises us the right to pursue it, along with other forms of happiness. As Professor Scott Altman puts it, institutions like marriage and parental rights protect a particular kind of pursuit of happiness, the "pursuit of intimacy." He writes, "I don't propose to assert a right to intimacy but a right to seek intimacy and be provided with background institutions that make success reasonably likely."[47] Just as law provides autonomous men with property and contract rules for policing their separateness, it also provides them with the background institutions of marriage and parenthood for pursuing happiness in the form of intimate connections.

The idea of *pursuing* intimacy is what distinguishes the lonely man's desire for connection from the "feminine" state of being born into a web of relationships. In Altman's description, individuals start out alone and must seek connection. Society is obliged to provide mechanisms, like marriage and parental rights, to help them along. Similarly, when Professor Kenneth Karst wrote an important early analysis of constitutional rights in relationships, he took for granted that the value of relationships derives from their being consciously pursued.[48] He thus held up marriage and a man's "legitimation" of an out-of-wedlock child as the highest forms of intimacy—conspicuously slighting the less freely chosen intimacy between a birth mother and child. In contrast, cultural feminists point to the mother and child to show that no one starts out alone. We are all already embedded in relationships, starting when we are born from a mother's body. Abby Lassiter and her son had an important relationship well before the law arrived on the scene to terminate it. What she needed was for the law to have greater respect for that relationship. The right to pursue intimacy described by Altman and Karst is different. The person starts out alone, in need of connection, and legal mechanisms like marriage and "legitimation" are means to that end.

Achieving that end requires another person's participation, which brings us to the fourth and final piece of this feminist analysis of what the law does and does not value: the hidden vulnerability of relationships, which is domination by other people. We saw in chapter 3 that the most well-established legal justifications for parental rights treat the child as a creature of the parent. Either the child is the parent's property, or the child's purpose is to propagate the parent's religion and other beliefs. The child is thus a vehicle for fulfilling the parent's need for connection, the means to the parent's ends.[49] Women in patriarchal society are similarly at risk of having their lives hijacked as means to someone else's ends. Unlike the autonomous man who needs the law to provide institutions that foster connection, the relational woman is more likely to need the law to help her escape domination within those institutions. Just as the autonomous man values his freedom but is vulnerable to loneliness, the relational woman values her relationships but is vulnerable to becoming a mere vehicle for the needs of another.

West described this last quality as being at risk of "invasion"—for example, by rape or forced pregnancy, which are both examples of how one person can be used by others for their own ends. The fear of invasion is similar to but not quite the same as the desire for autonomy. West explains that "the autonomy praised by liberalism is one's right to pursue one's own ends," but for a person at risk of invasion:

> I do not fear having my "ends" frustrated; I fear having my ends "displaced" before I even formulate them. . . . I fear that my ends will not be my own. . . . I fear I will never feel the freedom, or have the space, to become an ends-making creature.[50]

While cultural feminists focus on lifting up the positive, relational qualities associated with women, another group—known as dominance feminists and led by MacKinnon—focus on the invasions. Cultural feminism and dominance feminism are usually thought of as separate, incompatible schools of feminism. The tension between them is apparent in MacKinnon's comment that cultural feminists needed to get patriarchy's foot off their necks before celebrating their different voice. But in "Jurisprudence and Gender," West claimed dominance feminism as cultural feminism's grim sister. The two schools share a belief that the liberal feminism enshrined in law has missed the point. Both contend that the deepest problems of sexism are problems of difference, which sameness equality misses when it gives a lawyer to Gideon but not to Lassiter and when it fails to see the sex discrimination in pregnancy discrimination. As Professor Becker explained, "It is the systemic creation of hierarchy—out of real or perceived differences—that forms the core of discrimination. To see discrimination, you must focus on differences between men and women, because that is often where social practices create inequality."[51]

Just as American law values preserving autonomy over protecting relationships, it provides institutions like marriage and parenthood to address the need for connection but does little to protect against invasions. The *Geduldig* court, for example, didn't even acknowledge that Jackie Jaramillo's pregnancy was involuntary, which made it just as much an injury as the other disabilities the state was willing to compensate for. Whole law review articles have been written trying to explain that pregnancy can be an injury, and lawyers who argue for the right to abortion struggle to justify the right, instead, in the language of autonomy. Professor Khiara Bridges notes that even when the Supreme Court protected the right to abortion, it did so not because it acknowledged the injury of involuntary pregnancy but because it believed "a woman's pregnancy may occur during a time when she is incapable of taking pleasure in its inherently wondrous nature."[52] Similarly, feminists have extensively documented how the institution of marriage sacrifices women's individuality for the sake of men's need for intimacy. As Professor Katherine Baker explains, the law of marriage "provides men with a forum for intimacy and connection, but discounts the potential dangers to women of that interdependence and intimacy."[53] For example, the law justifies its reluctance to criminalize domestic violence and marital rape because of the need to protect "marital privacy." As with the beating of Joshua DeShaney, the privacy being protected belongs to the person who has power within the household, most often the husband and father. "In marriage," the legal maxim held, "the husband and wife are one—and the one is the husband."[54] The law fails to protect women (and children) within marriage because it is too preoccupied protecting the autonomous man's haven for connection. Women in family law are constantly at risk of becoming the Eve of Genesis—technically a person, but one who exists solely to redress the loneliness of the autonomous man.[55]

In sum, we have a four-part system of values that the law does and does not promote. This system is gendered, meaning its parts are identifiably feminine or masculine, even though the connection to any individual's sex or gender varies by circumstance. We have, on the one hand,

1. a masculine ideal of **preserving autonomy,** with freedom and the ethic of justice as its highest values; this requires legal systems like property and contracts to mediate interactions with other autonomous individuals;
2. but these autonomous individuals experience great loneliness and need to **pursue new connections** with others; institutions like marriage and parental rights help them do so.

On the other hand,

3. the feminine ideal starts out **existing in relationships** with others, which fosters values like intimacy and the ethic of care; the people in these relationships need protection for their relationships—protection against being separated from each other;
4. but they are also vulnerable to **invasion,** the hijacking of their lives by others, and thus they need legal tools that support their ability to separate from others when necessary.

American law speaks the language of preserving autonomy and helping to pursue new connections much more fluently than it speaks of protecting existing relationships and guarding against invasion. *Gideon* and *Lassiter* announced the law's preference for autonomy over relationships by expressly holding that the loss of autonomy (Gideon's going to jail) was more important and thus deserving of a free lawyer than the loss of a relationship (Lassiter's losing her child). Traditional marriage and parental rights are examples of how the law enables new connections, but from the perspective of a wife or child who is beaten or abused, those institutions exacerbate the invasion and domination of their lives by the husband or father.

CLASSIFYING THE UNWED FATHER CASES

Where do the Unwed Father Cases and their biology-plus-relationship test fit into this system of values? And why should we care? Earlier, I tentatively classified the Unwed Father Cases as protecting existing relationships, rather than preserving autonomy. That matters because over the next three chapters, I'll use the biology-plus-relationship test as a test case for relational feminism. My aim is to demonstrate how the legal system perpetuates its skewed value system—its preference for the "masculine" values over the "feminine" ones. The biology-plus-relationship test was a casualty of that value system. Because courts don't put enough value on relationships, they transformed the test from a tool for protecting existing relationships into a biological father's right to pursue new connections. They made that right so strong that it invaded the rights and lives of birth mothers. That harm went unnoticed because the law doesn't habitually acknowledge the "feminine" need for protection against invasion. In short, what started out as an impulse to protect one of the "feminine" values couldn't survive in a legal system committed to the "masculine" ones.

It's important to my argument that the Unwed Father Cases started out as an (uncharacteristic) effort by the Supreme Court to protect existing relationships. When I proposed that classification earlier in this chapter, we hadn't yet discussed the hidden vulnerabilities. Now that we've seen the full, four-part system one could argue that the biology-plus-relationship test was actually a mechanism for pursuing new connections in the form of parental rights. One would point out that the cases arose at a time when the institution of marriage seemed to be crumbling. By expanding fathers' rights to children born outside marriage, the Supreme Court shored up men's access to children. On this reading, the Unwed Father Cases expanded the benefits of marriage to a disadvantaged class of men, those who had been unable to acquire connections through marriage itself. Because they gave men a new way to create relationships with children, the Unwed Father Cases could be seen as serving the "masculine" need for legal doctrines that help lonely men pursue new connections.

While some aspects of the Unwed Father Cases support this reading, the better reading is that they protected existing relationships. At the end of chapter 2, I argued the cases should be considered feminist decisions for three reasons. First, they defined parenthood in terms of day-to-day caretaking for the child. In other words, they protected existing relationships. Unwed dads like Peter Stanley and Abdiel Caban weren't claiming a right to *pursue* intimacy, with the intimacy to be experienced in the future, as described by Altman. They were not staking a claim to a woman's future children, as a man does with marriage. They had already formed relationships with their children before the law arrived on the scene. They had made themselves vulnerable by caring for their children without the shelter of an institution like marriage or formal parental rights. The Supreme Court's rulings protecting them were thus a relationship-protecting move. Second, the Supreme Court used a feminine norm by taking pregnancy as the model for establishing parental rights. This model was based not only on female biology but also on the ideologically "feminine" ideal of protecting relationship. Finally, the decisions were feminist because they accommodated sex differences rather than insisting that women and men could be equal only to the extent they were the same. The best understanding of the Unwed Father Cases is thus that, unlike the usual run of cases, they prioritized the neglected "feminine" value of protecting existing relationships. The caretaking language in the Unwed Father Cases represented a foothold for placing value on relationships in the law, an opportunity to balance the protection of autonomy with more protection for relationships.

Unfortunately, the reverse happened, and the four-part system explains why. When the Unwed Father Cases protected caretaking relationships, they were in a sense speaking in a language that's foreign to the American legal system—they were in a different voice. When lawyers and judges started reading and applying those precedents, they highlighted and built on the parts that made sense to them. And what made sense to them were the need to preserve autonomy and provide the right to pursue new connections. The next three chapters trace how, as a result, fathers' rights were increasingly defined in "masculine" terms. Although the Unwed Father Cases grounded fathers' rights in their caretaking relationships with children, states and lower courts undermined that caretaking principle by giving rights to fathers based on genes alone. Genes became like marriage, another basis for pursuing connections with children (and controlling women). Instead of protecting fathers who had taken care of their children, the law defined fatherhood in terms of genes, paperwork, and money. Meanwhile, courts used the idea of sex equality in parental rights to invert the biology-plus-relationship test. Instead of basing men's parental rights on an analogy to pregnancy, which is to say an analogy to women's biology, the law switched to defining women's parental rights in terms of *men's* biology, with the contribution of genes trumping the relationship of pregnancy. The fate of the biology-plus-relationship test is thus proof of concept for relational feminism. It shows how the law acts on its preference to preserve autonomy and provide the means to pursue new connections rather than to protect existing relationships and guard against invasion.

PART TWO

The Collapse of Caretaking

FIVE

Expanding Fathers' Rights
against Mothers

THE SUPREME COURT GETS TO decide big questions, like who should have parental rights, and create rules for making the decisions, like the biology-plus-relationship test. The job of implementing its decisions, however, falls to lower courts in the tens or hundreds or thousands of cases that follow. Inevitably, those lower courts emphasize some aspects of the Supreme Court's decision while ignoring or even contradicting others. After the Unwed Father Cases, lower courts expanded biological fathers' rights well beyond the biology-plus-relationship test. They focused on the biology prong much more than the relationship prong, which meant they defined fatherhood mainly in terms of genes. Courts so embraced this genetic definition of fatherhood that they started giving parental rights to men who became genetic fathers through rape. While most states now have laws that let the victim terminate the parental rights of a rapist in some cases, those fixes cover only a subset of cases where the biology-plus-relationship test ought to apply instead of the genetic definition of parenthood. In terms of the system of values from chapter 4, defining fatherhood in terms of genes means giving the father a right to pursue connection with the child even when there's no existing relationship between them to protect. Courts enforce this right to pursue connection without regard for the invasion of the birth mother's life, such as when they make her rapist her legal co-parent. Instead of using the biology-plus-relationship test to protect caretaking relationships between fathers and children, courts turned genetic fatherhood into a tool for genetic fathers to force connections with both children and their birth mothers.

GENETIC ESSENTIALISM AND THE RISE
OF FATHERS' RIGHTS

The biology-plus-relationship test had barely crystallized as precedent before it began to crack under the pressure of two opposing forces in the lower courts. First came the advent of reproductive technology, especially in vitro fertilization. New ways of making babies coincided with popular and legal fascination with DNA, a fascination that became an ideology known as *genetic essentialism*. Genetic essentialism is the belief that genes constitute a person's true essence and that genetic connections are therefore the most important factors in family relationships.[1] The rise of genetic essentialism strengthened the perceived rights of fathers who had genetic but no other ties to children. Pushing in the opposite direction, however, was the second force: an adoption crunch. In the late twentieth century, adoptable infants were in short supply, demand for the healthy newborn ones was increasing, and a new private adoption industry was rising to profit from the gap. The unmet demand for adoptable infants pressured lower courts to limit the rights of biological fathers when the mother was willing to place the child for adoption.

Broadly speaking, states resolved the conflict between these two opposing trends by enshrining genetic essentialism in their definition of parenthood but then creating procedural hurdles to sideline poor fathers in adoptions.[2] This chapter focuses on the first trend: how states used the definition of parenthood to expand the rights of genetic fathers at the expense of mothers. Chapter 6 will discuss the second: how poor fathers were selectively excluded from this expansion of rights.[3]

You may recall that until the Unwed Father Cases in the 1970s, unmarried genetic fathers were rarely legal parents at all. Fatherhood came through marriage, not biology. In the cases from *Stanley v. Illinois* to *Lehr v. Robertson*, the Supreme Court demanded only that unwed fathers be recognized as legal parents *if* they had caretaking bonds with their children. All states must (in theory) honor parental rights in cases like *Stanley*, where the father had lived with and helped raise the children until their mother's death. However, no state limits fathers' rights to those men who have relationships with their children. Instead, simply being the genetic father is almost always enough for full parental rights.[4] What started out as protection for the relationship a man formed by caring for his children has become a form of genetic ownership of children instead.

To begin with the easiest example, a *married* genetic father's parental rights remain unquestioned. All states recognize some form of the marital presumption of paternity, the old English rule that ensured any child born to a married woman would be considered "legitimate."[5] If the husband is the genetic father, his parental rights are as unassailable as the mother's. For husbands who are not genetic fathers, recall that in *Michael H. v. Gerald D.*, Michael and Carole were Victoria's genetic parents, but Carole had reconciled with her husband Gerald and wanted to raise Victoria with him. The Supreme Court allowed the state to give priority to Gerald, even though Michael had also established a caretaking relationship with Victoria. Since that decision, however, the rise of genetic essentialism has eroded the parental rights of husbands who aren't genetic fathers. Most states today would consider *Michael H.* a more difficult case to decide. Gerald and Michael would both be considered "presumed fathers," Gerald by virtue of marriage and Michael by virtue of genes, regardless of whether either of them had ever met Victoria. Faced with two presumed fathers, a court would most likely bestow parental rights on whichever father the judge thought would be best for Victoria. (A few courts might consider recognizing both as fathers, giving Victoria a total of three parents.) In addition, being married would limit Carole's options in some states. If genetic-father Michael were out of the picture but Carole didn't want to raise Victoria with husband Gerald, she wouldn't be allowed to challenge Gerald's paternity, even with genetic evidence that he wasn't the biological father. A court would refuse to question Gerald's paternity unless Carole had Michael waiting in the wings, ready to acknowledge his paternity and step in as father. Only Michael, not Carole, would be allowed to point to genes to displace Gerald.

Outside of marriage, parents can now use a "voluntary acknowledgement of parentage" form to establish legal parenthood in the delivery room. If the birth mother and putative father sign the VAP together, its effect is similar to the marital presumption of paternity. The couple still aren't married to each other, but the VAP makes them co-parents to the child unless proven otherwise by a DNA test within a specific amount of time (from sixty days to two years, depending on the state). There's some uncertainty about the role of genes in this process. As with the marital presumption, some parents use VAPs intentionally to establish the parenthood of someone who is definitely *not* the genetic father. For example, many lesbian couples sign VAPs together, and, less conspicuously, many men in opposite-sex relationships sign VAPs despite not being the genetic fathers. (Some know they aren't the father, others do not.) Some states welcome these non-genetic VAPs as a way to formally designate the child's second legal parent. Although VAPs serve many purposes, the main reason states have them is to make the second parent liable for child support. Most states aren't eager to look a gift father in the mouth and would rather focus on his wallet than on his genes. However, in some states, especially those hostile to same-sex parents, it may be illegal to sign a VAP if you know you are not a genetic parent.[6]

Both marriage and a VAP require the birth mother to consent, at some point, to the other person becoming a co-parent to her child. With marriage, her consent was implied at the wedding, which may have been in in the distant past, but as a starting point it seems fair for the state to assume that a married woman giving birth expects her spouse to be her co-parent. Similarly, a VAP records everyone's beliefs and expectations at the time of birth.

However, it turns out the birth mother's consent to a VAP is in some ways a formality. Although signing the VAP at the hospital is the easiest way to establish paternity, a determined genetic father can still bring a paternity lawsuit if the mother refuses to sign the VAP. He will win under almost all circumstances.[7] As long as the mother isn't married, no state requires any sort of relationship with the child in order for a man to obtain parental rights, nor does it matter whether the mother wants him in her life. All he needs is a blood test proving genetic paternity. As far as the law is concerned, a baby whose birth mother is her only legal parent has a defect in her family, a blank space that needs to be filled. Moreover, even if the father doesn't sue for paternity, if the mother receives certain public benefits the state will require her to identify the likely father, on pain of losing her benefits. The state will then try to establish paternity in order to collect child support—perhaps for the benefit of the child but more likely to reimburse the state welfare program.[8] An unmarried woman who wants to raise her child on her own (or with someone other than the genetic father) won't be allowed to do so if the genetic father wants to participate or if she needs help from the state. Unless the birth mother has a husband (or maybe a wife) to compete for the empty space labeled "father" that courts perceive in a mother-child family, the biology-plus-relationship test disappears and biology alone establishes a father's rights.

After the Unwed Father Cases, states also gave unwed fathers broad power to block adoptions sought by birth mothers. Unlike in *Caban v. Mohammed*, *Quilloin v. Wolcott*, and *Lehr v. Robertson*, in which the mothers wanted their new husbands to adopt their children, later disputes involved birth mothers' wanting to place newborns for adoption by unrelated couples. State laws varied widely in what a genetic father had to do to prevent the adoption of a newborn. Most states gave the genetic father a veto over adoption regardless of whether he had a caretaking relationship with the child, so long as he complied with procedures like putting his name on the putative-father registry.[9] When states required something more, they emphasized financial support rather than caretaking relationships. For example, Utah has a reputation for being hostile to unwed fathers' rights. Yet a father there can prevent an adoption merely by filing paperwork to assert his claim of paternity, with no caretaking of the child beyond offering to pay a share of the cost of childbirth.[10] In some states, the burden runs in the opposite direction. It is the birth mother, the adopting couple, and the adoption agency who are expected to find the genetic father and offer him a chance to block the adoption.

When the parties don't follow these procedures, enforcement of fathers' rights has sometimes been unyielding, with the father's genetic rights counting for more than the birth mother's decision that adoption is best for her child. Genetic rights have also at times counted for more than any caretaking relationship the adoptive parents may have formed with the child. In two high-profile cases in the 1990s, courts vindicated fathers' genetic rights by ordering "Baby Jessica" and "Baby Richard" transferred from their adoptive parents to their biological fathers at the ages of two and four, respectively. Both fathers won their cases, despite never having met the children before suing for custody, because they hadn't received proper notice before the adoptions. Professor David Meyer provides this description of the culmination of the Baby Richard case:

> The last day of April 1995 had dawned just like any other for four-year-old Richard Warburton. It was a Sunday, chilly and gray, a perfectly average day in what passes for spring in suburban Chicago. By three o'clock that afternoon, however, Richard was fighting desperately to cling to the fragments of his life as they dissolved around him. Though his parents had told him a few hours earlier that he would be going on a "sleep over" at the home of a family he did not know, even at four years old he plainly sensed that something more life-altering was about to take place. After all, the belongings of his childhood, the silver bicycle with training wheels, his basketball, the blue toy box, his clothes, were already neatly collected near the front curb and a crowd of reporters and neighbors numbering into the hundreds had amassed on the front lawn. Inside the house, crying convulsively, oblivious to his national fame as the "Baby Richard" caught up in a well-publicized custody battle, young Richard Warburton pleaded with each member of his family

to protect him. When his mother, wracked with tears, was unable to answer, Richard turned next to his father, and finally to his seven-year-old brother, begging each of them in turn to come with him. "I'll be good," he sobbed, "Don't make me leave. I'll be good."

Less than an hour later, after brief and awkward introductions to the biological parents he had never met, Richard was carried out before the television cameras and the weeping crowd to a waiting van. As he sobbed and clung to his adoptive mother, his heart racing and pounding against her chest, a family friend gently pried his fingers from her neck and shoulders so that he could be wrested into the hands of his biological father. With that, he was whisked away from all he had known to join a new home and family. The mandate of the Illinois Supreme Court that he be transferred to the custody of his biological [father] "forthwith" was fulfilled.[11]

In cases like Baby Richard's, courts adhered to the "masculine" value from chapter 4 at the expense of the "feminine" one. The Illinois Supreme Court treated the genetic father's right to pursue a connection with his offspring as absolute, with no regard for the existing relationship between Richard and the adoptive parents who had raised him nearly since birth.

In the other case from the 1990s, Baby Jessica's birth mother, Cara, decided to place Jessica for adoption without telling the genetic father. She listed a different man as the father on the paperwork, and he signed off on the adoption. Just five days after the birth, Cara changed her mind, but she had already signed the papers relinquishing her rights. She then notified the true genetic father, Daniel, and he asserted his parental rights in court. Cara also filed claims in which she argued that her consent to the adoption was invalid. State law required giving a birth mother at least three days after the birth before she signed the final papers relinquishing the child, and Cara had signed after less than two days. She also claimed to have been misled in some way about the papers or the adoption process, but the specifics of those claims aren't clear from the record because the courts never reached them. Cara's claims were mired in procedural technicalities and some murky language in the statute about the three-day waiting period. Daniel's claim, on the other hand, was clear, and he prevailed solely on the basis of being the genetic father. If that had happened within a few weeks of Baby Jessica's birth, then one might welcome at least the outcome of the case as vindicating a birth mother's right to make a fully considered and informed decision about adoption, even though the vindication came through the back door of the father's genetic entitlement. Unfortunately, the courts took two years to resolve the case, and they let the adoptive parents keep the baby in the meantime. The denoument of Baby Jessica's case was thus the same as Baby Richard's: a young child yanked from the only parents she had known on the strength of the biological father's genetic rights.

A third, similar case reached the Supreme Court in 2012 under the title *Adoptive Couple v. Baby Girl*.[12] (The bizarre title is because of some ancient legal customs you can learn about in your first semester if you go to law school.[13]) In that case, Christina Maldonado was pregnant but wanted to break up with her boyfriend, Dusten Brown, and place the baby for adoption with a couple she'd chosen. Dusten wanted to get married. He told Christina that if she wouldn't marry him, he wouldn't pay child support and would prefer to give up his parental rights. He later claimed he'd only said that to pressure her into marrying him. Amazingly, some commenters thought this admission cast him in a favorable light, because he had offered to marry her. Those same commenters also thought it unfair to Dusten that, when he followed through four months after the birth by signing papers to relinquish his parental rights, he didn't realize the baby would be adopted. He assumed Christina would be raising her.[14] As soon as he realized the forms he had signed would allow the girl to be adopted, he tried to revoke the relinquishment of his rights, apparently so he could continue trying to use the now-four-month-old child to coerce his ex-girlfriend into marrying him.

To this point in the story, Dusten had not satisfied the biology-plus-relationship test (he'd never taken care of the baby), but that isn't why he ended up losing his genetic rights under state law. His mistake was refusing to pay child support. States have shown little interest in men's caretaking for their children, which was the focus of the biology-plus-relationship test, but they are very interested in men's pocketbooks. Because Dusten hadn't paid for any of the child's expenses, he lost the right to block the adoption under state law.[15] His case also had some additional procedural twists that we'll examine in chapter 6. The result of those twists for Baby Girl was that she ultimately suffered the disruptions of Baby Jessica and Baby Richard combined. Even though Dusten had waived his genetic rights under state law by failing to pay child support, a lower court initially ruled the adoption agency's procedures were improper for other reasons, so the adoption was invalid. Therefore, like Baby Jessica, Baby Girl was removed from her adoptive home at the age of two and given to Dusten, without regard for her existing relationship with her adoptive parents. Two years later, the Supreme Court disagreed with the lower courts and found the procedures had been adequate. So Baby Girl switched families again at age four, just like Baby Richard. By that time, of course,

Dusten had established a caretaking relationship with Baby Girl, so he satisfied the biology-plus-relationship test. But even at that late stage, as they ordered the second upending of the life of a four-year-old child, the courts ignored the existing relationship. Dusten may have tried to manipulate Christina into marrying him, but that doesn't mean the caretaking relationship he had formed with his daughter by the time the case reached the Supreme Court didn't deserve protection. In the first instance, however, Christina, not Dusten, was the parent who satisfied the biology-plus-relationship test and should have been allowed to decide about the adoption.

Consider, in sum, the options for a pregnant woman who doesn't want the genetic father to acquire parental rights. Perhaps he has abused her, or perhaps she doesn't want to parent with him for some other reason; he might be irresponsible or a bad role model or just someone she doesn't want as her co-parent. I have argued that under the Unwed Father Cases, especially *Lehr v. Robertson,* where Jonathan Lehr tried very hard to claim parental rights but lost anyway, the absence of a caretaking relationship should be fatal to the genetic father's claim to parental rights. Even if I'm wrong, however, the most an unwed father should be able to claim under *Lehr* is the right to be heard in court on the question of what would be best for the child. That was the system New York had in place and the Supreme Court approved in *Lehr.* If Jonathan had sent his postcard to the putative-father registry, he would have been informed of the hearing date for the adoption case and would have been allowed to speak at the hearing. He would *not* have had an automatic right to block the adoption based on his genetic tie to the child. Instead, the court would have asked what was best for the child, which means Lorraine, the birth mother, would have been able to argue her case for why making Jonathan the legal father would not be best. As I mentioned in chapter 2, we don't know what Lorraine's reasons were, and we don't know what reasons the court would have considered acceptable, but at least the court would have considered her arguments.

But courts have ignored those aspects of the Supreme Court's decision in *Lehr* that limit the father's genetic rights. Instead, when they see a mother-child family, with an empty space where they think the father belongs, they dispense entirely with the relationship prong of biology-plus-relationship. That means that, for the pregnant woman who doesn't want the genetic father to acquire rights, the only certain option is to have an abortion (if she can). Otherwise, the best defense is a husband; if the birth mother is already married to another man, a court might allow the husband to displace the genetic father, as in *Michael H.* Depending on what state she lives in, a wife might be able to do the same. Next-best is an adoption plan, again depending on the state. Although genetic fathers generally have the power to block an adoption, there are time limits and other rules, like the requirement to pay child support, that vary by state; it's possible the genetic father, like Dusten Brown, will make a mistake and lose his rights. But no state requires the father to have an actual caretaking relationship with the child in order to have parental rights. No state applies the biology-plus-relationship test when the genetic father seeks rights against the mother. A woman with only herself to offer as the baby's family has virtually no chance of defeating the genetic father's claim if he or the state chooses to assert it. Although the Unwed Father Cases seemed to make a caretaking relationship the touchstone for parental rights, states and lower courts responded by embracing genetic essentialism and fathers' rights, which took away the birth mother's ability to decide who her baby's family should be.

GENETIC ESSENTIALISM AS FAKE SEX EQUALITY

Part of how genetic essentialism has acquired such power in family law is by masquerading as sex equality. Courts and scholars talk about "equality" for biological parents, a sleight of tongue that equates biological motherhood with biological fatherhood, as if gestating and ejaculating were equivalent reproductive functions. While it's true they are biological counterparts and that each creates a biological connection, gestating is a much greater contribution that includes a large social-emotional component—a caretaking relationship. As we saw in chapters 1 and 2, despite this difference between biological motherhood and biological fatherhood, the Supreme Court required the law to make up the difference for biological fathers. The court created a special path for men to do something comparable to gestation: the biology-plus-relationship test. Courts have yet to give such consideration to the disadvantages of female biology. Women are entitled to maternity leave only to the extent Congress grants it, are still paying luxury taxes on tampons, and are now subject to forced pregnancy and childbirth in most of the country. But with the biology-plus-relationship test, men have constitutionally protected parental rights on equal terms with women.

As I explained in chapter 2, my criticism of this double standard doesn't mean I think the Supreme Court should have taken away the biology-plus-relationship test and denied men the ability to acquire parental rights. That would have amounted to giving men the "*Geduldig* treatment" of refusing to take their biology into account when designing the rules for parenthood, just as *Geduldig v. Ailleo* refused to take women's biology into account when designing the rules for the workplace. Instead, a court that cared about sex equality would fix the double standard in the other direction, by overruling *Geduldig*. But giving men parental rights based on genes alone exacerbates the double standard rather than fixing it. The *Geduldig* approach would have said that if the state defines parenthood in terms of gestation and birth, that's just tough luck for men. "Equality" would mean only pregnant persons have initial parental rights at the moment of birth. The better approach, which the Supreme Court used in the Unwed Father Cases, is the biology-plus-relationship test. Under that approach, "equality" means men can have the same parental rights as women, which they achieve by meeting a test that is roughly comparable to how a birth mother achieves her rights. What we have instead is "equality" that insists on men having equal parental rights without having to meet any standard at all. That is fake equality because it ignores an important biological difference for the sake of making sure men can automatically get what women have.

Despite men's having received an unprecedented accommodation of their biological disadvantage, many legal scholars, including feminist scholars, perceive men as discriminated against—or even systematically subordinated to women—when the law requires something more than genes to confer parenthood. Professor Michael Higdon complains that such a rule renders men "powerless" and "at the mercy of the mother," and Professor Martha Davis argues that the old legal maxim—"the husband and wife are one, and the one is the husband"—has been reversed in the law of parenthood, with the law now erasing men's existence. Professor Marjorie Maguire Shultz says modern women's independence from men has led them to "exploit their natural procreative advantages," making men's biological disadvantage "more visible and more distressing." Professor Jeffrey Parness titles an article "Systematically Screwing Dads," a construction in which men who lose parental rights to children they've never met are "screwed"—metaphorically fucked as if they were women.[16] A bar journal offering practice tips for lawyers conveys a similar sense of sexual anxiety. The article is about the importance of using the putative-father registry, because a man who fails to register can lose his automatic genetic rights. The article is titled "The Putative Father Registry: Behold Now the Behemoth," and it opens with this quotation:

Look at the behemoth.
What strength he has in his loins,
What power in the muscles of his belly!
Under the lotus plant he lies,
Hidden among the reeds in the marsh.[17]

Here, the putative-father registry itself is personified as a virile male creature who lies in wait, threatening to cut off the genetic father's . . . well, let's just say his rights. These descriptions of men's grievances don't suggest the loss of an intimate relationship with a treasured child. They suggest anxiety about men losing power. When one group has historically subordinated another, it's easy to confuse the loss of unjustly held power with "reverse discrimination." The claim that equality requires men to have genetic rights to children—or else they will be wrongly subordinated to women—makes that mistake. The biology-plus-relationship test creates equality by leveling nature's field, which is already a better deal than the law gives women when nature disadvantages them. Moreover, as we will see in future chapters, defining parenthood in terms of genes denigrates gestation, which in turn denigrates women as a class and caretaking as an activity.

That is not to say that fathers are all treated fairly in the law of parenthood. Chapter 6 will discuss how certain fathers are treated unfairly and some of what could be done about it. What many reformers want done about it, however, is to keep expanding fathers' genetic rights. What they too often fail to address is that the expansion is paid for in the rights of birth mothers. Perhaps this cost is worth paying if it serves some worthy end, like improving the lives of children, but it shouldn't be papered over with superficial claims of "equal" biological parenthood.

Some feminists believe stronger rights for fathers *would* be better for children, and for women, because having stronger rights might encourage fathers to be more involved in raising their children. Feminists have long been frustrated that even though formal sex equality in the workplace is the law of the land, equality at home—in housework, childcare, and general willingness to sacrifice individual priorities for family ones—has been more elusive. Furthermore, inequality at home makes actual equality at work harder to achieve because women are saddled with the double workload of a full-time job plus primary responsibility at home. Feminists call this quagmire "the stalled revolution"[18] and have pursued two strategies to try to pull out of the stall. One strategy is to keep reforming the workplace. If workplaces were more family-friendly, then perhaps women would be more able to succeed despite inequality at home, and perhaps men would do more at home if they were safe from losing out at work. Everyone would "have it all." The second strategy aims at the home directly by encouraging men to be more involved as fathers. The feminist case for genetic rights is that they are part of the second strategy. The idea is that granting automatic parental rights to genetic fathers sends a message, letting men (and women) know the law sees fathers as real parents.[19] This message is supposed to encourage men to take the steps necessary to meet the biology-plus-relationship test (and force women to let them do so). It follows, hopefully, that men will establish closer relationships with children, and women will get relief from the double load.

Encouraging men to identify more strongly as fathers and to define fatherhood to include caretaking, not just breadwinning, is a worthy cause. However, there are many ways to provide that encouragement. The United States notoriously lags behind other wealthy countries in enacting family-friendly labor laws like paid parental leave and subsidized day care. In contrast, the United States notoriously surpasses other wealthy countries in incarcerating both mothers and fathers. Slight progress has been made in preserving children's relationships with mothers who are in prison, but even less has been done in the face of the mass incarceration of fathers.[20] More prosaically, public men's rooms remain bereft of diaper-changing tables, and community organizations from hospitals to libraries sponsor a raft of week-day-morning parent-toddler programs known as "Mommy and Me" classes, often with government funding. Parallel programs for fathers are about holding down a job while making time to teach your kid to throw a baseball.[21] After divorce, a mother's custodial time with children is treated as her obligation while the father's time is his right, to be used at his option.[22] In light of all society could be doing to reshape and support fatherhood in ways that would also support mothers and children, it is premature to reach for genetic rights, which shift power from women to men and define fatherhood in the narrowest possible terms.

It's also not clear why automatic rights should be expected to encourage greater involvement by fathers. That's not how incentives usually work. One does not give the reward first in the hope it will somehow induce the desired behavior. In fact, we've already seen the results when this cart precedes this horse. Similar arguments about getting fathers more involved with children were the basis for equalizing custody after divorce. "Equalizing" meant giving men joint custody and equal time, regardless of how much caretaking they'd done before the divorce. The result was "a legal system that empower[ed] fathers" by giving them extra leverage in divorce litigation.[23] Women who had been primary caretakers were put in a position to bargain away property and support rights in order to keep their children. Courts also started holding mothers responsible for the father-child relationship.[24] When a father who had performed little caretaking before divorce was nonetheless awarded equal custody, courts blamed the mother if the children resisted going with the father.

Similarly, when courts define fatherhood in terms of genes, they demand that women facilitate fatherhood even while they are still pregnant. Courts criticize pregnant women for failing to alert men of the fact of pregnancy or keep them apprised of their fetus's whereabouts. They worry that if courts don't impose these duties on women, men will be "forced" to stalk their ex-lovers in order to keep tabs on their reproductive property.[25] This threat is based on the canard that a man who has sex with a woman thereby acquires an automatic right to the child she may bear. That's an assumption the law should reject. Encouraging men to embrace fatherhood and caretaking is a worthy goal, but automatic genetic rights are not the way to go about it. Even if they were, feminists shouldn't promote this strategy without acknowledging the cost it deducts from women's rights as birth mothers.

THE COST: SINGLE MOTHERS' RIGHTS

Ordinarily, there's nothing wrong with states protecting individual rights more strongly than the federal Constitution requires. For example, we saw in chapter 1 that even after the Supreme Court said, in *Geduldig v. Aiello,* that pregnancy discrimination wasn't sex discrimination, the court allowed Congress to ban pregnancy discrimination. The court also allowed California to mandate maternity leave in *CalFed v. Guerra,* and it allowed Congress to enact the Family and Medical Leave Act, which includes a range of benefits but was largely aimed at helping women with their double burden of work and family responsibilities.[26] Legislatures are allowed to protect women from sex discrimination in the form of pregnancy discrimination, even though the Supreme Court doesn't think the Constitution requires them to do so. So states can go further than the Constitution requires to protect our individual rights. But parental rights are not strictly individual rights. They are rights held in relation to another person, the child, and they are inherently shared with anyone else who has parental rights to the same child. It's one thing for a state to recognize rights more generously than the Constitution requires, but it's another to do so at the expense of other people's constitutionally protected rights.[27] When state courts expand the rights of genetic fathers, they do so at the expense of birth mothers.

When a genetic father claims parental rights, courts don't even recognize that the birth mother has rights at stake; much less do they protect her rights. When courts see a single mother with a child, they see a blank space waiting to be filled with a father. For example, in 1992, the California Supreme Court faced the question of what happens when a father has failed to satisfy the relationship prong of biology-plus-relationship because the mother has denied him access to the child.[28] In *Adoption of Kelsey S.*, Kelsey's birth mother, Kari, had decided during her pregnancy to place her baby for adoption, a decision the genetic father, Rickie, opposed. Rickie wanted to raise the child. As usual, we don't know why Kari wanted to place the baby for adoption rather than raise him with Rickie, because the court considered that information to be irrelevant. Rather, the court said it would be "improper to make the father's rights contingent on the mother's wishes." The court thus treated the question of legal fatherhood as entirely separate from the relationship between mother and child—paternity was a blank space to be filled. On this view, even in the context of infant adoption, a man's interest in his genetic child grants him an automatic legal right against the child's mother. Even a man who becomes a father through a one-night stand thereby acquires complete parental rights to any resulting child, based on genes alone, so long as he files the right paperwork and is willing to pay child support. Parental rights protect a form of genetic ownership rather than an existing parental relationship.

Kelsey S. presented one of the questions left open after the Unwed Father Cases: whether the father must have an actual relationship with the child in order to block an adoption, or whether it's enough that he tried to form a relationship but the birth mother rejected him. The choice between adoption and keeping a child is a choice that parents, and only parents, get to make. Although colloquially we sometimes refer to "giving up" a baby for adoption, placing a child for adoption is not at all equivalent to abandoning it. It is a parenting decision, not a failure to parent. Adoption can also include the birth parent's choosing the adoptive parents, staying in contact over the years, and giving the child the eventual option to meet the birth parent. I argued in chapter 2 that the most logical reading of the Unwed Father Cases is that a man who lacks any relationship with the child also lacks parental rights, so if the mother denies access, he won't be able to acquire rights. Instead, the birth mother's existing relationship with the child should give her the superior right to make parental decisions for the child, including the decision to place the child for adoption.

In other contexts, courts recognize that giving rights over a child to someone who is not a legal parent takes rights away from the legal parent. The Supreme Court made this clear in a 2000 case called *Troxel v. Granville*.[29] Tommie Granville had two daughters with her partner, Brad Troxel. When they separated, Brad moved in with his parents, Jenifer and Gary, so the girls saw their grandparents frequently during their father's weekend visitation time. Two years after the separation, Brad died. At first, Tommie kept bringing the girls to see the Troxels frequently. Eventually, however, she became engaged to a man who also had children from a prior marriage, and she wanted to focus on the new family. She told Jenifer and Gary she would still bring the girls to visit, but not so often and without staying overnight, because they needed to spend more time with their new stepfather and stepsiblings. Jenifer and Gary sued in Washington state court for a visitation order.

Usually, there are only two circumstances when a judge takes over this kind of decision from parents. One is if the judge finds the parent to be unfit, meaning the parent has abused or neglected the child and it isn't safe to leave the parent in charge. In that case, the judge might appoint a guardian or foster parent, or the judge herself might make decisions about the child's life. The other circumstance is when the parents are divorced or were never married and they can't agree. Then a judge will decide using the "best interests of the child" standard. In short, most of the time, parents are allowed to decide what's best for their children, including how often they ought to visit their grandparents. Judges have a role only when the parents are proven inadequate or they reach an impasse.

Nonetheless, the Washington judge mostly sided with the Troxels. He did so because the state had passed a law telling judges they could issue a visitation order *whenever* they thought it would be in the best interests of a child. Such laws are commonly known as grandparent visitation laws, but the Washington law actually allowed *anyone* to file for visitation and ask the judge to second-guess the parents. Applying the best-interests standard, the judge in *Troxel* opined that, in general, it was good for kids to spend time with their grandparents. He also thought the girls would benefit from seeing their cousins more and from some unspecified musical opportunities at the Troxels' house. He therefore ordered Tommie to bring the girls to visit their grandparents one full weekend a month, one week in the summer, and on Jenifer and Gary's birthdays.

On appeal, the Supreme Court struck down that order, holding the judge had gone too far in second-guessing Tommie's decisions. The views of a parent, said the Supreme Court, must receive "special weight" in a dispute with an outsider, even a grandparent. Although the trial court had applied the familiar "best interests of the child" standard, that standard properly applies only in disputes between adults who each have equal claim to the child, such as two legal parents. A stronger constraint binds judges when they interfere over the objection of the only legal parent. A court cannot overrule the parent just because the judge disagrees about what's best for the child. The court must, according to *Troxel,* give special weight to "the wishes of the parent or parents." That still leaves plenty of room for grandparents to seek visitation if the parent tries to cut them out completely. But the parent's decision is at least entitled to some deference from the judge.

One thing that ought to be clear after *Troxel* is that "the wishes of the child's parent or parents" have equal weight regardless of whether it is "parent" or "parents" who are making the decisions. However, because states have ignored the relationship prong and defined fatherhood in terms of genes, no state has applied *Troxel* to the situation in which the birth mother wants to prevent the genetic father from obtaining rights. At the time of birth, the birth mother often is the only parent with constitutionally protected rights, since she and no one else has met the biology-plus-relationship test. In *Troxel,* the Supreme Court made clear that Tommie's rights as a single mother were the same as the rights she and Brad held jointly while he was alive. A widow and her children are a family. There is no blank space that needs to be filled at the behest of the state or anyone else. Like a widow with children, an unmarried mother and her newborn child are also a family. When a genetic father has not met the biology-plus-relationship test—such as with a one-night stand—the mother is like Tommie Granville. She has fully protected parental rights, which she shares with no one. The genetic father, on the other hand, is similar in some ways to a grandparent. He is a person society considers special with respect to the child, but he doesn't have constitutionally protected parental rights.[30] Following *Troxel* would mean deferring to the birth mother about whether the genetic father should join the family—or at least giving her view "special weight."[31] When states ignore *Troxel* in this context and instead give the genetic father automatic parental rights, they deny the single mother and child the status of being a family.

Following *Troxel* would also mean giving a single mother at least as much deference as states still give to married couples through the marital presumption. When the mother is married and her husband is willing to claim the child as his own, courts will sometimes refuse even to look at genetic evidence from another man. At a minimum, if a purported genetic father tries to claim a child and the married mother objects, the court will consider her objections. In contrast, courts are harshly critical of unmarried women who try to avoid sharing their pregnancies and newborns with genetic fathers. When Professors Mary Burbach and Mary Ann Lamanna analyzed how courts talk about unwed mothers' and fathers' rights, the most common theme they identified was "Lie/Deception" by the mother, meaning courts criticized birth mothers for lying about the child's paternity or hiding the pregnancy or adoption from the genetic father.[32] One court expressly rejected the holding of the Unwed Father Cases, that a caretaking relationship is needed to establish parental rights, because establishing that relationship requires the mother's cooperation. The court said it was unwilling to make the father's rights "dependent upon the whim of the unwed mother."[33] The court thus assumed that an unwed mother makes parenting decisions on the basis of "whims." Under *Troxel*, that's an unconstitutional assumption: parents must be presumed to act in the best interests of their children. This disparity—calling an unmarried woman fickle and deceitful for objecting to a father's genetic claims, while giving the law's protection to a married couple who close ranks against the wife's lover who is in fact the genetic father of her child—reveals a commitment to the patriarchal family rather than to caretaking relationships. A husband's (biologically false) acknowledgment of paternity counts for more than a single woman's parental rights.

THE WAGES OF GENETIC ESSENTIALISM: PARENTAL RIGHTS FOR RAPISTS

The most extreme manifestation of the genetic definition of parenthood is when male rapists are given parental rights to the children who result from their crimes. For example, in a Pennsylvania case, a woman who had been raped repeatedly since childhood by her stepfather saw him convicted, but when she tried to terminate his parental rights to the resulting child, she was met with a law requiring her to have a replacement father lined up and ready to adopt before the genetic father could be cut off.[34] In a Massachusetts case, a judge *ordered* a convicted rapist to establish paternity, apparently in the belief that suing his victim for parental rights would be a good way for him to take responsibility for his crime.[35] A rapist's paternity suit can serve as a tool for rapists to control their victims, such as by offering to drop the paternity suit in exchange for the victim's dropping her criminal complaint. Or it can lay the groundwork for seeking full or partial custody. For example, a teenager in Louisiana gave birth to a daughter after being raped in 2005. Although no charges were ever brought on the violent aspects of the rape she alleged, simple math proves it was statutory rape. Six years later, the rapist found out about the child. He established paternity and won shared custody. In 2021, when the girl was about the age her mother had been when she was raped, the girl started alleging that her father was abusing her. In early 2022, a doctor "confirmed that there was evidence of forced entry congruent with sexual assault."[36] The father, however, alleged that the mother had bought a cell phone for her daughter, which the judge had apparently instructed her not to do. Treating the mother's disobedience to this ridiculous order as a greater parental sin than allegedly sexually assaulting one's child, the judge awarded sole custody to the father.

Amid public outcry over such cases, Congress enacted the Rape Survivor Child Custody Act of 2015, which offers modest grants to states if they put in place "a law that allows the mother of any child that was conceived through rape to seek court-ordered termination of the parental rights of her rapist with regard to that child."[37] To receive the RSCCA grant money, the state must make conception-by-rape an explicit basis for termination of a father's parental rights under a standard of proof called "clear and convincing evidence," which is easier for a victim of rape to meet in court than the proof beyond a reasonable doubt required for a criminal conviction. A few states already had such laws, and more than half have them now because of Congress's encouragement. Others require a criminal conviction of rape to trigger termination of parental rights, and a few have only generic rules for when parents can be declared unfit.[38]

The RSCCA responded to a problem that shouldn't exist in the first place. The Supreme Court already rejected the idea that genes alone should give rise to parental rights. That's why it created the biology-plus-relationship test in the Unwed Father Cases. States have nonetheless defined parenthood in terms of genes, which opens the door to rapists' paternity claims. The RSCCA, unfortunately, accepts this definition of parenthood as given. It treats genetic fathers as automatically entitled to parental rights, which can only be cut off by proving the rape in court. Consider how the RSCCA applies to cases of what Susan Estrich sarcastically called "real rape": the stranger-with-a-knife scenario, which is what Congress had in mind with the RSCCA.[39] In this scenario, the pregnant victim who gives birth will have custody by default at the time of birth. Under the biology-plus-relationship test, the genetic father shouldn't have any rights until he establishes a caretaking relationship with the child. The victim should thus be able to protect herself from his paternity claim by denying him access to the child. Instead, in the cases that inspired the RSCCA, the rapists were able to file paternity claims and win parental rights based solely on genes. The RSCCA could have helped the victims by re-affirming the biology-plus-relationship test and telling states to stop giving fathers parental rights on the basis of genes alone. Instead, the RSCCA accepted the premise that genes alone give a man rights to the child, which can only be taken away by special legislation and a court hearing. The RSCCA gives the mother a defense if the rapist files a paternity suit, which is a step in the right direction. But if he doesn't, and she decides to keep the child, she must either sue him herself and prove the rape or live with the constant possibility that he will assert his rights. If she wants to place the child for adoption, she may first have to go to court to prove her RSCCA claim. The RSCCA unfortunately confirms and thereby strengthens the background assumption that genetic fathers have automatic parental rights.

Despite this shortcoming, the RSCCA is an improvement on the genetic definition of parenthood because it doesn't pretend that biological motherhood and biological fatherhood are "equal." The RSCCA is conspicuously sex-specific: it protects only women victims of rapes by men. Yet women sometimes commit rape, of both the statutory and the forcible kind, and they sometimes become pregnant as a result. If the point of the RSCCA were that *all* rapists are unfit to parent, Congress would have told states to terminate the rights of rapist mothers, not just rapist fathers. It didn't. Or, if the point were that all rape victims should be able to keep and raise their resulting children without interference from their rapists, the law would have extended that right to men who become fathers from being raped. It didn't do that either. What, then, is the point? The RSCCA is sex-specific because its aim is to protect *the birth mother* from continued domination by a rapist. Congress's official findings in support of enacting the RSCCA included:

(8) A rapist pursuing parental or custody rights forces the survivor to have continued interaction with the rapist, which can have traumatic psychological effects on the survivor, making it more difficult for her to recover.

(9) These traumatic effects on the mother can severely negatively impact her ability to raise a healthy child.

(10) Rapists may use the threat of pursuing custody or parental rights to coerce survivors into not prosecuting rape, or otherwise harass, intimidate, or manipulate them.[40]

Nowhere did Congress suggest that its concern was for the child or for the father's fitness as a parent, except indirectly in finding (9). Rather, Congress sought to prevent the father from using his genetic rights to further invade the mother's life. Unlike most parentage laws, the RSCCA recognizes that a paternity suit brought by a genetic father is not just about the child. It is also about the mother's parental rights and the course of her life. Awarding automatic parental rights to a genetic father inherently diminishes the preexisting parental rights of the birth mother.

Male and female rapists' parental rights are asymmetric under the RSCCA because biological parenthood is asymmetric. A genetic tie is different from a relationship created through gestation and should not give rise to the same parental rights. But states have ignored that difference and given fathers rights based on genes alone. Only in the most extreme cases, where the mother can prove the conception resulted from rape, has Congress stepped in to protect the mother's rights.

When a teenaged boy becomes a biological father through statutory rape, the question arises whether he must pay child support to his rapist. The universal rule is that he must, and men have also been ordered to pay child support after being forcibly raped when they were drugged or unconscious.[41] Many commenters have bemoaned the unfairness of this legal rule, but I cannot find any who propose that the teenaged father should instead be given custody by default. That, I hope, sounds cruel and absurd, but it is the same default used for pregnant female victims who forego or can't have an abortion. A female rape victim has custody by default as soon as the baby is born. But when the male is the victim, the female rapist routinely retains custody of the resulting child.[42] Imagine if the RSCCA made things "equal" by demanding the same approach for female victims. The state would reassure the pregnant rape victim that her rapist would take custody of the child immediately after birth. That would also be cruel and absurd. Why? Because regardless of who raped whom, the mother's parental relationship exists at the time of birth in a way the father's does not, and taking away the baby she bore in order to hand it over her rapist is an outrage. The female victim has custody by default, but so does the female perpetrator, because the two situations are crucially different. Imposing a rapist father on his victim and child is wrong in a way that allowing a female rapist to keep her child is not.

The asymmetry of the RSCCA is an increasingly rare instance of the law recognizing that birth mothers and genetic fathers are differently situated at the time of birth. Elsewhere, the shibboleth of "equality" for biological parents prevails. Relational feminism explains why. As we saw in chapter 4, the legal system's primary value is preserving autonomy, and it helps people use their autonomy to pursue new connections through institutions like marriage. The biology-plus-relationship test modified the old parentage rules in order to serve a different value: protecting existing relationships, which is an unfamiliar and less valued goal for the law. In the course of implementing the test, lower courts transformed it into something more familiar: a tool for pursuing new connections, with genes substituting for marriage as the basis for the right to connect to a child. The collateral damage of invading birth mothers' lives and families didn't even register to courts as a harm, because the courts perceived an empty space where they ought to have seen a family.

SIX

Sidelining Inconvenient Fathers

AS THE LOWER COURTS TRANSFORMED the biology-plus-relationship test from a shield for protecting existing relationships into a sword for forcing new connections, they made genetic fathers' rights strongest against birth mothers but weakest against husbands, adoptive parents, and especially the state itself. When fathers' rights were inconvenient for the state, rights that ought to have existed in theory disappeared in practice. In many situations, states and the federal government continued denying rights to fathers who had raised their children, either on their own or with the mother. They emphasized the father's formally acknowledging the child and paying child support rather than the caretaking the Supreme Court had emphasized in the Unwed Father Cases. The rights that came with genetic fatherhood were thus ratcheted up or down to limit women's independence from men while still denying rights to disfavored men.

FATHERS' RIGHTS AGAINST MOTHERS, BUT NOT AGAINST THE STATE

While states whittled down the relationship prong of biology-plus-relationship to the point where even a rapist could claim parental rights to a child born from the rape, they simultaneously disregarded men's actual caretaking relationships with children. In doing so, they blatantly flouted the Supreme Court's decisions in the Unwed Father Cases. For example, Professor Josh Gupta-Kagan describes a rule in child-protection law called the One-Parent Doctrine:

A child's mother abuses her, state child welfare authorities file a petition in family court seeking custody of the child, and the mother admits her abuse. The child's father lives apart from the mother, has shared custody of his child, and is not responsible for the mother's abuse. The father seeks custody of the child. The father has not been proven unfit, so one would expect the court to grant the father custody. But under the "One-Parent Doctrine," adjudicating the mother alone unfit gives the family court authority to place the child in foster care, severely invading the father and child's constitutionally protected relationship.[1]

The situation Gupta-Kagan describes here is nearly identical to *Stanley v. Illinois,* the first of the Unwed Father Cases. An unmarried mother is unable to care for her children (in *Stanley* because she was dead; in a more typical case because she has been accused of neglect). The father has an established relationship with the child, but the state nonetheless takes the child, places her or him in foster care, and insists it has the right to do so without so much as a hearing for the father. This complete disregard for fathers' relationships with their children has been plainly unconstitutional since *Stanley* was decided in 1972. Yet it was standard practice in family courts until at least 2014, when the Michigan Supreme Court told its family courts to cut it out, kicking off a trend of courts around the country belatedly recognizing the One-Parent Doctrine as an egregious abuse.[2]

You may be wondering how state courts could get away with ignoring Supreme Court precedent for decades. Professor Gupta-Kagan tried to answer that question.[3] The most important reasons he found were lawyers—more precisely, the absence of lawyers. We saw in chapter 4 that, in *Lassiter v. Department of Social Services,* the Supreme Court held parent-child relationships weren't important enough for a parent to be entitled to a free lawyer when the state tried to take away the child. Almost none of the fathers who have lost their children to the One-Parent Doctrine could have paid for a lawyer on their own, and even if they could, the small market for lawyers defending parental rights meant that for many years there were few lawyers with expertise on the topic. States eventually started providing lawyers for poor parents voluntarily (even though *Lassiter* said they didn't have to), but it took decades for this field of legal practice to become fully established. By then, *Stanley* was apparently long forgotten. The direct result of the Supreme Court's denial of the right to counsel in *Lassiter*—because the court deemed relationships less important than freedom—was the unconstitutional denial of untold numbers of fathers' rights under the One-Parent Doctrine.

The state family courts that created and enforced the One-Parent Doctrine were not alone in placing little value on fatherhood. Federal law also disregards the caretaking relationships of fathers with their children. Although the states are in charge of the core of family law—questions of marriage, divorce, and child custody—many federal laws have family-law components. For example, family relationships are important to immigration and citizenship. You probably know that a child born in the United States is automatically an American citizen.[4] When a child is born outside the country to an American parent, the situation is more complicated. Congress has adopted various rules and tinkered with them over time. Traditionally, those rules distinguished between mothers and fathers in their ability to pass citizenship to their children. If you were born outside the US and had only one citizen parent, whether you were a citizen could depend on whether you had an American mother or an American father.

The Supreme Court faced one of the distinctions between mothers' and fathers' ability to transmit their citizenship to their children in a 2017 case called *Sessions v. Morales-Santana,* in which the government was trying to deport Luis Morales-Santana.[5] When Luis was born in 1962, the law in effect at that time allowed an unmarried woman to transmit US citizenship to her child born abroad as long as she was a US citizen who had lived in the US for at least one year before the child's birth. An unmarried father, however, could transmit his US citizenship only if he had lived in the US for at least *ten years* before the birth, and five of those years had to be after he turned fourteen years old. The ten-year residency rule also applied to a female or male US citizen who married a non-citizen and had a child with her or him abroad. The ten-year rule thus applied to married mothers, married fathers, and unmarried fathers, but unmarried mothers were treated differently and needed only one year. In addition, an unwed father had to be formally declared the father, either by a court or by his own sworn affidavit, before the child turned eighteen years old.[6]

Luis's father, José Morales, was born and raised in the United States, but he took a job in the Dominican Republic a few weeks before his nineteenth birthday. That meant he was a few weeks short of having lived in the US for five years after age fourteen. His son Luis was born in the Dominican Republic. José later married Luis's mother and formally acknowledged Luis as his son, and they all moved back to the US when Luis was a teenager. A quarter century later, when Luis was facing deportation, he tried to claim he was a US citizen. When his case reached the Supreme Court, the court struggled to articulate any sensible reason—even a stereotype—for why fathers (and married people) would need all those extra years of absorbing American-ness in order to transmit it to a child. The court's answer was that when one of a child's parents is American and the other is not, Congress imagined the two parents to be competing for the child's patriotism. Congress further imagined that an American parent who had spent more time in the country would be more likely to win that contest. With an unwed mother, on the other hand, Congress thought there was likely no father around to compete, so the child's loyalty to the United States was assured. The Supreme Court objected to this assumption that unwed fathers are always absent from their children's lives, and it held that unmarried mothers and fathers must be able to transmit their American citizenship under the same rules. Unfortunately for Luis, the court made things equal by striking down the one-year rule for unwed mothers instead of extending that rule to unwed fathers. In the mean-time, Congress had changed the rule to require only five years of residency, with at least two years after age fourteen, so that's the rule that now applies to all American parents who have a child abroad with a non-American part-ner. But Luis didn't benefit from that change either because it wasn't retroactive.

Under *Morales-Santana,* as in most family law, a mother and father are on equal footing once they're recognized as legal parents. But as in domestic family law, there's a prior question of *who counts* as a mother or father. Citizenship law, like family law, traditionally considered motherhood to be definitively proven when the mother gave birth to her child. Fatherhood required something more. The Supreme Court considered what that some-thing more could be in a 2001 case, *Nguyen v. Immigration & Naturalization Service.*[7] Tuan Anh Nguyen was the child of an American man, Joseph Boulais, and a Vietnamese woman. Tuan was born in Vietnam, but his mother disappeared shortly after his birth, and Joseph brought him to the United States when he was five years old. At the age of twenty-two, Tuan pleaded guilty to a felony, which prompted the INS to try to deport him. Like Luis Morales-Santana, Tuan tried to avoid deportation by claiming US citizenship. His father Joseph had the requisite years of residency in the US, but Joseph had never formally acknowledged Tuan in a sworn statement. The catch was the requirement that the acknowledgment has to be made before the child turns eighteen. Because Tuan was already twenty-two and Joseph hadn't yet signed the necessary statement, Joseph had missed his chance to make his son a citizen. Tuan argued the law discriminated against male citizens like Joseph by imposing this extra hurdle for transmitting citizenship to their foreign-born children, a hurdle all the more onerous because the ability to jump it had an expiration date.

The circumstances of this case are, again, a lot like *Stanley*. The mother is out of the picture, and the government invokes a statute that means, in effect, that the father's caretaking relationship doesn't matter because he lacks a formal legal tie to the child, either by marriage to the mother or by sworn acknowledgment. As in *Stanley*, the government argued in *Nguyen* that the statute was justified because unwed biological fathers typically don't have meaningful relationships with their children. In *Stanley*, the Supreme Court had said that even if that were often true, the government couldn't assume it was true in every case. The Supreme Court wasn't necessarily bound to follow *Stanley* in *Nguyen*. *Stanley* was about the father's right to custody of the child, and the Constitution arguably gives Congress greater power over the rules for citizenship than it gives states when they are breaking up families. But in *Nguyen*, the government's own argument was that the goal of the statute was to make citizenship depend on whether the child had a meaning-ful family relationship with the citizen parent. The statute requiring formal acknowledgment of paternity *rather than* a lifelong caretaking relationship was thus contrary to the government's stated purpose. To serve that purpose, the Supreme Court should have followed *Stanley* and held in *Nguyen* that the father's actual caretaking relationship with his child made a formal acknowl-edgment unnecessary. That caretaking relationship also eliminated any dif-ference between the mother and father that might exist at the time of birth, in terms of whether they have a meaningful relationship with the child. The statute requiring Joseph to formally acknowledge he was Tuan's father, when he had raised him from birth as a single father, was unfair and served no purpose.

For a bureaucracy like the INS, a rule based on the existence or nonexist-ence of a particular piece of paper (a sworn acknowledgment or a marriage certificate) might be more convenient than a rule that asks whether a parent and child truly had a meaningful relationship. However, the INS routinely probes relationships in order to decide questions of immigration and citizen-ship. For example, you can't secure a green card for your spouse just by pre-senting a copy of your marriage certificate. The INS will demand documenta-tion to prove the relationship is "real"—items like wedding photos and joint bank statements. If INS officials are suspicious, they may question you and your spouse in separate rooms about details of your relationship, or they may show up at your house on an unexpected morning to make sure the guest bed hasn't been slept in. Proving whether a father participated in raising a child is easier than proving whether a marriage is sincere.[8] Congress didn't adopt the rule at issue in *Nguyen* to save the INS the trouble of investigating facts. Rather, Congress conceived of fatherhood as a matter of the father choosing to acknowledge the child, not as a caretaking relationship.

The majority of the Supreme Court in *Nguyen* had a similar idea about the importance of the father's formal acknowledgment of the child. The majority cited statistics about the number of American men who travel abroad, especially young men in the military. The court cast these men as the nation's prodigal sons, suggesting that both they and the country needed to be protected from claims for citizenship by the children they leave strewn about the globe. The court's priority was to ensure that American men retained the ability to *refuse* to acknowledge their biological children. This priority tracks with Professor Karst's idea from chapter 4 that acknowledgment of paternity is the most valuable kind of parental intimacy precisely because it is freely chosen by the father. The *Nguyen* court treated parental rights as a matter of a man's choice to pursue a connection with the child or not. The court's desire to protect that choice outweighed any appreciation it may have had for Joseph Boulais's lifelong caretaking relationship with his son.[9] The court therefore upheld the law defining fatherhood as a matter of a formal acknowledgment rather than a caretaking relationship, and it denied Tuan's bid for citizenship. Federal law under *Nguyen,* like state law under the One-Parent Doctrine, places no value on fathers' caretaking relationships with their children.

We saw in chapter 5 that a birth mother who wants to raise her child on her own has virtually no defense against a genetic father who wants parental rights to the child. Congress even had to pass a law prodding states to take automatic parental rights away from rapists. If a woman gives birth to a child fathered by a man who isn't her spouse, but she wants to raise the child with her spouse, it's her spouse's claim under the marital presumption, not hers, that has a chance of prevailing against an outside genetic father. But the genetic father's rights are much weaker when his opponent is the state rather than the mother. A genetic father with no other tie to the child can take half the mother's custody rights on the strength of his genes alone, but *Nguyen* and the One-Parent Doctrine allow the government to disregard not just his genes but also his caretaking, even when the father is a single parent like Joseph Boulais. A system that cared about protecting meaningful relationships would reverse this ranking between the mother and the state because, if anything, the mother's rights to the child should be stronger than the state's. If the father's rights are variable, they should be weakest against the mother but strongest against the state, and strongest of all in a case like *Nguyen* where the child has no other parent.

FATHERS' RIGHTS AND UNFAIR
ADOPTION PRACTICES

When the birth mother wants to place a newborn for adoption but the genetic father wants to raise the child, the birth mother and the state are typically on the same side, in favor of the adoption. Here the law of parenthood faces a conflict in its priorities. On the one hand, genetic essentialism—the idea that genes are the most important element of a parent-child relationship—demands respect for the father's claim against the mother if he wants to block the adoption. On the other hand, prospective adoptive parents generally have more money and higher status than birth parents, which means they can better navigate the legal system and lobby for rules that protect their interests. In addition, once a child has been placed with adoptive parents, their caretaking relationship also deserves protection. After the nation watched Baby Richard crying and screaming as he was pulled from his adoptive mother's arms, adoption agencies and adoptive parents lobbied states to find ways to terminate the rights of genetic fathers efficiently and permanently. The pressure to facilitate adoption was intensified by the scarcity of available infants. The first Unwed Father Case was decided in 1972, just a year before *Roe v. Wade* recognized the right to abortion. The contraceptive pill had become widely available, and the stigma of unmarried motherhood was declining rapidly, leading more women, especially White women, to keep their children rather than place them for adoption. (Black women had long been much more likely to keep an unplanned child.)[10] Despite misplaced rhetoric about the nobility of "saving" a child through adoption,[11] adoptable infants are much in demand, and the rights of genetic fathers are a hindrance on the supply.

Many states responded to this situation and to cases like Baby Richard's by cutting back on the ability of genetic fathers to block or disrupt adoptions.[12] States still defined fatherhood in terms of genes, but they made it procedurally tricky for a father to assert his rights (for example by requiring that he put himself on a putative-father registry) when the mother wanted to place the baby for adoption. Courts could then blame unwed fathers themselves for losing their genetic rights by not following the rules. That's what the Supreme Court did in *Lehr v. Robertson* from chapter 2. Jonathan Lehr had gone to great effort to try to obtain parental rights. He hired lawyers and investigators and filed a paternity case. But he didn't put himself on the putative-father registry, which the court mockingly pointed out he could have done just by "mailing a postcard" to the right government office.[13] The point of the postcard, of course, was to inform the courts of his claim, so they wouldn't grant an adoption without giving him a chance to be heard. But the court that granted the adoption in *Lehr* knew about his claim. The judge just decided to ignore it because Jonathan hadn't made it known with a suitably addressed postcard. Although courts are reputed to be sticklers for procedure, they typically disapprove when one party pounces on such a small technicality to avoid dealing with the merits of a case. But that's the example the *Lehr* Supreme Court set for lower courts dealing with unwed fathers.

In addition to postcard mandates, the new procedures for a father who wanted to block an adoption featured short deadlines, lack of notice about pending adoptions, and other legal technicalities unlikely to be fully understood or complied with by any but legally savvy or well-represented fathers.[14] States varied in how difficult it was for a father to claim genetic rights, so adoption agencies often advised their clients to ensure that births took place in the most adoption-friendly states. This practice, known as "forum shopping," defeats the point of a putative-father registry, since the father can't register with the state if he doesn't know in which state the child will be born. In addition, in many states, the test for parenthood became not "biology-plus-relationship" but "biology-plus-paying-child-support." We saw an example with Dusten Brown in *Adoptive Couple v. Baby Girl*.[15] Under state law, Dusten could have claimed automatic parental rights without any caretaking relationship, as long as he had helped pay for the costs of the pregnancy and birth. But because he had refused to pay, telling the birth mother, Christina, that she had to marry him first, he didn't qualify for rights under state law. Making rights contingent on payment makes it harder for poor men to claim rights. With these hurdles in place, states could define fatherhood in terms of genes while in reality sidelining poor genetic fathers in newborn adoptions.

The most prominent examples of unfair adoption practices are in cases governed by the Indian Child Welfare Act, known as ICWA.[16] The historic, genocidal removal of children from Native families is well documented. It includes the boarding schools mentioned in chapter 3, which were expressly intended to destroy Indian tribes by denying them the right to raise their children. This history convinced Congress in 1978 to enact ICWA, which provides extra protections when Indian children are removed from their birth families. In addition to those procedural protections for parents, ICWA gives tribes the right to weigh in on adoptions of Indian children. The Supreme Court most recently interpreted ICWA in Dusten Brown's case, *Baby Girl*. As I mentioned in chapter 5, his case had some extra procedural twists; those twists came from ICWA. Under ICWA, Dusten should have received much greater procedural protections before he signed away his parental rights. In particular, recall that Dusten signed the papers relinquishing his claim to the child while he was under the impression that Christina would be keeping the baby, not that the baby would be adopted by strangers. His motives for making that distinction were unsavory: he wanted to use the child to press Christina into marriage. But under ICWA his consent to the adoption was invalid if he didn't fully understand it, and that being the law, he should have received the benefit of it. ICWA also would have given Dusten's tribe rights to object to the adoption. The Supreme Court, however, read ICWA narrowly so it didn't apply to Dusten's case.

If you already knew something about the *Baby Girl* case, you were probably annoyed by how I described it in chapter 5. I didn't mention ICWA at all, instead emphasizing Dusten's manipulative behavior. I didn't tell you Dusten was a citizen of the Cherokee nation, which backed his efforts to prevent an Indian child from being adopted by a White family. In a racist and shabbily reasoned decision by Justice Samuel Alito, the Supreme Court limited ICWA's scope and stopped just short of striking the law down entirely. The court sent Baby Girl back to her White adoptive parents without any consideration of her best interests, even though by then she had been in Dusten's custody from age two to age four. The chapter 5 version of this story emphasized the dynamics between Dusten and Christina, the birth mother, while this chapter is concerned with the Supreme Court's disregard for the interests of both Dusten and his tribe. Both versions are partial, tendentious, and true. The chapter 5 version might ring especially true for Christina, who also had Native ancestry but identified as Hispanic and who chose the adoptive parents in part because of their shared religious beliefs. I stand by my argument from chapter 5 that strong rights for genetic fathers give them too much power over birth mothers, and that Dusten's behavior in trying to make Christina marry him is an example of why that's bad.

However, *given* that the law gives the genetic father the right to block an adoption even if he doesn't have a caretaking relationship with the child, it is also unfair to Dusten that he lost this right because he was confused about the papers he was signing. This is the trap I talked about in chapter 2, in which disadvantaged men are subordinated by being denied privileges that other men receive—in this case, the ability to exert control over the child and the birth mother based on genes alone. In this version of the trap, the law first declares what all men are supposedly entitled to expect, the right to claim paternity by virtue of their genes alone. But men who can't pay child support or hire lawyers to navigate the courts and check the paperwork for them lose out on this right. That seems (and is) unfair to disadvantaged men. The system thus pits the class-based unfairness of the procedural hurdles confronting men against the sex-based unfairness to women of defining fatherhood in terms of genes in the first place. The trick is to solve both those problems at once rather than solve the problem of procedures that are unfair to genetic fathers by exacerbating the problem for birth mothers of parental rights based only on genes.

Although ICWA is the only time Congress has admitted it, adoption has a long association with the wrongful removal of children from poor and minority families. Black children weren't considered adoptable by White families until the mid-to-late twentieth century, but they were nonetheless removed from their parents for other reasons, including post–Civil War "apprenticeships" that were slavery in all but name.[17] A "child-saving" movement of the nineteenth and early twentieth centuries was based on the belief that children from poor or immigrant families could be saved by being raised in institutions or in "better" homes.[18] The disproportionate removal of poor children and children of color continues today and includes both pressure to relinquish newborns for adoption and state intervention in the name of protecting children.

One example of the pressure birth mothers are under in the adoption process is that in the United States, a birth mother's consent to adoption can become irrevocable in as little as a few days; other countries allow as much as six months for her to change her mind.[19] Birth mothers in the US are thus under unique pressure to make a quick decision, and they are not always fully informed about some of the complexities of the process. Even the stated waiting period may be misleading. Consider a scenario based on a case in Louisiana: Immediately after the birth (perhaps while still under the influence of medication), a birth mother signs forms relinquishing the baby so it can be placed with the prospective adoptive parents right away. She is reassured that she can withdraw her consent to the adoption for up to thirty days after the birth. What she is unlikely to understand or be told is that "withdraw consent" is not the same as "get the baby back." It may mean only that she can appear at the adoption hearing and *argue* it would be best for the baby to be with her.[20] In other words, she will have to convince the judge to choose her—most likely a young, poor, unmarried woman who got pregnant accidentally and has already expressed doubts about her own ability to parent by signing the relinquishment papers—over the prospective adoptive parents, who've been evaluated by the agency and found to be stable, financially secure, and in all ways prepared to care for the child.

When women look for help navigating this process, or even just finding food and shelter during their pregnancies, they often encounter "crisis pregnancy centers." CPCs are best known as "fake abortion clinics" that pretend to offer women's health-care services but instead try to steer women away from abortion. Some CPCs also serve as fronts for Christian adoption agencies that use heavy-handed tactics to make sure women follow through on their adoption plans.[21] CPC volunteers might, for example, offer a pregnant woman a place to stay, but they thereby make her dependent on them, and they may threaten her with eviction if she wavers in her commitment to adoption. Birth mothers who rely on CPCs have also reported being promised regular updates about the child after the adoption, without being told those promises are unenforceable.[22] When one woman called her "counselor" from the hospital to ask if she could bring the baby home instead of turning it over to the adoption agency, the response was, "You're the one who spread your legs and got pregnant out of wedlock. You have no right to grieve for this baby."[23] This statement reflects the belief of some Christian proponents of adoption that an unmarried mother has no rights to her child. They claim the Bible uses the word *orphan* to mean a child without a father, from which they conclude God doesn't want unwed mothers to have any rights.[24]

The child-welfare system too often seems to agree, removing children from mothers whose alleged neglect of their children boils down to being single and poor.[25] A child-welfare system has an important role to play in protecting children from violent, abusive parents. In chapter 3, we saw the horrible injustice of the state's failure to act to protect Joshua DeShaney from his father, who beat his small son senseless and gave him severe, permanent brain damage. Most of the child-welfare caseload, however, consists of cases of "neglect" rather than "abuse." Again, in some of the neglect cases, children are in real danger, such as when the parent is so incapacitated by a drug addiction that she can't keep the child safe. Ideally, of course, society would prevent as many of those cases as possible by providing health care to prevent and treat addiction. A fence at the edge of a cliff is better than an ambulance down in the valley, but in American politics, fences are "socialism," and the child-welfare system functions at best as an ambulance.[26]

In many cases, however, child-welfare authorities remove children from their parents unnecessarily. Indeed, authorities are much more likely to remove a child from her home in response to an allegation of neglect than in response to an allegation of physical or sexual abuse.[27] For example, in the congressional proceedings leading up to the enactment of ICWA, Congress found that only 1 percent of removals of Indian children from their homes were due to allegations of abuse. The remaining 99 percent were for "neglect" or "social deprivation." The most common form of "neglect" was that the child was being cared for by an extended family network, rather than exclusively by a nuclear family consisting of a mother and a father. State officials believed that being cared for by extended kin "would cause Indian children to be confused about their own gender roles and create unhealthy role-modeling."[28] States were literally removing Native children from their families and putting them in White foster homes because the children had too many adults taking care of them.

Conversely, too little adult supervision is also a common basis for accusations of parental neglect. In chapter 3, I described the free-range–kids movement, whose proponents often clash with authorities over how much supervision kids need, and sometimes the authorities come off looking absurd. For example, in 2014, a woman in Florida was accused of neglect for letting her seven-year-old son walk less than half a mile home from a park. (He was even carrying a cell phone.) Free rangers would say the mom is in the best position to judge her child's abilities. But being able to perfectly calibrate your child's independence to his abilities is a luxury some parents don't have. That same year, another mother was similarly accused in South Carolina for leaving her nine-year-old daughter at a nearby playground during a few of the mother's shifts working at McDonald's. (The daughter also carried a cell phone.) That mother had also determined that her daughter could handle herself on the playground, but it wasn't the mother's ideal arrangement. Rather, it was a necessity created by a lack of childcare options and the demands of her job. Poor parents are much more likely to run afoul, out of necessity, of child-welfare agencies' over-zealous rules about constant supervision.

Parents lose their children to the foster-care system for many other reasons related to poverty. Perhaps the parent's apartment is too small, without a separate bedroom for each child; or the apartment is too dirty, and the state would rather take the child away than send someone to clean it; or the stress of poverty makes the parent impatient and quick to snap at or spank the child; or there's not enough food in the house; or the wiring is exposed; or the railings on the balcony are loose.[29] The best way to protect children from most of what the law currently classifies as parental neglect would be to eliminate poverty.

The system's disrespect for the integrity of poor families extends beyond the reasons for removing children to include court proceedings that also deny poor parents their rights. For example, even under ICWA's heightened protections, some participants in the child-welfare system have little regard for Indian parents' procedural rights. In 2015, the Oglala and Rosebud Sioux won an order from a federal court against a South Dakota judge and other state officials for shocking procedural abuses in cases removing Indian children from their parents. The judge and state prosecutors had illegally denied Indian parents the right to counsel, routinely falsified court documents, and held improper, off-the-record discussions.[30] The facts of *Baby Girl* illustrate some less extreme kinds of resistance to ICWA in state-court proceedings. The adoption agency in *Baby Girl* was supposed to notify the Cherokee tribe promptly of the pending adoption, but the agency dragged its feet and didn't notify the tribe until after placing Baby Girl in the custody of the adoptive parents in another state. When the agency sent the notice, it misspelled Dusten's name and listed the wrong date for his birth.[31] Those errors led Cherokee officials to initially conclude the father was not a member of the tribe, which meant their objection to the adoption was delayed. While these errors may have been mere clerical mistakes, critics who know the history behind ICWA have good reason to distrust and instead infer bad faith. Even if not intentional, the mistakes are the sort of shoddy compliance with procedure that suggests lack of regard for ICWA's aims.

The ultimate decision in *Baby Girl* made clear the Supreme Court also disdained ICWA's goals. Couching its decision in vague, unfounded suggestions that ICWA's definition of "Indian child" might be an unconstitutional racial classification, the majority seized on the allegation that Baby Girl was only "3/256 Cherokee."[32] This figure probably understates Baby Girl's Native ancestry, but regardless of its accuracy the figure is irrelevant.[33] To be an "Indian child" is a political status that refers to eligibility for tribal membership. (That's why I've been using *Native* to refer to the racial group but *Indian* to refer to the legal category.) Baby Girl is 100 percent Cherokee in the same sense that Senator Ted Cruz is 100 percent American. Cruz was born in Canada to an American mother and a foreign father. Baby Girl's Cherokee citizenship, like Cruz's American citizenship, came not from her place of birth but from her citizen parent. By harping on Baby Girl's blood quantum, the Supreme Court, as Professor Bethany Berger has written, rejected "the possibility that a child could remain politically Indian after generations of intermarriage"—a rejection that promoted "the assumption that Indian tribes would eventually disappear" due to intermarriage.[34] The court also portrayed being classified as Indian as a burden, since having to comply with ICWA could in theory slow down the adoption process.[35] The real harm, in the court's eyes, was that a White girl was being treated as Indian.[36]

With hostility to ICWA from state courts all the way up to the Supreme Court, the long history of the government wrongfully removing Indian children from their parents and tribes continues. Similar continuing histories loom in the memories of other minority and poor communities. Some of the abusive practices that perpetuate this history fall most heavily on fathers, such as the One-Parent Doctrine, which states use to bypass fathers and place children in foster care based on the mother's alleged abuse or neglect. Similarly, although most of the abusive adoption practices described above are directed at birth mothers, the procedures can also be unfair to fathers, from Jonathan Lehr's mistake with the postcard to Dusten Brown's confusion about what he was signing. Many calls for reform of the adoption system therefore ask for stronger rights for genetic fathers, including perhaps a national putative-father registry.[37] The fact that abusive practices exist, however, doesn't mean stronger genetic rights for fathers are a good solution. Whatever the rules for fatherhood are going to be, they should be fairly enforced and administered. But fatherhood shouldn't be defined in terms of genes alone. Instead, reforms to protect families should rein in the systems that unnecessarily remove children from their homes and discount the importance of existing caretaking relationships with both mothers and fathers.

Regarding adoption, reforms should include ensuring women have access to contraception and abortion, so they can choose whether and when to give birth, and eliminating poverty so no one ever feels compelled to relinquish a child in order to meet the child's basic needs. The adoption process itself must ensure birth mothers receive accurate information and freely consent to the adoption. And birth mothers need a reasonable amount of time to make a final decision about adoption.[38] These sorts of protections for birth mothers would help avoid some of the legal cases that are nominally based on fathers' rights. In many of the contested-adoption cases that have arisen in state courts, the birth mother as well as the genetic father is challenging the adoption. For example, in Baby Jessica's case from chapter 5, the birth mother changed her mind about the adoption just five days after the birth. Few other countries would have denied her rights to the child at that point, but in Iowa she was two days too late. That meant her best option for getting the baby back was to enlist the genetic father. He had never met the child, but his genetic rights hadn't been properly terminated under state law, so his rights were stronger than her right to change her mind.[39] This chain of events is not unusual. Birth mothers actually initiate many of the cases that vindicate fathers' genetic rights, relying on the fathers only because their own rights have been lost.[40] Reforms to adoption procedures, such as giving mothers more time to decide and making sure they understand the process better, would help prevent these cases from arising in the first place.

José Morales, Joseph Boulais, Dusten Brown, and the fathers shut out of their children's lives by the One-Parent Doctrine have all been treated unfairly by the legal system. That unfairness is not merely the unfairness of faceless bureaucracies that inevitably skip a step here or miss a nuance there. As we saw in chapter 3, disrespect for parent-child relationships is often part of race- or class-based subordination. Reforms, however, should support fathers' caretaking relationships with children. They shouldn't make the mistake of trying to cure race- and class-based subordination by adding to gender-based subordination. The genetic definition of parenthood does exactly that by turning the father's genes into a right that trumps the birth mother's caretaking relationship formed through gestation.

SEVEN

Leveling Down to Genes

THE SUPREME COURT'S STARTING point in the Unwed Father Cases was that there was a difference between biological motherhood and biological fatherhood that was relevant to parental rights. The court then created the biology-plus-relationship test to make up for the disadvantage to fathers, who could not establish a caretaking relationship with the child through gestation but could after birth. The court used that test to protect fathers' existing relationships with children when they had them. But lower courts transformed the biology-plus-relationship test and made it a right to claim new connections with children based on genes. These courts also continued to place little value on men's existing relationships with children, as with the One-Parent Doctrine in child-protection law and *Nguyen v. INS* in the law of citizenship. Eventually, the courts even rejected the original starting point: that pregnancy and birth create a parental relationship. The culmination of the legal system's resistance to the biology-plus-relationship test was when courts switched to defining motherhood, like fatherhood, in terms of genes.

In vitro fertilization, in which eggs and sperm are combined in a lab (fertilization occurs *in vitro,* meaning *in glass,* rather than in the body), made it possible to split biological motherhood into two parts, genetic and gestational. This technology led to much debate over which contribution, genes or gestation, is the true essence of biological motherhood. Genes won. When courts today say "biological mother," they mean the genetic mother, not the gestational mother. Even many feminists use the term this way because it is "equal" in the sense meant by sameness equality. The law achieves sameness equality by treating women the same as men to the extent they are the same (both contribute genes) and ignoring the rest (gestation). To define parenthood in terms of genes is, conceptually, the same as defining the rules of the workplace as if workers never got pregnant. In chapter 1, we saw the Supreme Court hold in *Geduldig v. Ailleo* that women were equal at work when they were treated the same as men in the sense that everyone had disability insurance for circumcision but no one had it for childbirth. Similarly, biological parents now have equal rights in the sense that both mothers' and fathers' rights are defined in terms of genes, not gestation. Increasingly, courts consider it improper stereotyping to recognize any difference between a birth mother's and a genetic father's relationship to a newborn, despite the fact that the birth mother gestated, gave birth to, and thereby formed a relationship with the child.

DOWNGRADING GESTATION TO DEFINE
MOTHERHOOD IN TERMS OF GENES

Fear of such stereotyping dominated the opinions in *Nguyen v. INS*.[1] We already saw that in *Nguyen,* the Supreme Court upheld the rule that an unwed father must formally acknowledge his child in order to be considered a legal father who can transmit citizenship. To do so, the court came up with a novel rationale that was different from how the INS had defended the rule. The INS had argued that the citizenship rules for mothers and fathers had to be different for two reasons. The first was the need to prove biological parenthood. A birth certificate, said the INS, proves motherhood but not fatherhood. Fatherhood must be proved by a marriage certificate, a sworn statement, or a court order. This is obviously silly. The best way to prove biological fatherhood is with DNA from a cheek swab. A man's acknowledgment of paternity is proof of his willingness to assume the social role of a father, not of his biological paternity.

The INS's second argument was that citizenship should pass from parent to child only when the two have a "meaningful relationship." A mother, said the INS, has a meaningful relationship with her child by virtue of gestation and birth. A father might not even know the child exists, so something more than biology is needed. Based on the Unwed Father Cases, which made the same assumption that a birth mother necessarily has a meaningful relationship with her child but a genetic father may not, the INS probably thought it was on solid ground so far. The Unwed Father Cases, however, held that in order to determine whether a meaningful relationship exists between father and child, the law should look at the actual relationship, not whether there's a sworn statement on file. That was the whole point of *Stanley v. Illinois*.[2] When Joan Stanley died, Peter Stanley had no official paperwork saying he was the children's father—no marriage license, no sworn statement, only a life together, which the Supreme Court held the state was obliged to respect. In *Nguyen*, however, the INS convinced the Supreme Court to do in immigration law what state courts had already done in domestic family law: replace the relationship prong of biology-plus-relationship with a bureaucratic formality. Rights would be determined by paperwork rather than parenting.

As we saw in chapter 6, the *Nguyen* Supreme Court, led by Justice Kennedy, was more concerned with keeping out the unwanted foreign babies of US soldiers and businessmen than with protecting caretaking fathers like Joseph Boulais, Tuan's father in *Nguyen*. The court thus wanted to uphold the law, but it was wary of being seen to endorse what it saw as a gender stereotype that mothers but not fathers have meaningful relationships with their children. Rather than seem to endorse that view, the court rejected the premise that a *mother* has a meaningful relationship with her child at the time of birth. To replace that premise, the court made up its own justification for the law. While refusing to say birth mothers have meaningful relationships with their newborns by virtue of having gestated them for nine months, the court allowed that mothers are different from fathers in one small way: their *opportunity* for a meaningful relationship with the child. Sex differences in reproduction, according to the court, boiled down to the fact that when a child is born, the mother is necessarily in the same room at the same time. Mother and child therefore have an opportunity to meet and *perhaps* form a meaningful relationship. A father doesn't necessarily have that opportunity. The court upheld the law on the basis of this difference in opportunity, which it said was a function of the mother's necessary "presence at the birth." It ignored the relationship the mother had been forming in the nine months she spent creating the child before they met as separate people after the birth. By downgrading maternity from a "meaningful relationship" established by gestation to an "opportunity for meaningful relationship" due to being present at the birth, the *Nguyen* majority seemed to think it had purged the citizenship law of any stereotypes about women as caretakers. Thus was the process of gestating and delivering a child reduced to being present at its arrival, as if babies were dropped in their mothers' laps by storks.[3]

Sadly, the dissent in *Nguyen*, written by Justice Sandra Day O'Connor, adhered to this stork-based model of reproduction. Justice O'Connor rightly pointed out that the majority's made-up justification—protecting the opportunity for a relationship—was much less weighty than what the INS had argued, which was the need for an actual, meaningful relationship. Moreover, if a parent's presence at the birth was what mattered, there was no reason not to give rights to fathers who could prove they'd been at birth and thus had the same opportunity to meet the child. The majority had thus failed to provide a convincing rationale for the law. But like the majority, the dissent refused to acknowledge any meaningful difference between the biology of motherhood and the biology of fatherhood, even at the time of birth. All nine justices thus signed on to the proposition that a birth mother, like even the most absent genetic father, has only a *potential* relationship with her child. The majority's discussion of the opportunity granted the mother by her presence at the birth even echoed some of the language of the Unwed Father Cases, which spoke of the need for a man to "grasp the opportunity" presented by biological fatherhood in order to gain parental rights.[4] The discussion of "opportunity" in *Nguyen* suggested, disturbingly, that a new mother also had no parental rights until she grasped the opportunity and took additional steps to establish a post-birth relationship with the infant at whose birth she happened to be present. Just as mothers and fathers are equally genetic parents, they are, according to the Supreme Court in *Nguyen*, equally lacking in any meaningful relationship with the newborn child.

The trouble here is that the premise of the Unwed Father Cases was that the birth mother already has a relationship with the baby at the moment it becomes a separate person by being born. The *Nguyen* justices seemingly thought this premise depended on stereotypes about mothers' roles after children are born. But recognizing the relationship created by gestation is not stereotyping. It is evenhanded application of criteria for women and men claiming parental rights. The court's biology-plus-relationship test, designed to define legal parenthood "in terms the male can fulfill," was based on pregnancy—which includes both biology, in the form of genes and gestation, and a caretaking relationship in the form of gestation. It is thus also a test the female can fulfill. Today, she can fulfill it in two possible ways. With technology like IVF, she can fulfill it in the same way as the male: by contributing her genes without gestating the child, then taking care of the newborn in the same way a genetic father can. Or she can fulfill the test in the way that was the model for it in the first place: by gestating and giving birth. Equality should mean that the law recognizes the mother's parental rights when she meets the criteria that would earn parental rights for the father. Under those criteria—biology plus relationship—a birth mother's parental rights are fully established (by gestation) at the time of birth. But according to the entire Supreme Court in *Nguyen,* a newborn child is alone in the world, a small but noble savage waiting for someone in the room to grasp the opportunity for a relationship.

By denying that a birth mother has a meaningful relationship with her baby at the time of birth and by refusing to account for the relationship between Joseph Boulais and his son Tuan, *Nguyen* undermined the relationship prong of the biology-plus-relationship test, just as state courts had done. But *Nguyen* also narrowed the biology prong in a way that scrunches the law of parenthood into the ideologies of sameness equality and genetic essentialism. Equating biological motherhood with biological fatherhood means that what matters about them is how they are the same, so both have to be defined in terms of what biological mothers and fathers have in common: genes. Indeed, in the *Nguyen* court's telling, genes seem to be the only things that distinguish the birth mother from the midwife, the doctor, or anyone else who happens to be present at the birth. In the name of avoiding sex stereotypes and because gestation has no analog in biological fatherhood, the Supreme Court disregarded nine months of caretaking to write gestation out of the parentage formula for which it was once the model.

GENETIC ESSENTIALISM

Until the late twentieth century, the law hadn't had to worry much about defining biological motherhood; proving biological fatherhood was the challenge. But then fatherhood became easy and motherhood became a puzzle, both because of technology. Genetic testing could identify a biological father with near certainty, but in vitro fertilization could split biological motherhood between two women. Which, judges and litigants demanded to know, was the true mother? King Solomon aside, this question was first posed in the law around the same time sex equality was becoming a constitutional principle—and was taking the form of sameness equality. Defining motherhood in terms of genes was appealing because it meant parenthood would be the same for women and men. For those who subscribed to non-stork-based theories of reproduction, genetic essentialism was also associated with exciting new scientific discoveries, which made it appealing in a society that values fancy new technology over messy natural processes like gestation. Science, however, can't answer a question like "Who is the true mother?" because that question actually means "Whom should society recognize as the legal parent entitled to custody of this child?" Science can explain a lot about the world, but it doesn't answer *should* questions. For that you need Solomon.

Genetic essentialism nonetheless took hold in the law of motherhood, in which there are two kinds of disputes. The first are cases involving surrogacy contracts, which raise the question of motherhood when the surrogate refuses to surrender the child after giving birth to it. The second are cases in which fertility clinics make mistakes. Clinic staff occasionally mix the wrong sperm and eggs or put the wrong pre-embryo into a woman. (Scientists and doctors refer to the fertilized cells created by IVF as "pre-embryos" to distinguish those cells from the small part of the pre-embryo that later develops into the fetus.[5]) In the US, two early surrogacy cases set the stage for defining motherhood in terms of genes rather than gestation. A decade later, at the turn of the millennium, a third case set the same standard for cases of mistakes by clinics. These three cases were all in different states and weren't binding on other states, but as the firsts of their kinds in a field with relatively few cases being litigated, they had enormous influence on the course of surrogacy law in the United States.

FULL SURROGACY

The first of the two surrogacy cases was *In the Matter of Baby M,*[6] which reached the New Jersey Supreme Court in 1988, two years after Baby M's birth triggered a custody battle that captured the attention of the nation. Mary Beth Whitehead had agreed to serve as a "full surrogate" for William and Elizabeth Stern. A full surrogate is one who is both the genetic and the gestational mother of the child. She is also sometimes called a "traditional surrogate" because she becomes pregnant either sexually or by assisted insemination, so this kind of surrogacy was possible long before the invention of IVF. (The biblical story of Bilhah, Rachel, and Jacob, which was the basis for Margaret Atwood's *The Handmaid's Tale,* was a case of full surrogacy.) In *Baby M,* the contract called for Mary Beth to become pregnant through assisted insemination with William's sperm. In exchange for $10,000, she would carry and give birth to the child, then give up her parental rights. Because Mary Beth was married, her husband, Richard Whitehead, was also a party to the contract. He agreed to give up his parental rights under the marital presumption, which ordinarily would have made him the legal father of any child born by his wife.

For the Sterns, surrogacy was a solution to a conflict between their two interests. William "very much wanted to continue his bloodline," a desire that took on special significance because most of his family had been killed in the Holocaust. Elizabeth, however, was a doctor and believed she might have multiple sclerosis, which makes pregnancy riskier. According to the New Jersey court, "Her anxiety appears to have exceeded the actual risk, which current medical authorities assess as minimal. Nonetheless that anxiety was evidently quite real." The surrogacy contract allowed them to have a child who was genetically William's without Elizabeth's having to be pregnant.

While still in the hospital after giving birth, Mary Beth realized she couldn't bear to give up the baby, whom she named Sara Elizabeth. When the Sterns told her they planned to rename the baby Melissa Elizabeth, she broke down in tears and told them she didn't know if she could part with the child. She brought the baby to the Sterns' house three days after the birth only to return two days later saying she couldn't live without her child. She begged them to let her have the baby for a week. Fearing Mary Beth would otherwise take her own life, the Sterns relented. But a month passed with Mary Beth refusing to return the child, and the Sterns obtained a court order for custody. The Whiteheads fled to Florida, passing the baby out a back window while police were entering their house to enforce the custody order. By moving every few days, the Whiteheads evaded authorities for three months, which ended when Florida police found them and returned the baby to the Sterns.

Faced with these facts, the New Jersey Supreme Court emphatically refused to see the surrogacy contract as anything other than an adoption for money, which was "illegal and perhaps criminal." Adoption, like surrogacy, is expensive for the adopting parents. They pay large sums to agencies, lawyers, and brokers, and they often pay some of the birth mother's expenses during the pregnancy. It is a crime, however, to buy or sell a baby, so adopting parents can't offer money specifically in exchange for the birth mother's parental rights. In *Baby M*, William Stern argued he was paying not for a baby but for "gestational services." The court responded by pointing out that the contract called for Mary Beth to receive nothing if she lost the pregnancy before the fourth month and only $1,000 if the child were stillborn, "even though the 'services' had been fully rendered." Clearly, the contract was for the product. The court also rejected William's argument that Mary Beth was analogous to a sperm donor because she contributed the biologically female components of reproduction (egg and gestation), just as a sperm donor contributes the male component. The court said it was "quite obvious" that female biological parenthood was "not parallel" to male biological parenthood. Finally, the court said the contract violated state policy that adoption cases should be driven by what's best for the child. The court implied that a birth mother has both a right and a duty to evaluate prospective adoptive parents for her child. It chided Mary Beth for not doing much to investigate the Sterns' quality as potential parents before signing the contract, but it ultimately held that this feature of surrogacy contracts—that they may be signed before the birth mother "has the slightest idea of what the natural father and adoptive mother are like"—was yet another reason to declare such contracts illegal. In sum, the contract was invalid and the parties lucky not to be charged with human trafficking.

With the contract thrown out, *Baby M* became just another custody dispute between unmarried parents. In that dispute, the court chose William Stern to have primary custody. Its decision raised some legitimate concerns about, for example, Richard Whitehead's alcoholism, but it also placed a troubling emphasis on the Sterns' relative wealth. The court gave Mary Beth Whitehead the right to have the child for two days every other week, plus two weeks in the summer. William and Mary Beth remained Melissa's legal parents until she turned eighteen, when she went to court to terminate her relationship with Mary Beth and have herself adopted by Elizabeth Stern.[7]

GESTATION-ONLY SURROGACY

Five years after *Baby M,* in 1993, the California Supreme Court confronted surrogacy for the first time.[8] Anna Johnson and Crispina and Mark Calvert had met through a mutual acquaintance after Crispina had a hysterectomy. Anna offered to be a surrogate for them. The pre-embryo would be created through IVF with the Calverts' egg and sperm, making their contract a case of gestation-only surrogacy rather than full surrogacy. Unlike Mary Beth Whitehead, Anna Johnson wouldn't be the genetic mother of the child she gestated. Anna's contract with the Calverts called for the Calverts to pay $10,000, in installments, and to buy a life insurance policy for Anna. Their relationship, however, broke down even sooner than the relationship between the Whiteheads and the Sterns. Early in the pregnancy, Mark learned Anna had previously had several miscarriages, a fact he thought she should have disclosed. Anna was upset that the Calverts failed to buy her the promised life insurance policy. In addition, when she was hospitalized with complications from the pregnancy, Anna blamed it on the Calverts' causing her stress. At one point she sent them a letter demanding the rest of the $10,000 immediately, threatening not to give up the child unless they complied, and accusing them of "fetal neglect" and "moral depravity." The Calverts asked a court to declare them the legal parents of the yet-to-be-born child.

As with New Jersey in the *Baby M* case, there was no statute in California telling courts whether they should enforce surrogacy contracts. When *Johnson v. Calvert* reached the California Supreme Court, the court tried to resolve the case using the existing parentage laws, but that led to an impasse. California law allowed a woman to prove her maternity either by proving she had given birth to the child or by proving her genetic relationship with a blood test. In this case, Anna could prove maternity by the first method, Crispina by the second. The court needed a tie-breaker. It chose "intent," by which it meant the terms of the surrogacy contract. To explain this choice, the court quoted Professor John Lawrence Hill, who had argued that parenthood should be defined by what the parties intended before the baby was conceived because people like the Calverts were "the first cause, or the prime movers, of the procreative relationship."[9] Because it was their desire for a baby and their instigation of the contract that brought the child into being, they were the child's creators and thus his parents. Think of an artist who oversees a workshop full of apprentices. If Michelangelo has an idea for a sculpture and gives instructions for carving it to one of his apprentices, he might still claim credit for the artistic inspiration and present the sculpture to the public as one "by Michelangelo."[10] The Calverts brought their baby into existence in similar fashion and thus, according to both Professor Hill and the California Supreme Court, deserved to be recognized as his legal parents.

The *Johnson v. Calvert* court insisted the intent rule was necessary because in other cases, the genetic parents might change their minds and refuse to take the child. If the law considered the gestational mother to be the true mother, then the contracting parents would be off the hook and the surrogate would be stuck with the child. The court's argument on this point commits a logical error in assuming that one rule—genes, gestation, or contractual intent—must control in all cases. To the contrary, one might well conclude, as New Jersey did in *Baby M,* that a birth mother shouldn't make a final decision about giving up a child until after the birth but *also* conclude that someone who has contracted for a child shouldn't be allowed to walk away.

The *Johnson v. Calvert* opinion had several other logical flaws. First, the court wrongly assumed that Mark's rights as the father were beyond dispute and that the case was a contest between Crispina and Anna for the "mother" slot. Second, rather than trying to apply statutes written before anyone ever considered the possibility of gestation-only surrogacy, the court should have looked to the biology-plus-relationship test, which captures the essence of why the law protects parental rights in the first place. And third, *after* assessing each party's claim under the biology-plus-relationship test, the court should have grappled with questions about the surrogacy contract itself, questions the court evaded by adopting the "intent" rule.

1. Whose Parenthood Was at Issue?

In chapter 5, I described courts treating single mothers with children as defective families, with an empty space needing to be filled by a father. In *Johnson v. Calvert,* the California Supreme Court did something similar. In *Johnson v. Calvert,* however, the "father" slot was already filled and it was the "mother" slot that was in question. Because Mark was the only man, the court gave him the "father" slot—or rather, it just assumed the slot was his. The court's task, as it saw it, was to identify the true mother, either Anna or Crispina. When one of the briefs submitted in the case suggested that the child should have two legal mothers, the court responded that two mothers would be unacceptable because giving any rights to Anna "would diminish Crispina's role as mother." In the court's eyes, any parental rights Anna might assert could only come at Crispina's expense, not Mark's.

But by any fair analysis of their claims, Crispina and Mark were on equal footing. Their contributions to the child's creation were equivalent: both contributed genes. If anything, one could argue Crispina had a greater claim to the child, since the egg-extraction process she endured to contribute her genes was much more difficult and painful than what Mark went through to contribute his. There is no logical—at any rate, no non-sexist—reason for Mark's rights to be on firmer ground than Crispina's. The court's analysis therefore should have started with assessing all three parties' claims to the child, including Mark's.

2. How Would the Biology-plus-Relationship Test Apply?

The best way to evaluate the three parental claims in *Johnson v. Calvert* would have been to start with the biology-plus-relationship test. The court started instead with California's statutes on how to prove parenthood, which is how it ended up with a tie between Anna and Crispina. The statutes allowed Anna to prove her motherhood by proving that she gave birth and Crispina to prove hers with a DNA test. Those statutes, however, were rules of evidence, meant to tell courts what proof is needed to establish parenthood. The lawmakers who wrote them weren't anticipating a dispute over the actual definition of motherhood. The California legislature had not contemplated IVF and gestation-only surrogacy when it wrote those laws. When a situation arises that is so far from the original expectations behind a statute, courts routinely adapt the rules in light of larger policy considerations.

The best statement of the larger policy considerations at issue in *Johnson v. Calvert* was the biology-plus-relationship test. The purpose of that test was to articulate what, exactly, the Constitution protects when it protects parental rights. Before the Unwed Father Cases, the definition of "parent" had been taken for granted. "Parents" meant the birth mother, plus her husband if she had one. In order to extend parental rights to unmarried fathers, the Supreme Court had to ask itself what was so special about parents that gave them rights over their children. Its answer became the biology-plus-relationship test. Parents are special and have rights because they have a biological tie and a caretaking relationship. Surrogacy contracts presented the same general question as the Unwed Father Cases: who should count as a parent? Since the old statutes couldn't give the court an answer anyway (they produced the tie between Anna and Crispina), the best place to start would have been with the constitutional standard of biology-plus-relationship.

Anna's gestating and giving birth to the child satisfied the biology-plus-relationship test because gestation was the original model for the test. Admittedly, gestational mothers had previously always been the genetic mothers of the children they gave birth to. But gestation is also a biological tie. During pregnancy, the developing fetus was literally part of Anna's biology. They exchanged cells and DNA in ways that shaped how the eventual child's genes were expressed and that affected both Anna's and the baby's physiology and health over the longer term.[11] Gestation should thus satisfy the biology prong. It also satisfies the relationship prong because it necessarily entails substantial physical labor for the eventual child's well-being, and it is almost always an emotional labor as well. Therefore, Anna had a constitutionally protected relationship with the child.

Turning to the Calverts, their genetic contributions seem to meet the biology prong, assuming the method of conception doesn't matter.[12] The more difficult question is whether their involvement in the pregnancy should count for the relationship prong, or perhaps qualify them for parenthood in some new way. The California Supreme Court clearly thought their involvement was important, especially the fact that they were the "prime movers" whose desires initiated the process that led to the birth. Their role in the pregnancy raises one of the questions the Unwed Father Cases left open: whether it's possible for the genetic father to satisfy the relationship prong before the birth. I suggested in chapter 2 that even though he doesn't have a direct caretaking relationship with the child before the birth, he could participate by supporting his pregnant partner, and the attachment he forms in his own heart would be deserving of protection. The same argument could also apply to the Calverts. Their relationship with the baby Anna bore could then also qualify for protection under the biology-plus-relationship test.

3. What Should be the Effect of the Contract?

If all three adults have at least a plausible claim to parental rights under the biology-plus-relationship test, we should next turn to the contract. The California Supreme Court in *Johnson v. Calvert* skipped this step by defining parenthood in terms of the "intent" of the parties. By "intent," it really meant the terms of the contract, so in that sense it took the contract into account. But the court pretended the parties' intent existed independently of the contract, so their intent could be identified and enforced without considering anything else about the contract, as one would normally do in a case about enforcing a contract. There were at least three important questions the court failed to discuss before deciding to declare the Calverts the parents.

The first question was whether surrogacy contracts are legitimate contracts at all or whether, as the *Baby M* court argued, they amount to paying the birth mother for an adoption, which is a crime. While the court didn't address this question directly, its emphasis on Professor Hill's argument, that the contracting parents are the "prime movers" behind the child's existence, provides a clue to the court's views on the difference between surrogacy and adoption. The court defined parenthood in terms of the parties' agreed-upon intentions *before conception*, which distinguishes surrogacy from an adoption for money. The timing of the agreement seems to be important because of the "prime mover" idea that the contracting parents caused the existence of the child.

Second, if surrogacy contracts are legitimate contracts, how should they be enforced? There's a rule in contract law that lets you back out of a "specific performance" you've contracted to do. If you contract to do a specific thing but you then refuse to do it, a court will make you give back the money you've been paid, but it won't make you do the thing. That rule has exceptions. The question is, should surrogacy contracts be one of the exceptions? If so, then courts should enforce the surrogacy contract by forcing the surrogate to turn over the baby. If not—if the usual rule against specific performance applies—then enforcement of a surrogacy contract would just mean the surrogate's paying back any money she'd received.

Third and finally, ordinarily when both parties have breached a contract (Anna by refusing to turn over the baby, the Calverts by not buying the life insurance policy and allegedly treating Anna poorly), the court must consider how those breaches should alter the terms of the contract. If one party commits a serious breach, the other may have the right to cancel the contract. The *Johnson v. Calvert* court, however, ignored Anna's breach-of-contract allegations and instead characterized the litigation as having arisen from Anna's "change of heart." The court treated Anna's complaints about the Calverts as emotional, not legal, and therefore failed to analyze their contractual implications.

Because the court defined the Calverts as the parents by virtue of "intent," it never got around to applying contract law to the contract, such as by analyzing the question of specific performance or whether the Calverts were guilty of breach. Instead, the court let one term of the contract (the requirement that Anna give up her parental rights) define parenthood, regardless of any other terms of the contract and regardless of non-contractual, family-law principles like the biology-plus-relationship test.

. . .

The US surrogacy industry has boomed since *Baby M* and *Johnson v. Calvert* were decided. There's a range of approaches, from a near-ban on surrogacy in Michigan to enthusiasm for it in California, and states vary in many of the details of how they regulate surrogacy. But *Baby M* and *Johnson v. Calvert* foreshadowed one important aspect of how surrogacy developed across the country: there is a clear preference for gestation-only surrogacy (*Johnson v. Calvert*, with pregnancy achieved through IVF) over full surrogacy (*Baby M*, with pregnancy by assisted insemination). The states that are hostile to surrogacy generally consider full surrogacy to be "worse" than gestation-only surrogacy, and the pro-surrogacy states are mostly pro-gestation-only surrogacy. Broadly speaking, the law sees a surrogate as a mother if she provides the egg but not if she provides only gestation. This distinction tracks the distinction Professor Dorothy Roberts described, in chapter 1, between "spiritual motherhood" and "menial motherhood," where the spiritual tasks are the ones a good mother must perform herself but the menial ones can be hired out. In surrogacy, Roberts argued, the surrogate "provides the menial labor of gestating the fetus to term [while] the contracting wife is designated as the baby's spiritual mother."[13] Today, that spiritual connection is often attributed to genes.

In addition to the distinction between full surrogacy and gestation-only surrogacy, there was another difference between *Baby M* and *Johnson v. Calvert* that didn't make it into the courts' opinions but was important to feminists at the time. Many feminists feared the surrogacy industry would degrade and exploit women, especially women of color. The Whiteheads and the Sterns of *Baby M* were all White. The Calverts in *Johnson v. Calvert* were usually referred to as White in the press, although Crispina Calvert was Filipina American. Anna Johnson was Black. It isn't a coincidence that a White couple using full surrogacy (the Sterns), and thus giving the child the surrogate's genes, would choose a surrogate of the same race but a couple using gestation-only surrogacy (the Calverts) might not. As Professor Roberts also observed in her early critique of surrogacy, "In this society, perhaps the most significant genetic trait passed from parents to child is race."[14] That's not to say race is a genetic or biological category; it is a social category we create using heritable traits, such as skin color, along with other building blocks. Roberts argued that genetic essentialism, which leads judges to see so crucial a difference between full surrogacy and gestation-only surrogacy, is bound up with the ideology of race. Gestation-only surrogacy allows White aspiring parents to hire women of color to produce children, while ensuring the children will be considered White. Roberts and other early feminist critics of surrogacy worried that *Johnson v. Calvert* opened the door to creating "a caste of breeders, composed of women of color, whose primary function would be to gestate the embryos of more valuable white women."[15] They feared the surrogate was a new, more extreme version of the wet nurse or nanny, a role that shifts the menial work of reproduction onto poor women, especially women of color, while reserving the "spiritual" status of being the true mother for wealthier White women. As we'll discuss in chapter 9, the worst of these fears haven't come to pass. (Some feminists would say they haven't *yet* come to pass.) But racism has nonetheless shaped the law of surrogacy, including its preference for the genetic definition of parenthood.

INVOLUNTARY SURROGACY

The role of race is submerged in most court decisions about surrogacy. In *Baby M* and *Johnson v. Calvert,* the New Jersey and California Supreme Courts didn't mention race. But race surfaces when fertility clinics make mistakes by mixing up genes or transferring pre-embryos into the wrong woman. The first widely known case of such a mistake was *Perry-Rogers v. Fasano* in New York in 2000.[16] Deborah Perry-Rogers and Robert Rogers, who were Black, and Donna and Richard Fasano, who were White, all submitted eggs and sperm for in vitro fertilization at the same clinic. IVF was successful in the lab for both couples, and the clinic implanted pre-embryos in both women. Donna Fasano became pregnant; Deborah Perry-Rogers did not. About a month later, the clinic notified both couples that there'd been a mistake. The upshot was the clinic didn't know which embryos were developing inside Donna. Later that year, Donna gave birth to two boys who were, as the appellate court that ultimately resolved their custody battle emphasized, "of two different races"—one Black and one White. The Fasanos took both boys home to raise. Although they knew of the clinic's error, it isn't clear whether they knew the other couple wanted custody of the Black child, whom they named Joseph and the Perry-Rogerses later renamed Akeil. The Fasanos may have believed that relinquishing Joseph would have made him a ward of the state.

Any uncertainty about the Perry-Rogerses' interest in the child was resolved when they sued the Fasanos for custody. In response, the Fasanos agreed to give the baby to the Perry-Rogerses in exchange for visitation rights. After some wrangling, the trial judge signed several orders that seemed to ratify this arrangement. She gave the Fasanos several days each month, one week in the summer, and alternating holidays with Akeil. Some months later she increased the Fasanos' visits to every other weekend. The Perry-Rogerses appealed the new schedule, and by the time they presented their arguments to the appellate court, they had decided to fight the entire arrangement of sharing Akeil with the Fasanos. They argued the Fasanos were legal strangers to Akeil and therefore had no rights to him at all.

The New York appellate court purported to endorse California's intent analysis from *Johnson v. Calvert*. It said,

> Application of the "intent" analysis ... would—in our view—require that custody be awarded to the Rogerses. It was they who purposefully arranged for their genetic material to be taken and used in order to attempt to create their own child, whom they intended to rear.

This argument makes no sense at all. The whole point of "intent" in *Johnson v. Calvert* was that the court resolved the case according to the original intent on which all parties had agreed before the child was even conceived. In contrast, *no one* intended what happened in *Perry-Rogers v. Fasano*. The Fasanos intended to make a baby from their genes and Donna's gestation. The Perry-Rogerses intended to make a baby from their genes and Deborah's gestation. What they all got was a baby made from the Perry-Rogerses' genes and Donna's gestation. The only way to deem that baby the product of the Perry-Rogerses' intent rather than the Fasanos' is to ignore the gestational aspects of each couple's intent. The court's reasoning assumes the *important* aspect of the couples' intent was that they each intended to have their "own" genetic baby, not that each of the women intended to create a child from her own body. By making that assumption about what was important, the court engaged in genetic essentialism, the belief that genes are the most important aspect of the parent-child relationship. Indeed, in the court's description of the parties' intent, gestation disappears into the passive voice. The court said the Perry-Rogerses arranged for their genes "to be taken and used," as if it didn't matter at all who was going to do the using (the gestating) in order to create the child.

In addition to assuming the desire for a genetic connection was the most important aspect of each couple's plans for making a baby, the court heaped blame on the Fasanos for inappropriately bonding with Akeil:

> The happenstance of the Fasanos' nominal parenthood over Akeil should have been treated as a mistake to be corrected a[s] soon as possible, *before the development of a parental relationship.* ... Defendants cannot be permitted to purposefully act in such a way as to create a bond, and then rely upon it for their assertion of rights to which they would not otherwise be entitled.

This is stunningly inhumane. Remember that Donna Fasano was one month pregnant when she was told one or both of the embryos she carried *might* have someone else's genes. How were she and Richard supposed to calibrate their feelings about the pregnancy to prepare themselves to give away one, both, or neither of the babies Donna would bear, depending on how the DNA tests turned out? In passing, the court admitted the possibility that a woman might develop a bond over the course of a pregnancy, but it apparently thought the burden was on Donna (and Richard) to stifle those feelings for the remaining eight months. The decision in *Perry-Rogers v. Fasano* was thus the ultimate repudiation of pregnancy and birth as the basis for defining parenthood as biology-plus-relationship. By virtue of gestating them, Donna Fasano had both a biological tie and a caretaking relationship with the two boys she gave birth to, but these forms of parenthood didn't matter to the court. The court also denied that the two boys created in Donna's womb could in any sense be considered brothers. The court said the boys were not siblings by either "whole or half-blood," using *blood* in the metaphorical sense to refer to overlapping genomes, as opposed to literally sharing a circulatory system for nine months. To be related "by blood," in the court's view, meant to share DNA. "The metaphorical blood of the genetic tie" supplanted "the real blood of the pulsing cord."[17]

Perry-Rogers v. Fasano was decided by a mid-level appellate court in New York, which means it is binding law only in New York, and even there it could be overturned by the state's highest court or the state legislature. No other state's appellate courts have weighed in on who gets parental rights when clinics make mistakes. Nonetheless, the fertility industry, lawyers who work in the field, and trial courts in the states where cases have arisen have accepted *Perry-Rogers* as the definitive word on the question. Trial court proceedings in such cases are sealed for the sake of privacy, but sometimes the genetic parents go to the media to plead their case as well. In every case I've found, the courts have reached the same outcome as in *Perry-Rogers*. For example, like Donna Fasano, the woman I called Mina Kim in the introduction went through IVF, became pregnant with twins, and gave birth to two boys.[18] Her two boys turned out to be the genetic children of *two* other couples whose pre-embryos had mistakenly been placed in Mina. Those couples went to court and to the press. The media uncritically described the babies as rightfully belonging to their genetic parents, and the trial court apparently agreed, as it ordered Mina to give them up.

In Mina's case, as in *Perry-Rogers*, the clinic's error was apparent at the time of birth because of racial differences. Mina was Korean American, and all four genetic parents were White. Like the court in *Perry-Rogers*, media accounts of Mina's case treated the difference between her race and the babies' as evidence that she wasn't the true mother. Professor Leslie Bender has analyzed the role race plays in such cases. She concludes that the New York court's apparent anger at Donna Fasano for bonding with a child she gave birth to was driven in part by the judges' unconscious rejection of cross-racial parenthood:

> My conclusion is that the court faults Fasano for being a white woman who bonds with her dark-skinned child. Once she saw that the child she bore was African-American, according to the court, she ought to have denied any natural bonds with him and given him away.[19]

Mina, like Donna, bonded with the children she was creating through gestation, a bond she didn't reject when she discovered they were racially different from her. The court, however, attached no value to her gestation or her bond and took the children from her.

By following the *Perry-Rogers v. Fasano* rule for cases of mixed-up embryos, courts turned their backs on the idea of parenthood at the heart of the Unwed Father Cases. In the Unwed Father Cases, the Supreme Court took the birthing woman as the model for legal parenthood, the key elements of which were a biological tie and a caretaking relationship established, for the mother, through gestation. For fathers, the biology prong consists of genes, but for mothers, "biology" ought to include the actual shared blood of gestation as well as the metaphorical blood of a genetic tie. Under sameness equality, however, "equality," as a concept, can apply only when two things are the same. Lawyers and judges accustomed to sameness equality ignored that the Unwed Father Cases embraced a different kind of equality, in which the law made up for men's disadvantage by leveling a field that nature had left uneven. Instead, they interpreted the goal of equality for mothers and fathers to require glossing over any differences in their biology with the rhetoric of "equal" biological parenthood. This rhetoric has been turned against birthing women in cases like *Perry-Rogers*. For if biological motherhood is equal to biological fatherhood in the sense of things being equal because they are the same, it follows that "biological" means "genetic" and gestation is an unimportant, menial contribution.

A few more words must be said in fairness to the *Perry-Rogers* court. In its decision, the court repeatedly denied that it was endorsing a genetic definition of parenthood. Like the California court in *Johnson v. Calvert,* the New York court in *Perry-Rogers v. Fasano* said it would use the intent rule in all cases—not just in surrogacy cases but also in egg-donation cases, where the intent is for the gestational mother, not the egg donor, to be the legal parent. That means, for example, that the *Perry-Rogers* court would have reached the same outcome as the court that decided *In re Marriage of Buzzanca,* a case from one of California's mid-level appellate courts.[20] Luanne and John Buzzanca had contracted with a surrogate to carry an embryo that was created with egg and sperm they had bought from donors. Neither spouse would have a biological tie to the child. Near the end of the surrogate's pregnancy, John filed for divorce and tried to deny any responsibility for the about-to-be-born child. The court held Luanne and John to be the legal parents based on their intent (meaning their contract) alone, despite their lacking any genetic or gestational tie to the child. In cases like *Buzzanca,* and in ordinary egg-donation cases where the intended mother buys the egg and gestates it herself, the *Perry-Rogers* court would recognize the parental rights of the intended, non-genetic mother.

However, the court's willingness to give rights to non-genetic parents in some circumstances doesn't absolve the court of engaging in genetic essentialism. The court gave no coherent explanation for why *Perry-Rogers* was an "accidental surrogacy" case rather than an "accidental egg-donation" case. The clinic's mistake meant all parties had their intent—the intent to conceive and give birth to their own child and only their own child—frustrated, so intent couldn't determine parenthood. Yet the court was confident the Perry-Rogerses were the rightful parents of Akeil because they had "purposefully arranged for their genetic material to be taken" in order to produce a child *for them,* wherever (as the court saw it) the child happened to be gestated. One could equally say the Fasanos intended to use Donna's uterus to produce a child, wherever its genetic material came from, *for them.* But that didn't matter to the court. Why not? The dynamic at work is that courts are defining parenthood in terms of genes, *with the proviso* that the genes can be bought and sold. Crispina Calvert, who gave her own egg to be gestated by Anna Johnson, was the mother because it was her egg. Luanne Buzzanca, who become a mother without either a genetic or a gestational tie, was the mother because she had *paid for* the egg. But in *Perry-Rogers*, because Donna Fasano hadn't paid for Deborah Perry-Rogers's egg and Robert Rogers's sperm, the court treated her not as if she was the mother of a child but as if she had stolen the Perry-Rogerses' property, or at least wrongfully kept it once it left her body in the form of a baby.

THE DIFFERENCE BETWEEN PROTECTING EXISTING RELATIONSHIPS AND ENABLING NEW CONNECTIONS

Some readers of *Perry-Rogers v. Fasano* find consolation in the fact that each couple ended up with a baby. Because Donna gave birth to "twins," the courts charged with choosing the true mother had it easier than King Solomon. They had two babies instead of one to split. One problem with that consolation, however, is that now, when pre-embryos get mixed up in the lab, courts follow *Perry-Rogers* and give the babies to the genetic parents even when there aren't enough babies to go around. Mina Kim had to give away both babies she bore. A more important problem is that babies are not fungible. The loss of one child is not diminished by the consolation that you still have one left. The parent of multiple children has not divided her love into pieces, safely storing each piece in a separate basket to spread the risk of loss.[21] Why would we expect the Fasanos to feel differently from any other parents who lose one of their two children? Yet the court resolved the case by chastising them for their attachment to Joseph/Akeil. *Perry-Rogers v. Fasano* was a tragic case, but the court's response—denigrating the relationship in which the Fasanos were entangled—was no solution.

Perry-Rogers v. Fasano required a choice between the Fasanos' existing relationship with their child Joseph and the Perry-Rogerses' longing to create a connection with their child Akeil. Both are important human needs, and the loss or frustration of either a heartbreak. The feminist theory from chapter 4 tells us that the court's choice to enforce a right to connect based on genes rather than to protect an existing relationship was predictable. So was the fact that the court, rather than admitting the difficulty of the choice, expressed contempt for the Fasanos' existing relationship.

In the last three chapters, we've seen three ways in which feminist theory proved correct that the biology-plus-relationship test would run aground against the law's preference for autonomy and new connections rather than existing relationships:

First, in chapter 5, courts and legislatures weakened the relationship prong of biology-plus-relationship to give genetic fathers more power relative to birth mothers. With this shift, courts turned the biology-plus-relationship test into a right to pursue a new connection rather than a right to have an existing relationship protected. Except in the extreme cases of rape-fathered children covered by the Rape Survivors Child Custody Act, the law doesn't even acknowledge that this right for the father invades the mother's life and her relationship with the child.

Second, we saw in chapter 6 that the rights of fathers in caretaking relationships often remained unprotected. The child-welfare system's One-Parent Doctrine ignored the letter of the law of the Unwed Father Cases by allowing the state to take custody of a child based on one parent's neglect or abuse, without even a hearing for the other parent. Decisions like *Nguyen v. INS* crushed the spirit of the Unwed Father Cases by allowing the federal government to define fatherhood in terms of paperwork instead of caretaking. From these examples, we see how the law can denigrate the "feminine" value of protecting existing relationships regardless of the sex or gender of the people in need of that protection.

Third, in this chapter, we've seen the definition of parenthood come full circle. *Johnson v. Calvert* and *Perry-Rogers v. Fasano* defined motherhood in terms of genes, rather than in terms of the biological and caretaking tie of gestation. These cases are also examples of courts' preferring the "masculine" value of enabling new connections over the "feminine" value of protecting existing relationships, regardless of the sex or gender of the people affected in a particular case. In these cases, the same was true for values that reinforce racial hierarchy. The courts used the genetic definition of parenthood both to deny rights to Anna Johnson, a Black woman working as a surrogate, and to grant rights to the Perry-Rogerses, a Black couple seeking parenthood. That doesn't make the genetic definition of parenthood neutral with respect to either race or sex. Over the run of cases, genetic essentialism reinforces a harmful, biological ideology of race, and it defines parenthood in male terms.

Both women and men can seek new connections through reproductive technology, and with IVF both can be genetic parents without gestating. Courts will deem their seeking and their genes more important than the relationship of a birth mother—whether a paid surrogate like Anna Johnson or an involuntary surrogate like Donna Fasano or Mina Kim—even though the caretaking relationship of gestation was the original model for the biology-plus-relationship test. The Perry-Rogerses longed for connection and sought to create it by exercising their autonomy through the services of the fertility clinic. The Fasanos did the same but found themselves entangled in a relationship with Joseph/Akeil that the court did not respect. With the decision in that case, the legal system completed its evisceration of the biology-plus-relationship model for legal parenthood.

This evisceration shows that relational feminist theory can predict and explain how the legal system perpetuates its skewed values. Even after the Supreme Court developed the biology-plus-relationship test in the Unwed Father Cases, the courts rejected using the law to serve the "feminine" value of protecting existing relationships. Courts distorted the relationship prong beyond recognition in order to protect rights to pursue new connections instead. They allowed this pursuit to invade the rights and lives of birth mothers without even really noticing the harm they inflicted, so unaccustomed are lawyers and judges to analyzing legal problems in light of "feminine" needs for protection from invasion. It is to the problem of invasion that we must next turn, in order to fill in some missing pieces about what the biology-plus-relationship model means for the law of pregnancy and motherhood.

PART THREE

A Feminist Approach

EIGHT

How to Reason from the Body

THAT BRINGS US TO THE ELEPHANT in the room: the right to abortion.

In the last few chapters, I've accused some feminists of abetting the destruction of the biology-plus-relationship test by embracing the genetic definition of parenthood. The Supreme Court based the biology-plus-relationship test on its belief that gestation creates a meaningful relationship between a birth mother and her newborn child that is more significant than the genetic tie between the child and its biological father. This idea, that gestation creates a parent-child relationship, sets off alarm bells for many feminists because they fear it could be twisted into an argument against the right to abortion.[1] Most feminists scrupulously avoid using the word *mother* to refer to a pregnant woman because anti-feminists equate pregnancy with motherhood as a way to portray women who seek abortions as mothers murdering their children.[2]

Relational feminists agree that a pregnant woman shouldn't automatically be called a mother. No one should be forced to carry a pregnancy to term and become a mother, so it's presumptuous to call her one. But relational feminists also think it's important to recognize the relationship that is *being created* over the course of pregnancy—and comes into existence at its end.[3] When feminists argue for abortion rights without recognizing the relationship created through gestation, they miss one of the most harmful aspects of forced pregnancy. Forced pregnancy doesn't just physically take over a woman's body. It forces the woman's body into creating a new person with whom her life is then intertwined. As we'll see, legal arguments that ignore the relationship created by pregnancy lead to weaker rights for pregnant women. Contrary to many feminist fears, seeing and valuing the relationship created through gestation strengthens rather than undermines arguments for the right to abortion.

REASONING BADLY FROM THE BODY

The Supreme Court's 1973 decision in *Roe v. Wade* was a feminist victory because the court held a pregnant woman had a right to have an abortion. It did so because it concluded that a woman's right to control her body was among the liberties protected by the liberty clause of the Fourteenth Amendment, the same clause we discussed in chapters 2 and 3 that also protects parental rights, free speech, and most of our other rights. (Remember, the Bill of Rights in the first ten amendments applies only to the federal government, so protection from state governments comes almost entirely from the Fourteenth.) However, *Roe* was *also* the first time the court held that the state had a legitimate interest in what the court called the "potential life" of a fetus or embryo. The court's endorsement of that state interest gave the state power to restrict abortion under some circumstances. In later cases, the state's power ballooned to include the ability to enact a gauntlet of restrictions on abortion, from waiting periods to mandatory ultrasounds and eventually, in *Dobbs v. Jackson Women's Health* in 2022, the power to completely ban abortion again.[4]

In a landmark 1992 law-review article called "Reasoning from the Body," Professor Reva Siegel criticized how the Supreme Court reasoned about women's bodies, even in *Roe* itself, in order to justify the state power to restrict abortion. She pointed out that the court never explained why the state should be able to force a woman to create a child. Instead, the court treated the fetus as a separate entity from the pregnant woman (not as something she was making), and it decided the state had a legitimate interest in wanting the fetus to be born. The court then asserted that the woman's rights over her body had to be balanced against this state interest in potential life, "without devoting a single sentence to explaining why this is so."[5] That is, the court never said why the state was allowed to conscript the woman in service to the potential life of the fetus. Siegel argued that any attempt to provide such an explanation would have revealed the sexism behind bans on abortion. Pregnant women are the only people the state treats this way. Not even the dead are legally required to donate their bodies to save others, nor are parents required to donate blood or organs to their children. But the Supreme

Court wrote *Roe v. Wade* as if it were "a mere happenstance of nature" that the fetus was inside the woman and therefore the rights of women had to be limited to vindicate the state's interest in fetuses.[6] Siegel called this logical slippage "physiological reasoning," or "reasoning from the body," because the court reasoned as if the duty to gestate followed automatically from the physiology of pregnancy. It never considered whether the state might have *illegitimate* reasons for forcing women to bear children, such as the desire to force women to comply with their traditional gender role.

Siegel traced this physiological reasoning about pregnancy to the nineteenth-century campaign against abortion in the United States. That campaign was led by medical doctors at a time when organized, professional medicine was a relatively new, male-dominated field that was competing with the female-dominated field of midwifery. The doctors' arguments against abortion were largely based on "normative judgments about women, not simply concern for the unborn."[7] By "normative judgments," Siegel meant that doctors portrayed abortion as an act of rebellion by White, middle-class wives who had been encouraged by feminists to betray their duty not only to their fetuses but also to their husbands and to the manifest destiny of the White race, which required more White babies. To fight this feminine rebellion, the doctors invoked their supposed scientific expertise to change how the public saw abortion, in ways the Supreme Court echoed in *Roe* and that are still with us today.

Previously, in the eighteenth century, the prevailing theory of reproduction among scientists had been that the child was already fully formed inside the head of its father's sperm.[8] It followed that a sperm was like a Russian nesting doll, with all the generations of humanity contained originally in Adam's sperm. Over the course of the nineteenth century, scientists moved on to other theories, especially after Darwin published *On the Origin of Species.* (Evolution by natural selection is inconsistent with the idea that every creature that would ever exist was preformed and tucked into the first ancestor's sperm at the dawn of creation.) The nesting-doll theory, however, continued to influence the doctors who campaigned against abortion. The doctors claimed a human embryo was more like a baby kangaroo or a nursing infant than a part of the woman. At times they claimed the embryo wasn't even attached to her. They depicted pregnancy as a passive response by the woman's body and "systematically discounted women's role in reproducing life."[9] The pregnant woman was literally a vessel for the already fully formed, albeit minuscule, new human, who needed the womb only to expand in.

Even though the nesting-doll theory was already outdated, the doctors used these arguments to give a scientific veneer to their demands that women submit to their proper role as mothers.

Today, purportedly scientific arguments against abortion are essentially unchanged since the nineteenth-century doctors' campaign. When does life begin? "Science informs us as to the answer," claim today's anti-abortionists,[10] who may have been forced by advances in biology to abandon the idea of the preformed child riding along inside a sperm but who have adapted by declaring that a child is created at the moment a sperm reaches an egg. A fertilized egg, they claim, is already a baby, and it turns into a recognizable baby by being left to its own devices, "undisturbed by external intervention."[11] This is the same genetic essentialism we've seen before: the belief that the essence of a person consists of their genes. Instead of a literally preformed baby in the head of a sperm, modern opponents of abortion portray the essence of the child-to-be as the genes it inherits from its parents. The baby that the mother makes over nine months' gestation is secondary. Either way, whether a preformed mini-baby or a baby-as-genes, this model of reproduction treats gestation as a menial and meaningless contribution to the creation of a new life.

We've already seen in chapters 5 through 7 how genetic essentialism leads courts to downgrade the value of gestation. Genetic essentialism lies behind courts' greater willingness to enforce contracts for gestation-only surrogacy than for full surrogacy. A full surrogate is the genetic mother and thus more likely to be the "true mother" in courts' eyes. A gestation-only surrogate isn't considered a "biological" mother, since courts take "biological" to mean "genetic," so they are more willing to force her to surrender the child. Genetic essentialism is also why the court in *Perry-Rogers v. Fasano* was so sure Donna Fasano should be forced to turn over Joseph/Akeil to his genetic parents, because he grew from their egg and sperm, even though he did so as part of Donna's body. Genetic essentialism tells the courts that the baby at birth *is* the egg and sperm, just more grown up. The pre-embryo belonged to the Perry-Rogerses, and in the court's eyes it still belonged to them after it had spent nine months unfolding in the vessel named Donna. The same ideology of genetic essentialism that led courts to answer the question "Who is the true mother?" in terms of genes is the basis for the claim that "science" tells us abortion should be illegal. This is eighteenth-century nesting-doll theory, popularized by nineteenth-century doctors and updated with only a nod to twentieth-century science.[12]

As I argued in chapter 7, science can't answer *should* questions, like "who should have custody of this child?" or "should women have the right to abortion?" But for anti-feminists and for the Supreme Court, the fantasized separate existence of the embryo provided a reason for forcing the woman to gestate it. It is that leap—from the embryo's imagined separateness to the woman's duty to gestate—that Siegel criticized as "reasoning from the body," meaning reasoning from the body *without* examining other factors, like stereotypes about women, that could explain why we have forced pregnancy for women but not forced organ donation for dead people. This kind of "reasoning from the body" is, more precisely, committing a logical fallacy based on false understandings of the body. It isn't true that the embryo is unattached to the pregnant woman's body, that she's irrelevant to its development, or that it doesn't need her "external intervention." Even if those claims were true, they wouldn't dictate the conclusion that the woman has a moral or legal duty to gestate. Women should have at least as much right as dead people to reserve their bodies for themselves. As Siegel demonstrated, in the nineteenth-century debates, the physiological arguments served as cover for banning abortion in order to force women into their role as mothers. In *Roe v. Wade*, the Supreme Court adopted that physiological perspective by holding that the state had a legitimate interest in the "potential life" of a fetus and by treating that fetus as a separate entity from the pregnant woman rather than something she was making. It adopted this perspective without looking to see what other, sexist agendas the bans on abortion might be serving. The *Roe* court thus reasoned *badly* about pregnant women's bodies—with stereotypes about women's roles driving its reliance on bad facts and bad logic—when it held the state had a legitimate interest in forced childbirth.

REASONING WITHOUT THE BODY

Roe v. Wade may have treated women's duty to gestate as a natural consequence of their physiology, but late-twentieth-century feminists shared the belief of nineteenth-century doctors that abortion was a sex-equality issue (the difference being that the feminists were in favor of equality and thus in favor of abortion). After *Roe*, with abortion rights constantly in jeopardy, feminists felt an urgent need to explain the connection between abortion and sex equality to the courts. Perhaps, they thought, even if the Supreme Court changed its mind about protecting abortion under the liberty clause of the Fourteenth Amendment, feminists could convince the court that abortion was necessary for sex equality. Then perhaps it would be protected by the

Fourteenth Amendment's equal protection clause. This argument, however, ran up against the ideology of sameness equality. How could banning abortion be sex discrimination if abortion was equally prohibited for women and men? The Supreme Court's view, as Siegel pointed out, was that pregnancy's taking place in women's bodies was "a mere happenstance of nature," not an equality problem. It was a natural, not an artificial, constraint. Just like with the pregnancy discrimination in disability benefits in *Geduldig v. Aiello* from chapter 1, for abortion to count as a sex-equality problem in constitutional law, the discrimination had to come from outside the body—from society, not from nature.

It was thus a feminist achievement when, in the 1992 decision in *Planned Parenthood v. Casey,* the Supreme Court acknowledged a link between abortion, societal discrimination, and women's equality. The equality argument the court accepted, however, was an anemic one. Drawing on briefs submitted to the court by feminist lawyers, the court gave this account of how abortion helped women achieve equality:

> For two decades of economic and social developments, people have organized intimate relationships and made choices that define their views of themselves and their places in society, in reliance on the availability of abortion in the event that contraception should fail. The ability of women to participate equally in the economic and social life of the Nation has been facilitated by their ability to control their reproductive lives. . . .
>
> An entire generation has come of age free to assume *Roe*'s concept of liberty in defining the capacity of women to act in society, and to make reproductive decisions.[13]

The court thus implied that women needed the right to abortion because being a mother conflicted with being able to succeed in a career and participate fully in public life. That was true,[14] and it will be true so long as the burdens of parenthood fall so disproportionately on women. Women's overwhelming share of the work of parenthood was the societal discrimination— the artificial constraint—that allowed the *Casey* court to see abortion as an equality issue. This argument for abortion rights, however, has a built-in sunset clause. It implies that once parenthood is equally shared with men, women won't need the right to abortion anymore because there will be nothing unfair about motherhood. A future society with complete sex equality and no right to abortion sounds like an oxymoron to most feminists, yet it is the implicit goal of the sex-equality argument the court accepted in *Casey.*

That's because the argument went to such lengths to avoid "physiological reasoning" that the woman's body disappeared. The court attributed the disproportionate burden of parenthood to society's stereotyping of women, not to the biological and emotional work of gestating a child. Once society rid itself of stereotypes, women would be freed from both inequality and the need for abortions.

This bodiless equality argument for the right to abortion opened the door for other arguments that badly misconstrued what was at stake for women in the right to abortion. One such argument is the "adoption not abortion" argument. If all that's at stake is whether women become mothers for the long term, not how gestation itself affects them, then women don't need the right to abortion because they can instead place their children for adoption. The Supreme Court used this argument when it abolished the right to abortion in *Dobbs,* citing a shortage in the "domestic supply of infants" available for adoption as a reason to force women to breed.[15] At the oral argument in *Dobbs,* Justice Amy Coney Barrett touted "safe haven" laws, which allow women to relinquish newborns for adoption anonymously.[16] The gist of this argument is that a woman who doesn't want to become a mother should just give birth and then drop the baby off at the nearest fire station. This argument trivializes the fact that before a woman can surrender a child, she must first create and give birth to it. The possibility of relinquishing a child for adoption doesn't reduce the physical burdens and risks that forced pregnancy imposes. In addition, a person forced through pregnancy is forced to engage in caretaking during gestation, which is likely to lead to emotional bonding and a sense of responsibility toward the born child—a relationship. That's one reason why few women who seek abortions end up choosing adoption even if forced to carry to term.[17] An embryo is not a baby, and wanting to abort a pregnancy is not the same as being willing to give up a baby. In addition, for those who choose adoption, formal adoption procedures, flawed as they are, can give a birth mother much more control over the process than is possible through safe havens. Birth mothers today often have the power to select their babies' adoptive parents, and they are gaining the ability to bargain for future information and possible contact with the child. Anonymous safe havens, in contrast, are meant as a last-ditch option for women in dire circumstances who might otherwise harm themselves or the baby. Justice Barrett's emphasis on safe havens rather than formal adoption implied that anyone seeking an abortion will lack interest in her born child, which is untrue. It is also misogynist, the view of a subset of proponents of adoption who see unmarried mothers as sinful, fallen women who aren't entitled to a voice in the adoption process.[18]

Another argument about abortion that trivializes gestation is the argument for a "male right to abortion." Before *Dobbs,* some legal commenters argued that men were victims of discrimination because pregnant women had the sole right to decide whether to have an abortion. A man claiming to be the biological father of an embryo that was part of a woman had the right neither to prevent an abortion nor to insist on one.[19] The male right to abortion would have consisted of a man's right not to pay child support if he asked the woman to have an abortion and she refused. Some proponents of men's abortion rights would also have given the man the power to block an abortion and force the woman to give birth, so long as he was "willing to legally commit to supporting and raising the child himself."[20] These arguments equate the invasion of being forced to gestate and give birth with the burden of writing a monthly check for child support. It's true that unwanted financial responsibility for a child is a burden, but that doesn't make it equivalent to forced pregnancy. The male-right-to-abortion argument treated pregnancy as merely a prelude to parenthood. It abstracted away the physical fact of the pregnancy happening in the woman's body to make a false equivalence between a pregnant woman and an expectant father. Contrary to this false equivalence, women's right to have the final say over abortion is a function of their bearing the burden and responsibility of pregnancy.[21]

It's not surprising that these two arguments—the adoption-not-abortion argument and the male-right-to-abortion argument—depend on misconstruing what's at stake in forcing a woman to gestate. Each is opportunistically using a bodiless idea of pregnancy to serve another agenda—an ultraconservative Christian agenda for adoption in the case of Justice Barrett and an anti-feminist, men's-rights agenda in the case of most proponents of a male right to control abortion.[22] However, the most comprehensive proposal for minimizing gestation in the law of pregnancy comes from the feminist side. In a 2019 article called "Unsexing Pregnancy," Professors David Fontana and Naomi Schoenbaum argued that the law should redefine the word *pregnancy* to mean not the state of gestating a child but the state of expecting to become a parent by any means—by gestating, by being married to a gestating person, by being party to a surrogacy contract, or by having had sex with someone who then became pregnant. Focusing largely on the Family and Medical Leave Act, they argue that many of that law's benefits for pregnant women should be extended to all expectant parents. For example, under the FMLA, a pregnant woman is entitled to take time off work to attend her prenatal medical checkups. But "if an expectant father wants job-protected leave to attend a prenatal appointment to view the ultrasound and bond with the child, this is not covered by the FMLA."[23] Similarly, the Affordable Care Act requires health-insurance plans to cover counseling to help pregnant women, and only pregnant women, quit smoking. Fontana and Schoenbaum argue that all expectant parents should be considered "pregnant" in that they might want to attend prenatal appointments, quit smoking, and participate in a wide range of other baby-prep activities.

Encouraging and supporting expectant fathers to do those things is a worthy goal. However, doing so by giving "pregnancy" rights under the FMLA to people who are not pregnant would raise many troubling questions. First would be the matter of identifying who is "pregnant" and thus entitled to benefits. For example, surrogate mothers, like other pregnant women, are already entitled to benefits under the FMLA. When a surrogate has a prenatal appointment, who should be entitled to take FMLA leave to go with her: her spouse or one of the contracting parents? both contracting parents? everyone? And why should it necessarily be any of those? After all, even a happily married pregnant woman planning to raise a child with her spouse might prefer a friend, her mother, or her sister as her main support person during pregnancy and childbirth. But "Unsexing Pregnancy" treats prenatal appointments as bonding opportunities for prospective parents, with all the focus on the fetus, rather than as health care for the pregnant woman. While it may be true that an expectant father would like to see an ultrasound in order to bond with the fetus, that isn't why they are done in doctors' offices. To channel the Supreme Court in *Nguyen v. INS*, there's only one person who must be *present* at a prenatal checkup. If others are to receive invitations, perhaps we could allow the pregnant woman to choose her own plus-one, rather than presume it should be the genetic father and/or her romantic partner and/or the person paying her to be a surrogate.

That brings us to a second problem. The law does not currently require a pregnant woman to legally identify the eventual parents of the child-to-be during the pregnancy. Legal parents are identified at birth or shortly thereafter because legal parenthood *doesn't exist* until birth. If the pregnant woman is married or has signed a surrogacy contract, society generally assumes it knows who the parents will be, but there is no official registry of pregnant people and their anticipated co-parents. There are putative-father registries in some states, but the key word there is "putative." "Unsexing

Pregnancy" expressly contemplates that genetic fathers should be entitled to "pregnancy" benefits, *even against the wishes of the pregnant woman* and even if the men are "one-night stands or ex-lovers."[24] But if a one-night stand or ex-lover claims to be "expecting," how does he prove it and thereby get his pregnancy benefits? The only options are to force the pregnant woman to submit to blood testing for paternity or to testify about her sexual history. Although courts already force women to do both of those things to ascertain paternity after a child is born, doing so during pregnancy would open a new front in the assault on women's bodily integrity.

Fontana and Schoenbaum try to limit this assault by making a distinction between those pregnancy benefits that "implicate the woman's body" and those that do not.[25] They would limit the unwelcome genetic father's rights to the ones they say don't implicate the woman's body. That means, for example, that the expectant father would have the right to benefits to help him quit smoking and otherwise prepare himself for parenting, and he would have the right to take time off work if the pregnant woman invited him to attend prenatal appointments. But if the pregnant woman didn't want him there, he wouldn't be entitled to come. With this distinction, Fontana and Schoenbaum argue their proposal could expand even the unwelcome father's participation in pregnancy without infringing on women's rights over their bodies.

This attempted distinction, however, is illusory in two ways. First, as I've noted, establishing a man's paternity *during pregnancy* necessarily implicates the woman's body. The pregnancy is happening in the woman's body, and any other person's connection to the fetus necessarily runs through her. Second, and more frightening, "Unsexing Pregnancy" relies on the (pre-*Dobbs*) law of abortion to justify giving pregnancy benefits to genetic fathers against the wishes of the pregnant woman. Before *Dobbs,* in cases like *Roe* and *Casey,* the Supreme Court held that women had the right to abortion, but that right could be limited by the state's interest in the potential life of the fetus. Abortion jurisprudence was about balancing the woman's right against the state's interest, so some restrictions were allowed but others were not. Fontana and Schoenbaum argue that there's no reason for "potential life of the fetus" to be the *only* state interest that can justify restricting a woman's rights during pregnancy. They propose that, in addition, women's rights could be curtailed for the sake of the state's interest in "the sex-equality benefits of encouraging paternal involvement in the pregnancy."[26] Just as states can regulate abortion for the sake of the fetus, they could regulate pregnancy and birth for the sake of making men feel like equal parents.

In *Dobbs,* the Supreme Court endorsed this kind of distressing creativity in finding new state interests that could justify regulating pregnant women.[27] Here's an example of how that could play out, with facts from two actual pregnancies. In 2018, a pregnant Tennessee woman named Jordan Cawman broke up with her boyfriend.[28] Even after the breakup, she tried to make him feel involved in the pregnancy by sending him an ultrasound image and pictures of her pregnant belly. He initially brushed her off but later filed a lawsuit demanding that she submit to a paternity test, that he be notified when she went into labor, and that he have the right to be present in the delivery room. In another case, a New Jersey man filed a similar suit against his ex-girlfriend, with the additional demand that the baby be given his last name. Disturbingly, the media reaction to these cases seemed to be shock when these men lost in court. One report announced that the New Jersey court had "made history" by ruling that a woman has the right to control whether her ex-boyfriend watches her give birth.[29]

Fontana and Schoenbaum's "Unsexing Pregnancy" provides a template for overturning those rulings. Witnessing a birth is a powerful emotional experience, surely on par with watching an ultrasound. It thus offers a bonding opportunity, which, according to Fontana and Schoenbaum's reasoning, will make the father more likely to see himself as an equal parent and thus more willing to do the work of parenting. Someone will have to explain to the next Jordan Cawman that while it may feel to her like an invasion when her ex shows up at the delivery room with a court order and a police escort, she should not complain, because the ultimate goal is to "*reduce* the burden on pregnant women" by making men feel more engaged in their parenthood.[30]

After laying out this template for trimming women's rights in the name of sex equality, Fontana and Schoenbaum attempt to impose their caveat that their argument shouldn't be used in situations that "implicate the woman's body." But "Unsexing Pregnancy" doesn't give a single example of when its *Roe/Casey* argument would apply but *not* implicate the woman's body.[31] It can't. The whole point of the state interest in potential life in *Roe* and *Casey* was to justify regulating women's bodies. You can't rely on precedent about the state's power to force women to give birth and then claim the argument somehow doesn't apply when the result would affect women's bodies. Fontana and Schoenbaum merely replace "the state interest in potential life" with "the state interest in sex equality," which in "Unsexing Pregnancy" means a state interest in giving men rights during pregnancy.[32] While they may prefer their rationale not be used to invade women's privacy, at least not too much, the only way to limit that invasion is to admit that, during a pregnancy, only one person is pregnant, and then to protect her rights over her body and her pregnancy accordingly.

REASONING BETTER FROM THE BODY

Defining *pregnancy* as merely the period of expecting to become a parent—the time when you are waiting for the stork—rather than as the physiological process of creating a new human being out of your body is, in essence, defining pregnancy in the way men rather than women typically experience it. It therefore isn't surprising that treating pregnancy as a waiting period leads to decreased rights for women (forced childbirth and no privacy rights while pregnant) and increased rights for men (the male right to abortion and the right to feel equally involved). A bodiless notion of pregnancy-as-waiting-before-parenthood erases both the invasion of an unwanted pregnancy and the relationship that arises from birth.

To say that gestation and birth create a relationship is not to say that an embryo or a fetus is a separate person. A relationship defined by caretaking necessarily develops over time. The act of birth creates the child as a separate person, and it makes a mother of the formerly pregnant woman.[33] Moreover, the relationship created by gestation is also part of the harm of a forced pregnancy and the consequent birth. To be compelled to give birth is to have one's whole self hijacked into motherhood. As Professor Kenneth Karst recognized, "coerced intimate associations are the most repugnant of all forms of compulsory association."[34] The intimate, caretaking relationship created by gestation and birth is part of why forced pregnancy is wrong and thus why the right to abortion is essential to women's lives.

It's also why relational feminism, with its emphasis on the importance of relationships and the harms caused by the law's skewed value system, provides the best theory for describing the importance of abortion to women's equality—but not in the instrumental way the court argued in *Casey*, where the right to abortion mattered because it could help women succeed in other parts of life. Rather, relational feminism explains that a legal system without a right to abortion is a legal system that doesn't recognize women's basic human needs. The right to abortion is not a tool for career success. It is an end in itself, necessary to women's equality because inherent to recognizing women's humanity.

In terms of the relational-feminist analysis from chapter 4, the right to abortion serves the "feminine" need for protection from invasion. Relational feminism argues that the law systematically favors the "masculine" needs (preserving autonomy, help pursuing new connections) over the "feminine" needs (protecting existing relationships, help escaping invasion). Although we've seen that a particular person can have either "masculine" or "feminine" needs, depending on the situation, the physical facts of pregnancy put the pregnant person in the "feminine" position. She needs *either* help escaping the invasion of an unwanted pregnancy *or* protection for the relationship created by gestation and birth. In previous chapters, I've argued that the legal system resists—indeed, can barely comprehend—the need to protect existing relationships. That's why courts transformed the biology-plus-relationship test into a tool for pursuing new connections, mainly (but not always) by genetic fathers. The legal system also resists—indeed, can barely comprehend—a pregnant woman's need to escape from invasion. For example, when courts started giving genetic fathers automatic parental rights (a tool for pursuing new connections), nobody even noticed that those rights invaded the birth mother's rights until it reached extremes like a rapist winning custody of his victim's child. Courts had shifted the biology-plus-relationship test from one category to another, from protection for existing relationships to a tool for pursuing new connections. Similarly, the faulty logic that Professor Siegel criticized in "Reasoning from the Body"—the unexplained logical leap from the state's interest in the fetus to the woman's duty to gestate—was possible because the court was blind to how the pregnancy itself invaded the woman's body and life.[35] Feminists arguing for the right to abortion had to shift from one category to another—from asking to be rescued from an invasion to asking to be left alone to exercise autonomy—in order to have any chance of winning in court. They had to present the right to abortion as a question of autonomy, not invasion, in order for it to count as one of the liberties protected by the Fourteenth Amendment.

That strategic shift distorted what was at stake in the right to abortion. It meant the problem with banning abortion wasn't that the government was failing to protect a woman from an invasion of her body by leaving her pregnant against her will. The problem was that the government was stopping the autonomous woman from doing what she wanted, which was to have an abortion. But to paraphrase Frederica Mathewes-Green, nobody wants an abortion as she wants an ice-cream cone or a Porsche. She wants an abortion as an animal, caught in a trap, wants to be rescued.[36] For some women, the difference isn't critical. If you can pay someone to rescue you from the trap, you can escape without the government's help. All you need is for the government to leave you alone while you hire a doctor to help end the pregnancy, so a right to autonomy is enough to protect your right to abortion. If you can't pay, however, the government's leaving you alone means either you stay in the trap (stay pregnant) or you gnaw off your own leg to escape (get an unsafe illegal abortion). The right to abortion from 1973 to 2022 meant the government was limited in how much it could interfere with a woman who had the money and wherewithal to obtain a safe abortion. Women who lacked the money or the wherewithal could stay pregnant or take their chances in the back alley. The government had to *let you* have an abortion, but it didn't have to *help you.*

The Supreme Court made this clear in 1977's *Maher v. Roe* and 1980's *Harris v. McRae*, in which the court refused to require Medicaid to cover even medically necessary abortions.[37] Medicaid is the federal health insurance program for poor people. In 1976, Congress enacted a provision known as the Hyde Amendment, which said Medicaid could pay for an abortion only if "the life of the mother would be endangered if the fetus were carried to term."[38] Congress re-enacts the Hyde Amendment every year, and in some years it includes exceptions for pregnancies that result from rape or incest, but it has never included an exception to protect the health of the pregnant woman. As Justice Thurgood Marshall explained in a dissenting opinion, in which he argued all medically necessary abortions should be covered:

> Numerous conditions—such as cancer, rheumatic fever, diabetes, malnutrition, phlebitis, sickle cell anemia, and heart disease—substantially increase the risks associated with pregnancy or are themselves aggravated by pregnancy.... By the time a pregnancy has progressed to the point where a physician is able to certify that it endangers the life of the mother, it is in many cases too late to prevent her death. There are also instances in which a woman's life will not be immediately threatened by carrying the pregnancy to term, but aggravation of another medical condition will significantly shorten her life expectancy.[39]

In our first post-*Roe* summer of 2022, the media reported many cases of pregnant women forced to risk hemorrhage, sepsis, heart failure, hysterectomy, and other complications because doctors weren't allowed to abort their pregnancies until death was sufficiently imminent. The strict abortion bans that are now the law in states like Texas are what the Hyde Amendment has been trying to impose on poor women since 1976.

Then as now, however, the majority of the Supreme Court was as unconcerned as Congress was about the plight of poor women. In sanitized language, the court explained:

> The Hyde Amendment ... places no governmental obstacle in the path of a woman who chooses to terminate her pregnancy, but rather, by means of unequal subsidization of abortion and other medical services, encourages alternative activity deemed in the public interest.[40]

Remember, this passage is about medically necessary abortions, so the "alternative activity deemed in the public interest" is for the woman to sacrifice her health, and possibly her life, on the altar of motherhood. An autonomy-based right gets you nowhere if what you need is help. It works well enough for women who have money and social resources and thus resemble the ideal man of liberal theory who wants the government to respect his autonomy and leave him alone. But abortion is a problem of invasion. A woman who is involuntarily pregnant needs to escape the invasion, and for that she needs help.

POSITIVE AND NEGATIVE RIGHTS

In law school, we learn that the right to abortion was only a right to get one *if you could* because the Constitution protects only "negative rights," not "positive rights." The Fourteenth Amendment says,

> No state shall ... deprive any person of life, liberty, or property, without due process of law; nor deny to any person within its jurisdiction the equal protection of the laws.

This passage, law professors tell their students, is "negative." It tells states *not* to do certain things, but it doesn't say they *must* do anything in particular. Other parts of the Constitution are similarly phrased in terms of what the government *shouldn't* do, for example that Congress shall "make no law" abridging the freedom of speech.[41] The Constitution thus prevents the government from unduly interfering with a person's freedom of speech or right to get an abortion. Those are negative rights: they keep the government away from you. But the government doesn't have to pass out megaphones or sponsor your podcast, nor must it provide medical care or otherwise help you by taking any positive action.

The distinction between negative and positive rights was the Supreme Court's justification for its decision in *DeShaney v. Winnebago County,* the case from chapter 3 in which state social workers did nothing while Joshua DeShaney's father beat him into a coma. In *DeShaney,* the court explained,

> While the State may have been aware of the dangers that Joshua faced in the free world, it played no part in their creation, nor did it do anything to render him any more vulnerable to them.... Under these circumstances, the State had no constitutional duty to protect Joshua.[42]

This argument that Joshua had no right to protection from violent abuse closely parallels the court's justification for denying the right to abortion to poor women in the Medicaid cases:

> Although government may not place obstacles in the path of a woman's exercise of her freedom of choice, it need not remove those not of its own creation. Indigency falls in the latter category.[43]

A poor woman is no more entitled to an abortion—in the sense of being entitled to the government's help in obtaining one—than Joshua was entitled to protection once the state knew he was being beaten. As every law student learns, we have a constitution of negative rights, not positive ones.

But that isn't true. In fact, the Supreme Court has a double standard for positive rights, and it's the same double standard we've seen before. The court favors "masculine" positive rights over "feminine" ones.

To understand how, first recall that in chapter 4 we saw the court's double standard for *negative* rights. In *Gideon v. Wainwright* and *Lassiter v. Department of Social Services,* the Supreme Court explicitly ranked the "masculine" interest in preserving autonomy over the "feminine" interest in protecting existing relationships. It held that sending James Earl Gideon to jail for any period of time was a greater harm than permanently taking away Abby Gail Lassiter's son, so Gideon was entitled to a free lawyer but Lassiter was not. The interests at stake in both cases were "negative" rights, meaning they were interests in being left alone by the government. Gideon wanted the government *not* to put him in jail; Lassiter wanted the government *not* to interfere with her relationship with her son. Although both cases involved negative rights, the Supreme Court interpreted the Constitution to give greater protection to the "masculine" negative right to autonomy than to the "feminine" negative right to preserve an existing relationship.

The Supreme Court applies the same double standard to positive rights, preferring the "masculine" need for help pursuing new connections over the "feminine" need for help escaping invasion. A woman who needs an abortion, like the animal caught in the trap, needs to be rescued. So did Joshua DeShaney. In cases like *DeShaney* and the Medicaid abortion cases, the Supreme Court has drawn a sharp line saying the Constitution doesn't oblige the government to provide this help. No one is entitled to rescue, no matter how clear the danger or how low the cost of rescue. The corresponding "masculine" need, however, is for help in pursuing new connections. As Professor Scott Altman put it, the lonely man of liberal theory needs a right to "be provided with background institutions that make success [in forming intimate connections] reasonably likely."[44] The preeminent example of such a "background institution" is marriage. The law provides that institution and the Supreme Court defends the right to marry. The double standard for positive rights is thus even more dramatic than the one for negative rights. The "feminine" positive right to be rescued from invasion doesn't exist at all, while the primary institution for pursuing new connections is one of the most respected rights in constitutional law.

In legal discourse, we hide this double standard by pretending that marriage is really a negative right, not a positive one. Altman's term, "background institution," is telling. The institution of state-sanctioned marriage is supposed to fade into the background so you don't notice the government is creating and maintaining it. Judges say the government may not unduly "interfere" with your freedom to marry, in the same way it may not unduly "interfere" with your freedom of speech. That makes marriage sound like a negative right. But what is the right to marry? Setting religion aside (as we must when discussing the state's role), marriage is a web of legal rights and duties, the terms of which of are written by state and federal governments in thousands of statutes and court decisions.[45] Maintaining the right to marry means requiring the state to issue marriage licenses, administer all of marriage's rights and benefits, and provide an elaborate and expensive dispute-resolution system (divorce courts) for when marriages end. When the government refuses to get involved by doing all those things, we call that "interfering" with the right to marry.[46] But if the state truly wished not to interfere with the right to marry, we would have only religious and other private marriages, not the vast, positive legal support for the institution that exists at every level of government. The masculine need for "background institutions" that help people pursue connections across the void is not only met; the meeting of it is rendered invisible when we pretend that the existence of a government-sponsored institution like marriage requires no positive action by the government.

In contrast, feminine needs to be rescued from invasion—a poor woman's unwanted pregnancy or Joshua DeShaney's abuse—are dismissed from constitutional law. The right to abortion is a matter of sex equality, not just liberty, because the law disfavors the entire *category* of human needs to which abortion belongs (protection from invasion), and those needs are disproportionately associated with women. In the case of abortion, the woman's need is a function of her ability to get pregnant, which the Supreme Court treats as the defining difference between the sexes. Shoehorning the right to abortion into the autonomy box, rather than recognizing a right to be rescued from invasion, had the predictable effect of denying the right to the most vulnerable women, those who couldn't afford an abortion. Autonomy rights are for people with the resources to exercise them.[47]

In chapter 4, we saw Justice Kennedy's ode to the institution of marriage and how it addresses the lonely man's need to pursue connections: "Marriage responds to the universal fear that a lonely person might call out only to find no one there."[48] I'm aware of only one Supreme Court opinion that expresses comparable empathy for a person who needs help escaping from invasion. It was a dissent by Justice Harry Blackmun. Blackmun wrote the majority opinion in *Roe v. Wade* in 1973, and it's a depressing read. It's mainly about doctors' rights, not women's, and it deserves all of Professor Siegel's criticism for "physiological reasoning" that virtually ignores the woman whose physiology is at stake. But after *Roe*, Justice Blackmun received more than seventy thousand letters from the public about abortion. He reportedly read as many of them as he could (from both sides), and his views on abortion changed more than those of any other justice. In his later opinions, he advocated passionately for abortion as a woman's right, including for it to be funded by Medicaid. I like to think all that practice in empathy led him to write this dissent in 1989:

> Today, the Court purports to be the dispassionate oracle of the law, unmoved by "natural sympathy." . . . Like the antebellum judges who denied relief to fugitive slaves, the Court today claims that its decision, however harsh, is compelled by existing legal doctrine. On the contrary, the question presented by this case

is an open one, and our Fourteenth Amendment precedents may be read more broadly or narrowly depending upon how one chooses to read them. . . .

Poor Joshua! Victim of repeated attacks by an irresponsible, bullying, cowardly, and intemperate father, and abandoned by [state officials], who placed him in a dangerous predicament and who knew or learned what was going on, and yet did essentially nothing except, as the Court revealingly observes, "dutifully recorded these incidents in [their] files." It is a sad commentary upon American life, and constitutional principles—so full of late of patriotic fervor and proud proclamations about "liberty and justice for all," that this child, Joshua DeShaney, now is assigned to live out the remainder of his life profoundly retarded. Joshua and his mother, as petitioners here, deserve—but now are denied by this Court—the opportunity to have the facts of their case considered in the light of the constitutional protection that [the Fourteenth Amendment] is meant to provide.[49]

More than any other justice, Justice Blackmun after *Roe* lived with constant reminders of how the court's decisions affected people's lives, especially those in need of rescue from an involuntary pregnancy. Joshua needed a different kind of rescue, but the empathy required to interpret the Constitution to respond to his plight was the same.

Justice Blackmun's reference to the Fugitive Slave Act at the beginning of the above passage is neither gratuitous nor incidental. The most important positive right in the Constitution is the Thirteenth Amendment: "Neither slavery nor involuntary servitude . . . shall exist within the United States, or any place subject to their jurisdiction." To say that slavery *shall not* exist puts a positive duty on the government to eliminate it, not just to refrain from maintaining it. It gives the government a duty to rescue. That duty was at the heart of what constitutional scholars call the second founding, meaning Reconstruction and the post–Civil War amendments to the Constitution.[50] The first founding gave us an assortment of negative autonomy rights known as the Bill of Rights. The second founding, however, began with the duty to prevent the powerful from hijacking the lives of other people through slavery. There's no reason, other than the Supreme Court's hostility to the prospect, that a duty to rescue the oppressed and trapped couldn't have become as powerful a force in our law as the duty to refrain from molesting the free. With some notable exceptions, however, the justices of the Supreme Court have opposed the second founding and fought to keep the Constitution of "masculine" rights—freedom from the government in the form of autonomy rights, plus the right to background institutions like marriage for pursuing connections, as solace for the lonely.

The exceptions are found mostly in dissents, like Justice Blackmun's dissent in *DeShaney*, but occasionally the feminine values slip into majority opinions. A partial right to abortion lasted almost fifty years by masquerading as an autonomy right. The biology-plus-relationship test was another one of the slips. When the Supreme Court formulated the biology-plus-relationship test, it reasoned well from the body, including when it assumed that childbirth gives rise to a parent-child relationship. The court recognized that biological motherhood was different not just biologically but also socially from biological fatherhood. Biological motherhood includes a social, caretaking relationship. The court made the birth mother the model for parenthood because that relationship was important to why it thought the Constitution should protect parental rights. At the same time, the court avoided the fallacies that come from fixating on physiology rather than on how that physiology is relevant to people's lives. The physiology of pregnancy matters, but not because science can answer questions like "who should be the legal parent of this child?" or "do women have the right to abortion?" The physiology matters because it is part of the pregnant woman's life.[51] Like other forms of caretaking (breastfeeding, changing a diaper, swinging a toddler in the air), it is both physical and social. Minds and hearts are part of bodies, and relationships are made from bodies interacting with each other, including when one body makes another through pregnancy. In the Unwed Father Cases, the Supreme Court recognized the relationship that results from gestation and childbirth not in a misty, sentimental way but simply as one example of an intimate, caretaking relationship that, once it exists, is worthy of protection.

NINE

The Body and Beyond

IF THE LAW HAD FOLLOWED through on the Unwed Father Cases and placed more value on the caretaking relationship formed through pregnancy, what would that mean for surrogacy contracts? In the early years of the surrogacy industry in the 1980s and 1990s, feminists feared surrogacy would usher in a *Handmaid's Tale*–style dystopia, only with women of color forming the underclass of gestators who would carry embryos made from the genes of White couples.[1] Those fears didn't materialize, and surrogacy seems to be here to stay. Therefore in recent years, feminists have focused less on whether surrogacy should be allowed and more on how it should be regulated. This new discussion should include the question of when a surrogate would be justified in refusing to hand over the baby.

Early feminist fears about surrogacy seemed to be coming true around the turn of the millennium, when India briefly emerged as a leader in international surrogacy before banning it in 2012. The Indian surrogacy industry featured live-in fertility clinics that catered to foreign clients and that critics described as "reproductive brothels."[2] The surrogates lived in the clinics for the duration of their pregnancies, and staff closely monitored their diets, activities, and medical care. The doctor who ran one clinic held all the surrogates' payments "in trust," dispensing their money only when the surrogate requested it for what the doctor deemed a legitimate purpose. The Indian government openly discussed building orphanages to house any children the foreign contracting parents decided they didn't want, as happened in Thailand in 2014: When an Australian couple arrived to pick up their twins born to a surrogate, they discovered that one of the twins had Down syndrome. They left him with the surrogate and went home with just one baby.[3] International surrogacy, with its long distances and extreme financial disparities between surrogates and their customers, showed surrogacy at its most starkly commercial.

On the other hand, the money a woman in the global South could earn as a surrogate could be life-changing. Feminist scholars like Professor Cyra Choudhury argued for regulating surrogacy through labor laws designed to protect the workers without denying them this opportunity.[4] The Indian clinic director described above argued that she held the women's money in trust to protect it from overbearing or irresponsible husbands. She claimed she would release the funds for a daughter's education or for a woman to start a business, but she wanted to keep the women's husbands from taking control of the cash. Surrogacy may have been disturbing to Western feminist sensibilities of the time, but it was less dangerous and more lucrative than many other options for poor women around the world, including poor women in the United States. In addition, it was clear surrogacy was going to happen whether it was legal or not. Extending the "reproductive brothel" metaphor, many feminists believed that criminalizing surrogacy, like criminalizing sex work, only made things worse for the women doing the work. Feminists therefore never pursued the suggestion from the New Jersey Supreme Court in *Baby M* that surrogacy should be prosecuted as human trafficking.

In thinking about how to regulate surrogacy, feminists were more concerned with the welfare of the surrogate than of the contracting parents. If anything, feminists were suspicious of the motives of the contracting parents, especially the mothers-to-be. Were wives being dragged along on husbands' quests for genetic parenthood, perhaps like Elizabeth Stern in *Baby M,* in which the surrogacy contract was the product of her husband's strong desire for genetic offspring and her fear of pregnancy? Or were the wives themselves the driving force behind the pursuit of parenthood, perhaps because they were under excessive social pressure to become mothers?[5] Either way, feminists worried about protecting the surrogate, not the contracting parents.

Later, however, many feminists came to see surrogacy as a matter of reproductive justice, especially for gay men. Some feminists even envisioned a "revolutionary alliance" of poor women of color helping gay men have babies.[6] They saw surrogacy as an opportunity to challenge the biological definition of the family and the law's preference for traditional, nuclear families. Others, however, thought surrogacy reinforced the traditional family by putting a high value on genetic ties. Lamenting this drift to traditionalism, Professor Michael Boucai recalled a past in which "queer politics, thought, and social life . . . reliably countered that love, not blood, makes a family," and he portrayed gay men's turn to surrogacy, and away from adoption, as an abandonment of those values.[7] But feminists still thought a ban on surrogacy would be unfair to gay men (and other aspiring parents who can't gestate), and they still worried a ban would end up hurting the women working as surrogates, so they found themselves in an uneasy alliance with the surrogacy industry. Rather than ban surrogacy, they wanted the law to regulate it, hopefully in ways that would protect the interests of the women working as surrogates.

As the industry developed, domestic surrogacy in the United States turned out not to replicate the racial structure and extreme financial disparities of early international surrogacy, nor did it mount much of a challenge to the hegemony of the traditional nuclear family.[8] Most contracting parents are straight married couples. The typical American surrogate is White, Christian, married to a man, and already a mother. She is less well off than the contracting parents, but she is not poor. Some of these characteristics are due to screening by the industry. Lawyers and brokers who negotiate surrogacy contracts believe a woman who already has children is less likely to change her mind about giving up the baby. Her husband, too, is a buffer against any wavering; the industry counts on him to oppose keeping a baby that isn't genetically his. After the early worries about exploitation of women of color, the whiteness of surrogacy in the US has left some scholars wondering why White aspiring parents *don't* seem to want women of color as surrogates.[9]

At least part of the answer is trust. Domestic surrogacy doesn't allow for the intense supervision offered at India's live-in clinics in the 2000s. Although surrogacy contracts often include provisions that restrict the surrogate's behavior—no smoking, no sex, no nonorganic food—compliance is hard to monitor, and at least some of those terms may not be legally enforceable. Instead, contracting parents rely on a relationship of trust with the surrogate, which White contracting parents may be more likely to develop with a surrogate who is also White and who is perhaps similar to them in other ways. Professor Pamela Laufer-Ukeles finds, "What starts with the desire to 'procure' a child, usually ends with familial collaboration and interconnectedness based on mutual respect and ongoing contact."[10] This quasi-familial relationship frequently includes the racial sorting that characterizes American marriage.

Many surrogates also experience the process in familial terms. Rather than bond with the eventual baby, surrogates who are satisfied with their experience report that they drew their satisfaction from their relationship with the contracting parents. When a surrogacy plan falls apart, the cause is likely to be conflict between the surrogate and the contracting parents rather than unexpected attachment to the baby. This pattern holds regardless of whether the contract is for full surrogacy (where the surrogate is also the genetic mother) or gestation-only surrogacy. Contrary to the split in American law, which favors gestation-only surrogacy, it is the surrogate's trust and confidence in the contracting parents, rather than the presence or absence of a genetic tie to the fetus, that makes the surrogate willing to surrender the child—or her lack of trust and confidence in them that makes her unwilling.[11] For many people participating in surrogacy, the relationship between the surrogate and the contracting parents thus has the quality of a family relationship.

SURROGACY AS A CONTRACT FOR FAMILY

As we saw in chapter 7, *Baby M* in New Jersey and *Johnson v. Calvert* in California were the leading cases that made genes a key distinction in the law of surrogacy. A full surrogate, who is the genetic as well as gestational mother, is usually considered a mother, while a gestation-only surrogate who becomes pregnant through IVF is more likely to be seen like a babysitter or nanny. In neither *Baby M, Johnson v. Calvert,* nor the laws and decisions in other states that followed them did the surrogate's reason for wanting to keep the baby factor into courts' decisions. Either the surrogate was the legal mother or she wasn't; nannies don't get to decide whether to give back the child at the end of the day. I suggested in chapter 7 that courts wrongly used this simplistic analysis to avoid grappling with the surrogacy contract itself, which would mean confronting the *reason* why the surrogate was backing out.

Courts didn't consider the reason for the surrogate's backing out because they assumed they already knew what it was. Courts see a surrogate who wants to keep the baby not as having changed her *mind* but as having had a change of *heart*.[12] They assume the reason she wants to back out is that she failed to predict her emotional bond with the baby and now can't bear to give it up. The question in the court's mind then becomes: Is an overpowering emotional bond with the child such an inevitable outcome of pregnancy that the law should refuse to enforce surrogacy contracts, in order to protect women from making this mistake? Professor John Lawrence Hill, on whose work the California Supreme Court relied in *Johnson v. Calvert,* argued that surrogacy contracts should be enforced because emotional bonding with a fetus was not biologically inevitable. He made the following observations, which sound like the field notes of a Vulcan trying to understand human emotion.[13] Here he is, for example, expressing something like surprise that a miscarriage could be distressing and sad:

> There is empirical support for the claim that women mourn after the loss of a baby, even a nonviable fetus.

And here he expresses a muted wonder that a woman could become depressed after being forced to surrender an infant for adoption:

> These experiences were reported even by women who were not permitted to see their babies upon birth. . . . In contrast to voluntary adoption, studies also suggest that the negative effects of relinquishment actually may be exacerbated by a compelled surrender of the child.

On the other hand, he cited the following as evidence that relinquishing a newborn shouldn't be difficult:

> Only 41% [of women] felt love during pregnancy. This response suggests that prenatal attachment is not an immutable biological imperative that supports a universal legal commitment to the priority of the gestational host.

Hill is claiming here that if 59 percent of pregnant women can avoid falling in love with their fetuses, then the law is justified in enforcing surrogacy contracts against a surrogate who decides she wants to keep the baby. ("Gestational host" means a gestation-only surrogate. I'm not sure whether that makes the fetus a parasite or a party guest.)

Setting aside whether 41 percent of women feeling love during pregnancy deserves the modifier "only," I offer my own story in rebuttal to Hill's interpretation of this survey. If I had participated in this survey, I would have been in the 59 percent who answered "no." I first felt something I would call love for my son on the morning after he was born. That doesn't mean I had no "prenatal attachment." It means I didn't yet think of him as a separate person. As I went to sleep a few hours after he was born, I thought of my own mother, who had her children when babies were whisked from the delivery room to the hospital nursery, only visiting their mothers at scheduled times. I imagined a nurse walking into the room to say, "It's time for the baby to go to the nursery so you can get some sleep." It was incomprehensible, as impossible as sending my leg to a different room for the night. My emotions hadn't yet caught up with the physical reality of my son's separate existence. That is, of course, my individual experience. There are many ways to experience the transition from solo person to pregnant person to person whom another person just came out of. A woman's emotions about a pregnancy and how it ends are undoubtedly influenced by the physiology of pregnancy, her wishes and plans, and even how society has told her she ought to feel.[14] But it's telling that someone so seemingly mystified by the idea of a woman's mourning a miscarriage or becoming depressed after being forced to surrender a newborn was also a primary authority for the California Supreme Court's decision to enforce surrogacy contracts.

In deciding to enforce surrogacy contracts, California and other states treated the surrogate's emotions as essentially irrational. They cordoned off those emotions and treated enforcement as an all-or-nothing question: gestation-only surrogacy contracts would either be enforced or not, without regard to the reason the surrogate gave for wanting to renege. In *Johnson v. Calvert,* the California Supreme Court attributed the breakdown in the surrogacy contract to Anna's "change of heart," even though it also noted that the Calverts had failed to buy the life insurance policy they had promised her and had allegedly acted callously when Anna went into preterm labor. The court cast Anna's allegations as emotional complaints rather than issues of contract law. In the court's description, Anna *felt* rather than *alleged* (as in, alleging a breach of contract) that the Calverts hadn't tried hard enough to get the insurance policy. It apparently never occurred to the court that the Calverts' alleged behavior could reasonably have affected Anna's views about making a baby for them. Perhaps Anna's "heart" had changed because the people she was making a baby for were acting like both she and the fetus she carried were disposable. Maybe that isn't fair to the Calverts, but the point is we have no way of knowing whether it's fair. It was, under the court's analysis, irrelevant. The court ignored the possibility that Anna's change of heart could be anything but arbitrary—that it could, for example, have coincided with a change of mind in response to new information about the Calverts.

The New Jersey Supreme Court, in *Baby M,* hinted at these sorts of problems when it bemoaned the fact that a surrogate typically signs her contract with very little information about the contracting parents. Mary Beth Whitehead, the surrogate in *Baby M,* may also have gained information during her pregnancy that made her less trusting of the contracting parents, William and Elizabeth Stern. Genetic reproduction was especially important to William because he had lost family in the Holocaust. At the time of entering the surrogacy contract, Elizabeth presented herself as medically unable to carry a pregnancy; she had diagnosed herself as possibly having multiple sclerosis. Depending on how much risk you think a woman should be willing to take for the sake of motherhood, you could interpret Elizabeth's actions as evidence of unwillingness, not inability, to carry the pregnancy. Mary Beth may have come to see it that way and may have concluded that Elizabeth was insufficiently committed to motherhood.

Something like that played out in a later case involving a surrogate named Danielle who gave birth in Cincinnati to triplets intended for James, a Cleveland man who was the genetic father, and his partner Eileen.[15] (The egg was from a donor.) Eileen already had grown children, and the couple had been unable to conceive with IVF. The triplets were born prematurely and hospitalized in intensive care for a week. Danielle began to have doubts about the couple because James visited the ICU only once during that week, and Eileen, who was busy babysitting her grandchildren while her daughter went on vacation, didn't visit at all. The trial judge in their case shared Danielle's doubts about James and Eileen and ruled that Danielle was "the better caretaker by far." But the Ohio Supreme Court, which had never before considered the issue of surrogacy, took just over two pages to rule that Danielle's lack of genetic tie to the triplets made the contract enforceable.[16] In both *Baby M* and the Cincinnati case, the contracting parents' turn to surrogacy seemed driven more by the husband's desire for genetic offspring than by the wife's interest in motherhood, which may have triggered doubts for both surrogates.

Consider one more example, the Iowa case from the introduction.[17] Tiana Baca, who was Black, agreed to be a surrogate for Christine and Peter Miller, who were White, with an embryo made from Peter's sperm and a donated egg. After Tiana became pregnant, the Millers started acting out feminist fears about White couples using surrogacy contracts to exploit Black women. Christine told Tiana that because the couple was paying her, they were in charge of her life for the duration of the pregnancy. Tiana's job was simply to say "yes, ma'am." Christine also called Tiana the N-word in an email. Peter used other racial slurs and profanity when talking about Tiana's husband on Facebook. Near the end of her pregnancy, Tiana decided not to hand over the baby. Perhaps she had formed an unexpected emotional attachment, but she may also have decided the Millers were unacceptable as parents; indeed, the latter decision could well have produced the former attachment. Because she was a surrogate, however, she wasn't entitled to assess the Millers' quality as parents. The Iowa Supreme Court enforced the surrogacy contract without even asking whether the Millers' racism and other bad behavior were grounds for breach.

The courts in all these cases treated the surrogates' "change of heart" as feminine weakness requiring no particular exploration or explanation. The question was merely whether to defer to that weakness, by holding surrogacy contracts unenforceable, or to enforce the contracts and make the women stick to the deals they had made. This way of posing the question puts feminists on the spot. Are women fully competent decision-makers who can assess their own interests and enter into contracts, or are they helpless victims of their emotions who need courts to protect them from their own choices? Put that way, the question answers itself.

That way of putting the question, however, overlooks important parts of the surrogacy bargain. As we've seen, a successful surrogacy contract is one in which the surrogate has a positive relationship with the contracting parents. That relationship helps give meaning to her labor, and it ensures that when she hands over the baby, she can be confident she's doing the right thing for the child. When a surrogacy agreement falls apart, it's usually because "one party to the contract feels the other has not met the expectations for emotional engagement"—such as Anna's feelings of abandonment by the Calverts or, in the other direction, when contracting parents feel the surrogate has shut them out.[18] When the cases go to court, however, judges ignore this relationship at the heart of the contract and focus only on ownership of the child. They define that ownership in terms of genes and the parties' intent. "Intent," as we saw in chapter 7, is a euphemism for the contract; courts use the euphemism to avoid doing any actual contractual analysis. Contract law, after all, has all kinds of ways to void, breach, cancel, modify, or otherwise get out of the terms of a contract. But if "intent," rather than the contract, made the Calverts automatically the parents from the moment of fertilization in the lab, then the court can ignore whether their alleged indifference to Anna's well-being violated important terms of the contract. If James and Eileen simply *were* the parents, then it was none of anyone's business whether they visited their babies in the ICU. And if genes and a contract made the Millers the irrefutable parents of the child Tiana Baca bore—well, no White person ever lost custody of their kids for being racist and abusive toward the domestic help.

What happens if we suppose, contrary to how courts decide surrogacy cases, that a surrogate who decides she wants to keep the baby might have a *reason* for changing both her mind and her heart? Then courts might have to ask not "should we defer to women's fickle emotions?" but "what kind of reason would justify breaching a surrogacy contract by refusing to surrender the child?" The contracting parents' genes (and money) shouldn't be a trump card against every possible reason the surrogate could give for keeping the baby.

One way to decide what reasons justify a surrogate's refusing to surrender the baby would be to say the surrogate gets to decide. That would mean courts would never force her to hand over the baby. In my view, this would be the best option. Consistent with the biology-plus-relationship test, this approach would effectively make the surrogate the legal mother by virtue of gestation and birth, and the contracting parents wouldn't have rights based on genes alone. It's a good thing for the surrogate to care and feel some responsibility for whether the contracting parents will be good parents of the child she is making for them. Admittedly, it may not be fair to the contracting parents to say their genes are their only contribution. I suggested in chapter 7 that the Calverts, for example, could get some credit toward the relationship prong of biology-plus-relationship based on their involvement in the pregnancy. Nonetheless, the balance of power between the surrogate and the contracting parents argues in favor of giving the surrogate the final say. Professor Julie Shapiro has persuasively argued that letting the surrogate decide is the better rule in light of how surrogacy in the US has developed. Since we now know that with "careful screening and counseling of the parties and the construction of a positive relationship between the surrogate and the intended parents," surrogacy can be successful, Shapiro argues that judicial enforcement is unnecessary.[19] In addition, making the contract unenforceable would create more incentives for the contracting parents to treat the surrogate well and for intermediaries, like fertility clinics and surrogacy brokers, to provide thorough screening and high-quality counseling to all participants in surrogacy.[20]

If the surrogate has the right to back out of the contract, some surrogates will surely do so for reasons I disagree with. Of the examples we've seen, the Iowa case provides the easiest basis for disliking the Millers and questioning whether they "deserved" the baby Tiana bore. *Baby M* and the Cincinnati case are harder, at least as I have conjectured about the surrogates' views of the facts, because the surrogates' objections to the contracting parents may have been based in part on stereotypes about mothers as primary parents. In Ohio, for example, if Danielle's ire was directed at Eileen, more than at James, for failing to show a mother's proper concern for the newborn triplets in the ICU, that seems unfair. On the other hand, the surrogacy industry sometimes relies on a sentimental vision of motherhood to recruit women to work as surrogates. Surrogates are encouraged to think of themselves as "not in it for the money" but for the sake of giving someone else the gift of parenthood. ("Surrogate mothers are amazing, selfless women who help make parenthood possible!"[21]) Often it is specifically to help another *woman* who has been unable to have a child. If the surrogate signed the contract because she was led to believe in the contracting mother's desire for and commitment to a baby, then perhaps she has cause for complaint if that desire and commitment were exaggerated. Indeed, the complaint I have hypothesized for Mary Beth Whitehead against Elizabeth Stern—that Elizabeth was unwilling rather than unable to carry the pregnancy—is one with which many lawmakers would apparently sympathize. In several states, surrogacy is allowed only when the contracting mother is medically unable to carry the pregnancy. The law thus declares that women capable of pregnancy aren't allowed to buy their way out through surrogacy. It isn't clear why the surrogate shouldn't be able to impose the same condition and consider it a breach of contract if she later learns the contracting mother would have been able to gestate with only whatever we have decided is the "normal" (and thus normative) level of risk from pregnancy.

If the surrogate isn't allowed to decide whether to complete the contract, then the alternative is to have a judge decide what counts as a valid reason. That would include asking questions like whether the surrogate is unfairly stereotyping the contracting mother, or whether she's entitled to do so because the contract rested on that stereotype. I'm not convinced judges will be better than surrogate mothers at answering those questions. We saw in chapter 3 that the most popular modern justification for parental rights, the best-for-the-child rationale, is based on the assumption that the person who has an intimate, caretaking relationship with a child is the best person to make decisions on behalf of that child. At the time of birth, that person is the birth mother, regardless of genes or contracts. However, given how established the surrogacy industry is in the US, it may be unrealistic to expect the law to cede back to surrogates the right to decide whether to surrender the baby. To the extent judges are instead called upon to make this decision, they should recognize that the relationship of trust among the adult parties is at the heart of a surrogacy contract. When the relationship and thus the contract fails, courts should ask who was responsible for destroying that trust rather than simply declare that the contracting parents are the legal parents.

The fact that the surrogate is being paid doesn't negate the caretaking relationship she forms through gestation, and she should at least have an avenue for arguing that the contract should be cancelled.

CARETAKING BEYOND THE BODY

In this book, I've argued that gestation establishes a caretaking relationship worthy of protection, but I've also said gestation is *not* inherently more valuable than other caretaking. That caveat is important to my claim that "essentially a mother" means simply that gestation satisfies the biology-plus-relationship test, rather than meaning that gestation is uniquely precious as a path to parenthood. Other parents who take care of children—genetic fathers, adoptive parents, and other non-gestational parents—have equally important relationships with their children.

At the end of the last section, I said the fact of payment shouldn't negate the caretaking relationship a surrogate forms through gestation. Gestation, however, is not the only form of caretaking that is bought and sold. Nannies, foster parents, and daycare workers all trade their caretaking for money. Often, they give and receive love in the process. Indeed, courts and other advocates for surrogacy often analogize surrogates to nannies or babysitters. They intend this analogy to minimize the surrogate's role and her claim to the child. The implication of being "like a nanny" is that the surrogate is *only* a nanny—a mere employee, not a mother. If all of my claims are correct— gestation establishes a protected relationship, that relationship is equal to but not better than other similar relationships, and payment does not negate it—then it follows that payment also does not negate the value of other, post-birth caretaking relationships. That is to say, if courts were to reconsider the law of surrogacy and give more protection to the relationship formed through gestation, they should also reconsider the law's refusal to protect other relationships formed through paid caretaking. They would need to ask, for example, whether a nanny who has effectively raised a child should be fire-able at any time, with no recourse to protect her relationship with the child.

Like contracting parents who hire surrogates, parents who hire a nanny want her to feel attached to the child in ways that benefit the child, but not to the point of displacing the parents. They want the nanny "to operate as a 'shadow mother,' acting like a mother during the day and then vanishing as soon as the real mother return[s], 'leaving no trace of her presence in the psychic lives of the children they shared.'" [22] From the nanny's side, the relationship she forms with the children in her care can be a source of both satisfaction and exploitation. A nanny or other childcare worker may think of her work as a form of mothering and may value the bonds she forms with children at work.[23] At the same time, employers who claim their nanny as part of the family may demand familial loyalty and correspondingly poor terms of employment.[24] (When I was a part-time nanny in college, the woman who hired me initially suggested that instead of hourly pay, I should just let her know when I needed money, "for pizza or something," and that she would give me her hand-me-down clothes.)

The race and class patterns that feminists feared would characterize surrogacy have long been true for childcare after birth, including the international component. Professor Arlie Hochschild describes how the organization of childcare can connect a string of women:

> Rowena Bautista... flew to Washington, DC, where she took a job as a nanny for the same pay that a small-town doctor would make in the Philippines.... Rowena's own children live in a four-bedroom house [in the Philippines] with her parents and twelve other family members—eight of them children, some of whom also have mothers who work abroad. The central figure in the children's lives—the person they call "Mama"—is Grandma, Rowena's mother. But Grandma works surprisingly long hours as a teacher—from 7:00 a.m. to 9:00 p.m.... Rowena's father is not much involved with his grandchildren. So she has hired Anna de la Cruz, who arrives daily at 8:00 a.m. to cook, clean, and care for the children. Meanwhile, Anna de la Cruz leaves her teenage son in the care of her eighty-year-old mother-in-law.[25]

This is the scaffolding of the "stalled revolution." At the top is the unnamed American woman in Washington, DC, who hired Rowena as a nanny for her child. American women have won equality of legal rights at work but not equality of obligations at home, relative to their husbands. But merely getting American husbands to do their share of the housework isn't going to solve the problem of children needing full-time care when parents have full-time jobs. The system that passes the work of parenthood down this chain of women is not just propping up the DC woman's professional opportunities (and possibly her husband's successful avoidance of equality at home). It is the product of an economic system that devalues caretaking. Hochschild describes what is being imported and exported in the international market for childcare, in which love and care have become the "new gold":

Today's North does not extract love from the South by force: there are no colonial officers in tan helmets, no invading armies, no ships bearing arms sailing off to the colonies. Instead, we see a benign scene of Third World women pushing baby carriages, elder-care workers patiently walking, arms linked, with elderly clients on streets or sitting beside them in First World parks.[26]

Like the surrogacy industry, the childcare industry trades money for caretaking and sometimes for love. The workers in both industries are expected to form parent-like relationships and may develop strong emotional attachments to the children they create or care for.

In the eyes of the law, a person who takes care of a child for free—such as a stepparent or grandparent—can eventually become a "quasi-parent." A quasi-parent is someone who is so important in a child's life that both the child and the quasi-parent are entitled to have the law protect their relationship, even against the legal parents.[27] It is someone who is less than a legal parent but more than a legal stranger. We saw an example of a quasi-parent rule in *Troxel v. Granville,* the grandparent-visitation case. In that case, the Supreme Court held the family court had to give "special weight" to the mother's decision to scale back the children's time with the grandparents, but *Troxel* didn't prohibit courts from ordering visiting time for grandparents or other quasi-parents. If parents completely cut off all contact with a grandparent or another person who is very important to a child, the state can still intervene.

Every state has some provision in its laws that allows for quasi-parents to ask for a court's help in maintaining their relationship with a child. The details and requirements vary across states, but all of them have exceptions that prohibit a *paid* caretaker from ever becoming a quasi-parent. The standard justification for this exception is as follows (as stated by a prestigious committee that makes recommendations to states about their laws):

> The law grants parents responsibility for their children based, in part, on the assumption that they are motivated by love and loyalty, and thus are likely to act in the child's best interests. The same motivations cannot be assumed on the part of adults who have provided caretaking functions primarily for financial reasons.[28]

This justification fundamentally misunderstands *why* parents are assumed to act in their children's best interests. As we saw in chapter 3, the parent's desire and ability to do what's best for the child *arise out of* the caretaking relationship. My mother's judgment about which of her children should keep taking piano lessons was better than anyone else's judgment because of the countless hours she spent hearing and watching us practice (or not), not because of her abstract status as our legal parent.

Moreover, it doesn't make much sense to say that paid caretakers must be excluded from quasi-parenthood because they're only in it for the money. The whole point of a quasi-parent claim would be that, for example, a nanny who has been fired is asking for unpaid time to visit the child and maintain the relationship. Her visiting time would no longer be paid, and it might consist only of the right to communicate with the child. Rather, the paid-caretaker exception is really about the power of money in a different way. The paid-caretaker exception lets parents hire a nanny without worrying about whether she can be dismissed at will, and it reflects an ideological commitment to the prerogatives of people with money. One of the contracting parents in the Cincinnati surrogacy case summed this up well. When Danielle, the surrogate, decided James and Eileen were unfit parents after they failed to visit the premature triplets in the ICU, the trial judge gave Danielle primary custody while the case was pending. At one of the hearings, James testified about Danielle, "The person who has [the babies] now has no connection them at all. We paid her." Obviously, it isn't true that Danielle had no connection to the babies she physically made and gave birth to. James's first sentence makes sense only in light of his second: "We paid her." James was expressing the belief that because he had paid for something—Danielle's gestational relationship with the triplets—it belonged entirely to him. The paid-caretaker exception to quasi-parent rules reflects the same belief about using market transactions to turn love and caretaking into commodities. If you pay her, it doesn't count.

But money changing hands doesn't make either a surrogate or a nanny merely a shadow of a legal parent. She is the person taking care of the child. In Professor Barbara Katz Rothman's words,

> Someone has to watch the children.... Whoever that person is ... must never be thought of as being there in place of someone else. The person who is there, is there.[29]

The person who is there is thereby forming a caretaking relationship with the child. Money can compensate that person for their time and effort, but it can't transfer the bond created through caretaking from the employee to the employer.

Every state has at least some provision in its laws for a quasi-parent status that gives grandparents and others with close relationships to children the right to continue those relationships. There is thus space in the law for a person who is not a legal parent but also not a stranger to a child. Especially after the Supreme Court's decision in *Troxel,* which required judges to give more deference to the legal parent, the bar to becoming a quasi-parent is high. A nanny seeking the right to visit a child after being fired by the parents would have to show that she had established a close caretaking relationship that the parents had arbitrarily cut off, and she'd probably have to show the child was suffering as a result. Given that the bar is already high even for unpaid quasi-parents, there's no need to categorically exclude her claim because she was paid for her time caring for the child. The fact of payment, whether in surrogacy or childcare, shouldn't automatically defeat the possibility of a relationship worth the law's protection. Caretaking is labor, but it need not be alienated labor that renders the worker a stranger to the person she helped create.

Conclusion

CULTURAL FEMINISTS OF THE 1980S correctly identified a pathology in American law. The law promotes an ideal of freedom for a man who, as Robin West observed, is "at best a sociopathic caricature of the 'individual' celebrated by classical liberals."[1] Feminists argued the law should equally promote an ideal of mutual obligations based on human relationships, with the relationship between mother and child as its model. West added the insight that each of these competing ideals implies that a person needs a particular kind of help from the state. The ideal man's lonely freedom drives him to pursue new connections, which produces his need for background institutions like marriage, which the law provides. The ideal woman's inherent connectedness to others makes her vulnerable to invasions like unwanted pregnancy or an abusive marriage. The state's response to these invasions ranges from neglect (as when it turns a blind eye to violence against women) to enthusiastic participation (as when it forces women to give birth).

Relational feminists took those insights and added that the "ideal man" and "ideal woman" are exactly that—ideals. When feminists describe the contrasting values of these ideals, they are describing the workings of the law, not the full humanity of any person. To the extent the ideal people correspond (in shifting and imperfect ways) to real people, they correlate with gender in part because gender correlates with power. Autonomy rights—the right to have an abortion, if you can pay for it; the right to speak your mind, as long as your boss won't fire you and your family won't shun you for it—are for people with money and personal security. Those same people are the least likely to have their lives invaded in ways they lack the resources to defend against. The correlation between gender and power doesn't have to be perfect for the preference for "masculine" values to reinforce the existing structure of power over the long term. A general preference for the values most useful to the powerful is enough.

For example, relational feminism explains why courts rejected the biology-plus-relationship test as the legal definition of parenthood, because placing value on caretaking relationships was a disfavored "feminine" value. As the test seeped through the courts, judges transformed it from a rule for protecting existing relationships into a tool for claiming new connections and invading the birth mother's relationship with the child. In making this transformation, judges didn't merely reject the possibility of defining fatherhood as a caretaking relationship. In the name of sex equality, they went further and eviscerated the definition of motherhood in the same way, ultimately toppling the assumption that giving birth to a child makes you a parent. Donna Fasano's and Mina Kim's nine months of caretaking that turned pre-embryos into children didn't count toward forming a parent-child relationship any more than Joseph Boulais's lifetime of caretaking for his son Tuan counted toward making Tuan a fellow American citizen.

The bloody consequences of the law's skewed value system are all around us, and they extend well beyond the law of parenthood. Joshua DeShaney spent his life severely disabled and died young because the law cared more about his father's right to possess him than about his need to be rescued. As I finished this book in the spring of 2022, heavily armed police officers loitered in a hallway while on the other side of an unlocked door, twenty-one children and teachers were murdered in a classroom in Uvalde, Texas, because the law protects individual freedom to wield military weapons but imposes no duty on the state to lift a finger in anyone's defense. One month later, the Supreme Court condemned untold numbers of women and girls to the invasion of forced pregnancy and an unknown but certain percentage of them to death, without even remarking on their sacrifice. Relational feminism explains how the law's skewed value system produces these outcomes. One way power works is through seemingly neutral legal rules that reliably favor people with power, which in these cases means favoring "masculine" needs over "feminine" ones.[2] The law favors the background institutions for pursuing new connections over a person's need to be rescued from abuse within those institutions, and so it favored the parental rights of Joshua's father over protecting Joshua from the dangers he faced in his father's free world. The law favors the sociopathic freedom to own heavy weaponry over schoolchildren's need to be rescued from the sociopath's free world, and so the first official report on the Uvalde massacre blamed the victims for leaving doors unlocked but never blamed the cowards who pass the laws and the profiteers who stoke the fears that flood our communities with weapons of mass murder.[3] And even when *Roe v. Wade* partially protected the right to abortion, the Supreme Court always treated abortion as a tragedy, never a boon that freed a woman from an unwanted invasion of her body.[4] The court never recognized what was at stake with the right to abortion: whether women were fully human in the eyes of the law.

The Supreme Court's refusal to incorporate women's humanity into constitutional law infects the court's entire jurisprudence of sex equality. In *Geduldig v. Aiello,* the Supreme Court held it was sex-neutral for the state to provide disability benefits for prostate surgery, gout, and circumcision but not for pregnancy. The court thereby endorsed a system of work that made pregnancy and childbirth incompatible with paid employment; pregnant women and mothers were to survive by being dependent on a husband. In *Dobbs v. Jackson Women's Health,* the court extended *Geduldig* to say bans on abortion were also sex-neutral. The court simultaneously insisted that the scope of protected liberty under the Fourteenth Amendment should be determined according to the beliefs of "eminent common-law authorities" like Matthew Hale, a seventeenth-century English judge who sentenced witches to be hanged and promoted the legal rule that raping your wife isn't a crime.[5] Truly are we now governed by a sociopathic caricature.

The genetic definition of parenthood is just as sex-neutral as pregnancy benefits and the right to abortion—meaning it isn't sex-neutral at all, and feminists should be just as scornful of claims that biological motherhood and fatherhood are "equal" as we are of the Supreme Court's ridiculous claims in *Geduldig* and *Dobbs* that imposing special burdens on pregnant persons has nothing to do with women's equality. The genetic definition of parenthood degrades women in the same way *Dobbs* does, by treating gestation as physically and emotionally trivial and as irrelevant to becoming a parent. It favors men over women because it turns a woman's consent to sex into consent to sharing her life and child with the genetic father. (It can even do the same without her consent to the sex, as when rapists obtain parental rights.) Including genes as *part* of the definition of legal parenthood at the time of birth makes sense because many parents and children find meaning in what they believe to be biological reflections of themselves in each other. But almost as soon as it was technologically possible to do so, the law endorsed the buying and selling of sperm and eggs. Courts and legislators hardly blinked as they extended the genetic definition of parenthood to include a person who paid for genes. The ease with which they made this transition gives away the game: The genetic definition of parenthood is less about the meaning parents attribute to sharing DNA with their genetic children than it is about defining parenthood from a male perspective that minimizes the importance of gestation. When the genetic definition of parenthood says birthing and non-birthing parents are the same at the time of birth, it means pregnancy and birth don't matter, which ultimately means caretaking doesn't matter either.

To resist the workings of power in the law of pregnancy, feminists must reason well from the body. In the law of parenthood, that means restoring the premise of the Unwed Father Cases that gestation and birth create a parent-child relationship worthy of constitutional protection. The person who gives birth to a child is that child's initial family. She is therefore also the person who should make initial decisions about who else should join that family. At a minimum, courts should give a single mother's decisions about her family the same "special weight" the Supreme Court held a widow was entitled to when the grandparents in *Troxel v. Granville* sued for court-ordered visits with their grandchildren. Currently, the law treats a single mother with a child as a defective family, in need of having the "father" slot filled. Courts fill that slot without regard to the mother's wishes, on the assumption that doing so is always better for the child. But under *Troxel,* what's best for children is supposed to be determined in the first instance by their parents, which at the time of birth means the birth mother. Courts should therefore defer to her decision about whether she and the genetic father should raise the child together or not. If not, courts should defer to her equally whether she chooses to raise the child herself or place it for adoption.

Genetic fathers should acquire parental rights by meeting the biology-plus-relationship test, which means establishing a caretaking relationship with the child with the cooperation of the birth mother. The state should honor that relationship as establishing fatherhood for any purpose. It should enable a father to transmit citizenship to his child, as the Supreme Court refused to allow in *Nguyen v. INS,* and give him custody rights to the child, meaning family courts must abide by *Stanley v. Illinois,* abolish the One-Parent Doctrine, and refuse to put children in state custody when their fathers are available to care for them. There are lingering questions about what a genetic father must do to satisfy the biology-plus-relationship test. As I said in chapter 2, I think the Supreme Court was too strict in at least one case, *Quilloin v. Wolcott,* in which the father never had day-to-day responsibility for the eleven-year-old boy, but the boy himself wanted to maintain their relationship. Daily responsibility is a good standard to use for an infant, but by the time the child is old enough to know a man as his father and express his attachment, that itself is persuasive evidence that the biology-plus-relationship test has been met. For infants, the biology-plus-relationship test protects the adult's attachment more than the child's. The birth mother, for example, has protected parental rights to her newborn because of the relationship she formed over nine months' gestation. Similarly, a genetic father could have parental rights at birth if the birth mother has involved him in the pregnancy and encouraged him to plan on being a father. But the genetic father's mere knowledge of the pregnancy and desire to raise a child should not be enough to establish parental rights. For example, in a case like *Adoptive Couple v. Baby Girl*, where Christina Maldonado broke up with Dusten Brown shortly after discovering she was pregnant, he should not have the right to demand access to either her or the child. Genes alone are not enough to invade the birth mother's family and claim a connection with a child.

The law of surrogacy should also use the biology-plus-relationship test to recognize the birth mother's relationship with the child she bears. The surrogate's relationship with the child is based on gestation and birth and is not a function of whether she is also the genetic mother. The law should therefore abolish the distinction between gestation-only surrogacy and full surrogacy. That distinction reinforces genetic essentialism, even though we now know the presence or absence of a genetic tie is not the key factor in the surrogate's willingness to go through with the contract. Rather, her willingness to surrender the child she made depends on her trust in the contracting parents. In addition, by favoring gestation-only surrogacy, the law effectively requires the parties to surrogacy contracts to undergo IVF. Full surrogacy is accomplished by assisted insemination, using one of the eggs the surrogate already has in her body. Gestation-only surrogacy requires the egg to come from someone else, which means it must be extracted from that other woman, fertilized in the lab, and then transferred to the surrogate. This process is much riskier and more physically burdensome to the egg donor and to the surrogate than assisted insemination. A woman undergoing egg extraction typically takes hormones orally and by injection over several weeks, which can trigger early-pregnancy symptoms like morning sickness. If the dose is a bit too high, the hormones can also cause painful swelling of the ovaries, and the long-term risks are unknown. The actual harvesting of the eggs requires heavy sedation, followed by deep abdominal cramping and bloating for about a week. Once the pre-embryos are created in the lab, the surrogate may also have to take hormones in order to become pregnant. In addition, the standard of care in most IVF procedures is to transfer only one pre-embryo to a woman at a time because of the serious risks to her and to the eventual children of a multiple pregnancy. If too many embryos begin to develop, the surrogate may have to undergo a reductive abortion to eliminate the excess ones. Surrogacy contracts, however, usually ignore safety guidelines about the number of pre-embryos to transfer.[6] In some parts of the country, contracting parents routinely bargain to transfer as many as four pre-embryos to the surrogate at once. The women involved in surrogacy contracts—the contracting mother or egg donor and the surrogate—are thus bearing the medical risks of adhering to a male-centered definition of parenthood based on genes. The law should not require them to bear those risks as the price of a valid surrogacy contract.

Like other birth mothers, a surrogate should decide who the baby's family should be because at the time of birth, she has the strongest claim under the biology-plus-relationship test. Shifting this power to the surrogate would encourage contracting parents, doctors, and surrogacy brokers to treat the surrogate well and to ensure high-quality screening and counseling for all the parties. If courts aren't willing to let the surrogate decide, then in the alternative they must at least be willing to consider a surrogate's reasons for wanting to renege. Courts should expect contracting parents to treat a surrogate as well as a good adoption agency would expect aspiring adoptive parents to treat a pregnant woman with whom they have a tentative agreement to adopt. An agreement for adoption is necessarily tentative during pregnancy because it is not enforceable in court, but most such agreements end up with an adoption as planned. There's no reason to think surrogacy contracts wouldn't have comparable or better success rates if they, too, weren't enforceable in court. Courts should recognize that a surrogacy contract is not an arm's-length, impersonal transaction. They should respect the relationships on which the contract depends—the relationship between the surrogate and the contracting parents and the relationship between the surrogate and the eventual child.

Finally, reasoning well from the body requires the right to abortion as protection from an invasion of one's self. Abortion should be safe, legal, and free. But when a "feminine" value like the right to abortion or the biology-plus-relationship test makes its way into the law of our fundamental rights, judges push back by first distorting the "feminine" principle and eventually by purging it from the law. Courts' commitment to "masculine" values shapes how they interpret and apply every legal doctrine, and it also shapes how litigants argue their cases. Suppose you are a feminist lawyer trying to defend the right to abortion. If you walk into court and start talking about the government's duty to protect women from the invasion of an unwanted pregnancy, you will lose, because your arguments will contradict precedents like *DeShaney*. If you talk about autonomy and the Fourteenth Amendment's liberty clause, you might win. The catch is that as soon as you choose the path of arguing for autonomy, you've effectively already lost the cases about Medicaid funding for abortion, because autonomy rights are for people with the resources to exercise them. That means you've already lost the right to abortion for poor women. A lawyer who chooses that course hopes that winning something now lays the groundwork for winning more later. But in this example, the logic of winning an autonomy right to abortion forecloses winning a right to free abortion later. Winning a partial victory in *Roe v. Wade* in 1973 and salvaging the remnants of it in *Planned Parenthood v. Casey* in 1992 required feminists to buy into a rationale rooted in preserving autonomy, which was contrary to the long-term goal of winning a right to abortion for all women.[7]

That's why it isn't enough to tinker with legal doctrines in the courts. The way forward for feminists must be to overthrow the value system that governs us but that belongs, in Martha Fineman's words, to "an eighteenth-century male citizen sheltered by institutions such as the patriarchal family and the privileges of a master–servant mentality."[8] That revolution will require reshaping our constitutional values through political action outside the courts. The courts, and especially the Supreme Court, have almost always been a reactionary force against women's rights. Women's gains have more often come from politics outside the courts. For example, when it came to the rules for pregnancy at work, the courts came up with the idea that pregnancy was unrelated to sex or gender and then the idea that lactation was unrelated to pregnancy. Congress responded with the Pregnancy Discrimination Act, the Family and Medical Leave Act, and provisions for breastfeeding in the Affordable Care Act. Similarly, the courts pioneered the genetic definition of parenthood and extended it to rapists. Congress checked them, at least a little, with the Rape Survivors Child Custody Act. Congress is also now the only hope for restoring the right to abortion. Many members of Congress and other legislators are lawyers, which means they've been trained to believe in the Constitution of "masculine" values and of purportedly negative rather than positive rights. But they are less insulated from women's political power than the courts are, and they ultimately have the power to constrain the courts. Questions about our fundamental values and how the Constitution should be interpreted to serve them are political questions, not legal ones. The Supreme Court and most of the lower federal judiciary currently represent the political views of a small faction of reactionary authoritarians whose disproportionate power over the rest of us depends on antidemocratic institutions like the Senate and the Electoral College. All of those institutions need to be reformed (the Supreme Court) or abolished (the Senate and the Electoral College) for the will of the people to have a chance of governing the nation.

Fortunately, the need to overturn the law's skewed value system also provides the basis for solidarity between feminists and anyone else fighting for a just society. For example, much of what I argued about the involuntarily pregnant woman who is caught in a trap and needs rescue in the form of abortion could also be said about someone who desperately needs the basics of life, such as food or medical care. A person who is denied basic necessities, like an involuntarily pregnant woman who is denied an abortion, is denied the ability "to become an ends-making creature," a denial Robin West described as the essence of invasion.[9] The same is true of a parent who lacks the resources to raise their child. Surely a feminist dream that includes the right to abortion—a positive right to escape from involuntary pregnancy, not just the right to get one if you can pay—can stretch to include the right not to suffer from hunger or curable disease and the right not to be forced by poverty to surrender a child. Similarly, in chapter 1 we saw debates over whether pregnancy should be considered a "disability" in the workplace. Feminists have a particular interest in designing the workplace to be compatible with pregnancy, which is distinct from designing it to meet the needs of people with disabilities, but feminists and disability activists can make common cause in their rejection of the idea that gainful employment is only for the "ideal worker" of the law's imagination. The same values that demand feminist reforms also demand a just world for all.

Relational feminism, through its critique of the value system we inherited from elite eighteenth-century men, provides a foundation for replacing that system. Laws, courts, and the Constitution must serve all four of the values in the system—the "feminine" values of respecting existing relationships and protecting people from invasion along with the "masculine" values of preserving autonomy and providing background institutions for pursuing new connections. It's possible, even likely, that these four won't be enough to achieve a truly just society, and we will discover more gaps and omissions in how the law responds to what people need. But as a starting point, honoring all four values would be better than honoring only two.

TIMELINE OF CASES

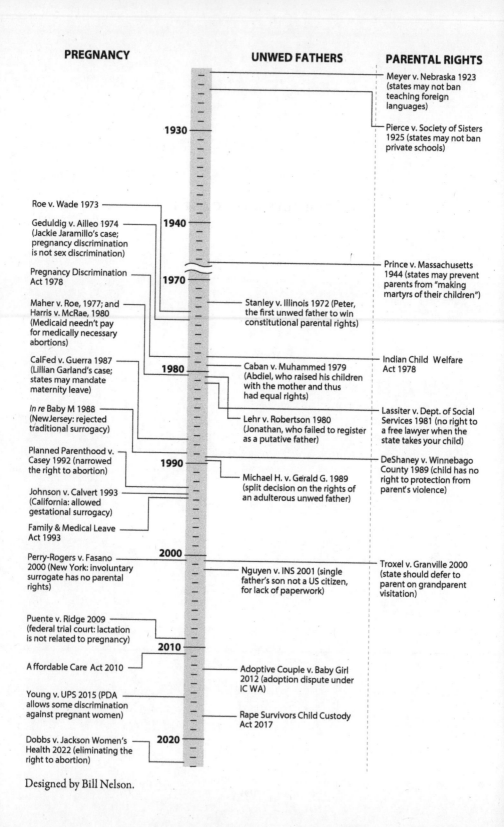

PREGNANCY

Roe v. Wade 1973

Geduldig v. Ailleo 1974
(Jackie Jaramillo's case;
pregnancy discrimination
is not sex discrimination)

Pregnancy Discrimination
Act 1978

Maher v. Roe, 1977; and
Harris v. McRae, 1980
(Medicaid needn't pay
for medically necessary
abortions)

CalFed v. Guerra 1987
(Lillian Garland's case;
states may mandate
maternity leave)

In re Baby M 1988
(NewJersey: rejected
traditional surrogacy)

Planned Parenthood v.
Casey 1992 (narrowed
the right to abortion)

Johnson v. Calvert 1993
(California: allowed
gestational surrogacy)

Family & Medical Leave
Act 1993

Perry-Rogers v. Fasano
2000 (New York: involuntary
surrogate has no parental
rights)

Puente v. Ridge 2009
(federal trial court: lactation
is not related to pregnancy)

Affordable Care Act 2010

Young v. UPS 2015 (PDA
allows some discrimination
against pregnant women)

Dobbs v. Jackson Women's
Health 2022 (eliminating the
right to abortion)

UNWED FATHERS

Stanley v. Illinois 1972 (Peter,
the first unwed father to win
constitutional parental rights)

Caban v. Muhammed 1979
(Abdiel, who raised his children
with the mother and thus
had equal rights)

Lehr v. Robertson 1980
(Jonathan, who failed to register
as a putative father)

Michael H. v. Gerald G. 1989
(split decision on the rights of
an adulterous unwed father)

Nguyen v. INS 2001 (single
father's son not a US citizen,
for lack of paperwork)

Adoptive Couple v. Baby Girl
2012 (adoption dispute under
IC WA)

Rape Survivors Child Custody
Act 2017

PARENTAL RIGHTS

Meyer v. Nebraska 1923
(states may not ban
teaching foreign
languages)

Pierce v. Society of Sisters
1925 (states may not ban
private schools)

Prince v. Massachusetts
1944 (states may prevent
parents from "making
martyrs of their children")

Indian Child Welfare
Act 1978

Lassiter v. Dept. of Social
Services 1981 (no right to
a free lawyer when the
state takes your child)

DeShaney v. Winnebago
County 1989 (child has no
right to protection from
parent's violence)

Troxel v. Granville 2000
(state should defer to
parent on grandparent
visitation)

1930

1940

1970

1980

1990

2000

2010

2020

Designed by Bill Nelson.

ACKNOWLEDGMENTS

My first thanks go to Tracy Brooks, University of Colorado Law School class of 2022, whose insights, efficiency, and knowledge of feminist theory were all incredible resources. Kristina Maude, class of 2024, joined us later and brought her pre–law school skills as an English teacher to bear on revising the manuscript to great effect. Both will be fantastic lawyers.

This book brings together ideas I've been exploring for many years, and I've benefited from being able to do so in print. Much of that work is listed in the bibliography, but I owe special thanks to the *William and Mary Journal of Women and the Law* for publishing my article "Essentially a Mother," which became the foundation for most of my work that followed, including of course this book.

More colleagues than I can count, let alone name, helped me improve the arguments in this book. I was honored to receive insightful global feedback from Susan Frelich Appleton and Barbara Katz Rothman. Ben Barton helped me work out the key points of "Essentially a Mother," the article, by reading a draft, finding the essence of the argument, and explaining it back to me. Martha Fineman's Feminist Legal Theory Project gave me time, space, and feedback for working out some of my early ideas, and Mae Quinn sponsored the Women's Writing Workshops that gave me many rooms of my own and taught me how to take them home with me. Cyra Choudhury organized a workshop at which she, Aziza Ahmed, Shelley Cavalieri, Leigh Goodmark, and Rachel Rebouché helped me figure out what the book was about. She also organized the Feminist Solidarity Project with Elizabeth MacDowell, Saru Matambanadzo, and Lua Kamál Yuille, who all keep me going when the fight for justice seems lost, as do my office neighbors and dear friends Paul Campos, Aya Gruber, and Ahmed White.

Many thanks also to my editor Maura Roessner and her assistants Madison Wetzell and Sam Warren for their commitment to the project, fielding of all my questions, and generosity with that final deadline, as well as to Lynda Crawford for punctilious copy editing.

Some of the best people I know appear briefly in the book. It was quite some time before I wanted to let my son, Elliott, sleep in another room, and I'm grateful every day to be his mom. Michael Hendricks, who kept playing the piano, and Steven Hendricks, who switched to the guitar, are the best brothers a girl could ask for. Mike is a neurobiologist who inspired chapter 8, on reasoning from the body, when I asked whether there was any evidence that some particular gender difference was "biological" and he replied, "All behavior comes from biology. There's nowhere else for it to come from."

And where would I be without my husband Steve Hendricks? Steve has been my compass since we met in my first year of law school. He helped me avoid becoming an ideal worker or otherwise getting sucked into the vortex of the law's skewed value system. He has supported my academic career with sacrifices big and small, most recently by editing this book. In between getting his most recent book out the door and starting on his next one, he coached me through everything from dangling modifiers to imposter syndrome. I can hardly believe my luck in having him by my side.

NOTES

INTRODUCTION

1. Isaac Stanley-Becker and Michael Brice-Saddler, "They Thought Their Embryo Didn't Take. Then Their Son Was Born to a Stranger across the Country, Lawsuit Claims," *Washington Post,* July 10, 2019 (Kim); Iulia Filip, "Rapist Given Paternity Rights to Victim's Child," *Courthouse News Service,* August 21, 2013 (Thornton); P.M. v. T.B., 907 N.W.2d 522 (Iowa 2018) (Baca and Millers).

2. See Fineman, *Neutered Mother,* 234–35 ("Men can and should be Mothers . . . in the stereotypical nurturing sense of that term—that is, engaged in caretaking.").

CHAPTER ONE: MOTHERS AT WORK

1. United States v. Virginia, 518 U.S. 515, 533 (1996).

2. See generally Molotch and Norén, *Toilet* (collecting essays on the politics of public bathrooms); Waldman, "Compared to What?" (discussing equality in the context of menstruation).

3. Geduldig v. Ailleo, 417 U.S. 484 (1974). In the discussion that follows, I use the phrase "pregnant and non-pregnant persons" instead of the court's phrase, "pregnant women and non-pregnant persons," because the latter phrasing seems to be confusing to modern readers accustomed to thinking of sex, gender, and biological capacities as distinct.

4. *Geduldig,* 417 U.S. at 499 (Justice Brennan, dissenting).

5. See Kay, "Equality and Difference" (presenting this critique as "episodic analysis").

6. Williams, "Deconstructing Gender," 822, 835–836.

7. See General Elec. Co. v. Gilbert, 429 U.S. 121, 161 n.5 (1976) (Justice Stevens, dissenting) ("The classification is between persons who face a risk of pregnancy and those who do not.").

8. More technically, for readers who are lawyers: In *General Electric,* the Supreme Court interpreted sex equality under federal employment law in the same way it had interpreted the equal protection clause in *Geduldig*—to allow discrimination against pregnancy. The PDA overruled *Gilbert.* Later, in *Nevada Dept. of Human Resources v. Hibbs,* 538 U.S. 721 (2003), the Supreme Court held the Family and Medical Leave Act was valid as a measure to enforce the equal protection clause. Some feminist scholars have maintained that *Hibbs* effectively overruled *Geduldig.* See, for example, Franklin, "Anti-Stereotyping Principle"; Siegel, "You've Come a Long Way, Baby." As discussed later in this chapter, the federal courts, including the Supreme Court, have remained hostile to pregnancy discrimination claims, have construed the PDA narrowly, and have yet to renounce *Geduldig*'s "sameness" theory of equality when it comes to discrimination based on women's reproductive biology. See also Manian, "Comment on *Geduldig v. Aiello,*" 189–90 (discussing *Geduldig*'s continuing influence); Dobbs v. Jackson Women's Health Org., 1 Gil. 3, 10–11 (2022) (slip op.) (doubling down on a broad reading of *Geduldig*).

9. Pregnancy Discrimination Act, 42 U.S.C. § 2000e(k).

10. California Fed. Sav. & Loan Assoc. v. Guerra, 479 U.S. 272 (1987).

11. Brief for Lillian Garland, 5, *CalFed* (No. 85–494).

12. Brief of the National Organization for Women et al., *CalFed* (No. 85–494). A group of smaller feminist organizations filed an opposing brief. Brief of Equal Rights Advocates et al., *CalFed* (No. 85–494). The competing arguments are elaborated in articles written by the principal authors of the two briefs: Williams, "Equality's Riddle," and Kay, "Equality and Difference."

13. See, for example, Claire Cain Miller, "When Family-Friendly Policies Backfire," *New York Times,* May 26, 2015; Case, "How High the Apple Pie?" 1759–61 (describing how family-friendly policies can incentivize discrimination against all women of childbearing age).

14. See Arnie Siegel and Nina Totenberg, "Amid Charges by Former Law Student on Gender Equality, Former Clerks Defend Gorsuch," NPR.org, March 20, 2017.

15. See Law, "Rethinking Sex and the Constitution," 963 (describing this "assimilationist view"). See, for example, Schultz, "Taking Sex Discrimination Seriously," 1066 (chastising feminists who "publicly dissented" from the view "that pregnant women are no different from other employees who receive or should receive workplace protections").

16. See Luna and Luker, "Reproductive Justice" (history and overview); Roberts, *Killing the Black Body,* 308–12 (theoretical foundations).

17. See Fineman, "Vulnerable Subject" (2008); *Autonomy Myth* (pioneering vulnerability theory, based on shared, universal dependency rather than the myth of an idealized, autonomous man like the ideal worker); Eichner, *Free-Market Family.*

18. Family and Medical Leave Act, 29 U.S.C. §§ 2601–54. Decades later, the Affordable Care Act of 2010 required a narrow class of employers to accommodate breast-pumping by employees. 29 U.S.C. § 207(r)(1).

19. See Brake, "On Not Having It Both Ways," 1006 ("Folding gender conflicts into universal frameworks does nothing to avoid the gender culture wars."); Bagen-

stos, "*Nevada Department of Human Resources v. Hibbs:* Universalism and Reproductive Justice," 203 ("Because the statute ties self-care leave together with parental and family leave, employer discontent with self-care leave has fed a backlash against the FMLA as a whole.").

20. In *Geduldig,* the dissent cited a report from the American College of Obstetrics and Gynecology estimating that disability due to childbirth typically lasts six to eight weeks. *Geduldig,* 417 U.S. at 500 n.4 (Justice Brennan, dissenting). For discussion of what accommodations for pregnancy are most effective, see Grossman, "Pregnancy, Work, and the Promise of Equal Citizenship"; Becker, "Care and Feminists," 78–82.

21. See Williams, "Reconstructive Feminism," 81 (characterizing sameness/difference debates as debates over "tomboy" or "femme" strategies).

22. See, for example, Muller v. Oregon, 208 U.S. 412, 421–22 (1908); Suk, "Gender Equality," 180 ("The constitutional protection of motherhood should be seen as a stepping stone to a gender-equal infrastructure for social reproduction.").

23. I explored this optionality in Hendricks, "Contingent Equal Protection," 426–40.

24. Carol Kleiman, "Court Victory in War on Sex Bias Was Not Without Serious Casualties," *Chicago Tribune,* June 22, 1987.

25. Guttmacher Institute, "Unintended Pregnancy in the United States," January 2019, https://www.guttmacher.org/fact-sheet/unintended-pregnancy-united-states; Centers for Disease Control and Prevention, "Understanding Pregnancy Resulting from Rape in the United States," February 27, 2019, https://www.cdc.gov/violenceprevention/sexualviolence/understanding-RRP-inUS.html.

26. Strebeigh, *Equal,* 96–97.

27. Rentzer v. Unemployment Insur. App. Bd., 32 Cal.App.3d 604, 606–07 (1973).

28. Compare McGinley and Cooper, "Intersectional Cohorts" (discussing the merits of characterizing "the trauma suffered by Black and Latinx students in poor, violence-torn inner-city communities" as a disability).

29. See Areheart, "Disability Trouble" (critiquing the disability/impairment binary with analogy to the gender/sex binary); Bagenstos, "Rational Discrimination," 859–60 (discussing the theoretical equivalence of discrimination and non-accommodation).

30. See Amy Joyce, "Yes, Duchess Kate Looked Flawless After Giving Birth. No, This Isn't Normal," *Washington Post,* April 23, 2018. At the time she gave birth the former Kate Middleton was formally known in the United Kingdom as Catharine, Duchess of Cambridge. In America, however, as soon as you marry a prince, you are a princess. See *Cinderella* (Walt Disney 1950).

31. See "Top Court Refuses Bid to Give Adoptive Moms Maternity Leave," CBC.ca, January 24, 2008.

32. American feminism is unusual in rejecting many protections aimed at mothers as such. See Suk, "Gender Equality," 153–54.

33. See Susana Kim, "Mom of Twins Born Via Surrogate Denied Leave," *ABC News,* September 2, 2011. Krill v. Cubist Pharmaceuticals, Inc., No. 1:11-CV-11519 (D. Mass. Sept. 6, 2012).

34. On the issue of inequitable leave for single parents and their babies, see Widiss, "Equalizing Parental Leave."

35. See Matambanadzo, "Fourth Trimester," 167–68 ("The fourth trimester framework conceptualizes pregnancy as a process that entails not only biological natural elements, but also social, emotional, and psychological elements.").

36. Quinn, "Fallen Woman (Re)Framed, " 464–67.

37. On the difference between accommodating breastfeeding and accommodating pumping, see Laufer-Ukeles and Barzilay, "Health/Care Divide." On the challenges of doing either in workplaces, see Boone, "Lactation Law."

38. Rothman, *Recreating Motherhood,* 249.

39. See Rimalt, "Maternal Dilemma" (discussing how pressures on both women and men reinforce traditional caretaking patterns); Case, "How High the Apple Pie?" 1756–65 (discussing how family-friendly policies can give men advantages over women without children); Justin Wolfers, "A Family-Friendly Policy That's Friendliest to Male Professors," *New York Times,* June 24, 2016.

40. See Widiss, "Shadow Precedents," 551–56; Brake, "On Not Having It Both Ways," 999–1003; Becker, "Caring for Children and Caretakers," 1517–18.

41. Puente v. Ridge, No. M-04-267, 2005 U.S. Dist. LEXIS 46624 (S.D. Tex. July 6, 2005), aff'd on other grounds, 324 Fed.App'x 423 (5th Cir. 2009).

42. Young v. United Parcel Serv., Inc., 575 U.S. 206 (2015). The Supreme Court remanded the case for consideration of evidence that, in practice, UPS accommodated almost all light-duty requests and had singled out pregnancy for disfavored treatment. For a detailed discussion of lower courts' treatment of PDA claims after *Young,* see Kessler, "Miscarriage of Justice," 11–32.

43. Affordable Care Act, 29 U.S.C. § 207(r)(1).

44. Affordable Care Act, 42 U.S.C. §§ 300–300a-8.

45. See Joel Bourne, "The Untold Story of the Daring Cave Divers Who Saved the Thai Soccer Team," *National Geographic,* March 5, 2019.

46. See Stevens, Patrick, and Pickler, "History of Infant Feeding," 36.

47. Roberts, "Spiritual and Menial Housework." See also Romero, "Unraveling Privilege"; Harbach, "Outsourcing Childcare."

48. See, for example, Williams, "Deconstructing Gender," 822–23.

49. See Carbone and Cahn, "Gender/Class Divide" (discussing class implications of expensive egg-freezing procedures). On the reliability of egg freezing, see Bayefsky, "Legal and Ethical Analysis."

50. Firestone, *Dialectic of Sex,* 227–28. I discussed the prospect of artificial gestation in Hendricks, "Not of Woman Born."

CHAPTER TWO: FATHERS AT HOME

1. Caban v. Mohammed, 441 U.S. 380, 397 (1979) (Justice Stewart, dissenting) (endorsed by a majority of the court in Lehr v. Robertson, 463 U.S. 248, 259–60 (1983)).

2. The first use of the term "biology-plus-relationship" to describe this test appears to be Schlackman, "Unwed Fathers' Rights in New York," 199. The shorter term "biology plus" was used in Zinman, "Father Knows Best," 972. I first made the central argument of this chapter in the article from which this book takes its name, Hendricks, "Essentially a Mother."

3. See Feinberg, "Restructuring Rebuttal," 250; Mason, *From Father's Property*, 24.

4. See Pirate v. Dalby, 1 U.S. 167 (Pa. Sup. Ct. 1786) (rejecting the argument that a child born to an enslaved woman was *filius nullius* and thus could not be presumed a slave).

5. See Mason, *From Father's Property*, 68.

6. Stanley v. Illinois, 405 U.S. 645 (1972).

7. Shortly after Joan's death, the state had removed the Stanleys' oldest child from the home and placed her in foster care. Although those proceedings formally accused Peter of "neglect," there may have been concerns of sexual abuse. Gupta-Kagan, "*Stanley v. Illinois*'s Untold Story," 781, 785. The case that went to the Supreme Court concerned only the two younger children.

8. Santosky v. Kramer, 455 U.S. 745, 748 (1982).

9. *Stanley*, 405 U.S. at 665–66 (Chief Justice Burger, dissenting). Although the quoted passage is from the dissent, the majority did not dispute this characterization of mothers and fathers but argued that men's typical irresponsibility should not control an individual case.

10. *Stanley* arose during the court's journey down the doctrinal cul-de-sac of "unconstitutional presumptions," so it phrased this question in terms of a presumption of unfitness. Illinois law, however, made it part of the definition of parent.

11. On the justices' disagreement about the reasoning in *Stanley*, see Gupta-Kagan, "*Stanley v. Illinois*'s Untold Story."

12. Quilloin v. Wolcott, 434 U.S. 246 (1978).

13. *Quilloin*, 434 U.S. at 248 ("*Stanley* left unresolved the degree of protection a State must afford to the rights of an unwed father in a situation, such as that presented here, in which the countervailing interests are more substantial."). The phrase "countervailing interests" appears to refer to the fact that the state's interest in *Quilloin* was to establish the child in the mother's new family, as opposed to removing the child to the foster system as in *Stanley*.

14. Caban v. Mohammed, 441 U.S. 380 (1979).

15. *Stanley*, 405 U.S. at 666 (Chief Justice Burger, dissenting).

16. *Caban*, 441 U.S. at 393.

17. Nguyen v. INS, 533 U.S. 53, 67 (2001).

18. See Feinberg, "Restructuring Rebuttal," 248; Milanich, "Certain Mothers, Uncertain Fathers," 24; Blackstone, *Commentaries*, 457.

19. See Appleton, "Presuming Women," 251; Roberts, "Genetic Tie," 269.

20. See Appleton, "Presuming Women."

21. Spitko, "Constitutional Function of Biological Paternity," 98.

22. See Joslin, "De Facto Parentage"; NeJaime, "Constitution of Parenthood" (arguing for constitutional protection of non-biological parents); Joslin and

NeJaime, "How Parenthood Functions." Compare Appell, "Virtual Mothers and the Meaning of Parenthood" (defending the biological basis of parenthood); Appell, "Endurance of Biological Connection" (same).

23. Mayeri, "Intersectionality," 402.

24. See Carbone and Cahn, "Parents, Babies, and More Parents"; NeJaime and Joslin, "Multi-Parent Families"; Higdon, "Quasi-Parent Conundrum."

25. Compare Black, *New Birth of Freedom,* 105 (proposing that state action should be unconstitutional if it constitutes "a heart-crushing blow to the pursuit of happiness").

26. Family law scholars are divided on whether the father can meet the relationship prong before the birth. Compare Purvis, "Origin of Parental Rights" (arguing that pre-birth labor proves "that the father intends to be an active and engaged parent"), and Woodhouse, "Hatching the Egg" (arguing for recognition of "gestational fathering"), with Baker, "Property Rules Meet Feminist Needs," 1588 ("The father has done and can do nothing to make his claim to a relationship any weightier at birth than it is prior to birth when the mother still has the right to abort.").

27. See generally the Uniform Parentage Act of 2017, § 301. The uniform act is written by a committee of lawyers, judges, and academics as a suggested model for state legislatures.

28. Lehr v. Robertson, 463 U.S. 248 (1983).

29. *Lehr,* 463 U.S. at 269 (Justice White, dissenting). There was some dispute about the facts. While Jonathan insisted he had done everything he could to find the child, Lorraine said he had refused to marry her and had shown no interest in the baby until she proposed the adoption by her new husband. Mayeri, "Foundling Fathers," 2364. For purposes of the Supreme Court's decision, however, the question was what legal rule would apply if Jonathan's version of the facts were true. If the court had ruled in his favor, the case would have returned to the state courts for determination of the facts.

30. See Meyer, "Family Ties."

31. Feinberg, "Parent Zero." See also Spitko, "Constitutional Function of Biological Paternity," 99 (describing the birth mother as the "initial constitutional parent").

32. *In re* Adoption of XX, 430 N.E.2d 896, 902 (1981).

33. See Michael H. v. Gerald D., 491 U.S. 110 (1989) (plurality opinion by Justice Scalia), and see, for example, Fineman, *Neutered Mother,* 85; Shanley, "Unwed Fathers' Rights"; Shultz, "Reproductive Technology," 318; Berger, "In the Name of the Child," 341; Roberts, "Genetic Tie," 252–57. See also Appleton, "Illegitimacy and Sex" (explaining the cases in terms of the regulation of sex).

34. Dolgin, "Just a Gene," 650.

35. Mayeri, "Marital Supremacy," 2354.

36. *Quilloin,* 434 U.S. at 256. See Spitko, "Constitutional Function of Biological Paternity."

37. June Carbone and Naomi Cahn have written extensively about these dynamics. See, for example, their *Marriage Markets* and "Triple System." See also Baker,

"DNA Default," 2071 ("To call adults who have had sex 'parents' because they had sex that produced a child . . . asks the law to respect and fortify many relationships that are exceedingly unlikely to survive."); Laufer-Ukeles, "Children of Nonmarriage" (arguing for focusing directly on the needs of children rather than imposing the trappings of marriage on unmarried couples); Blecher-Prigat, "Conceiving Parents" (arguing that the nature of the relationship between the biological parents is relevant to allocating parental rights).

38. *Quilloin,* 434 U.S. at 256. Compare, for example, Dowd, "Fathers and the Supreme Court"; Woodhouse, "Hatching the Egg."

39. Gupta-Kagan, "*Stanley v. Illinois*'s Untold Story," 804. See also Mayeri, "Intersectionality," 400 ("Reading Marshall's published *Jefferson* dissent and unpublished *Stanley* opinion together, it seems likely that the racial impact of Illinois's exclusion of nonmarital fathers from parental rights was on his mind.").

40. Between *Geduldig* and *Caban,* Justice Douglas retired and was replaced by Justice Stevens. Justice Douglas had dissented from *Geduldig,* voting for accommodation for women. Justice Stevens dissented in *Caban,* voting against accommodation for men. See also Freedman, "Sex Equality, Sex Differences, and the Supreme Court," 913 (stating that Brennan and Marshall's votes and opinions "reflect a recognition of the cultural origins of sex differentiation, the harms caused by sex discrimination, and the importance and feasibility of remedies").

41. Mayeri, "Foundling Fathers," 2298.

42. Anita Sarkeesian, "Damsel in Distress Part 1: Tropes vs Women in Video Games," Feminist Frequency, https://www.youtube.com/watch?v=X6p5AZp7r_Q. Sarkeesian says she did not coin this phrase but read it somewhere; neither I nor others have been able to track it down. See also Johnson, *Gender Knot,* 53 ("Although we usually think of patriarchy in terms of women and men, it is more about what goes on *among men.* The oppression of women is certainly an important part of patriarchy, but, paradoxically, it may not be the *point* of patriarchy."); Fineman, "Vulnerable Subject" (2010), 253 (describing "a perverse dynamic that often results in pitting one protected group against another").

43. Mayeri, "Marital Supremacy," 2378.

44. Michael H. v. Gerald D., 491 U.S. 110 (1989).

45. See generally West and Lithwick, "Paradox of Justice Stevens."

46. *Michael H.,* 491 U.S. at 132 (Justice Stevens, concurring). In *Troxel v. Granville,* 530 U.S. 57 (2000), the Supreme Court limited the permissible scope of nonparent visitation laws. Given that Justice Stevens's vote depended on the availability of that option, *Troxel* calls into question the continuing validity of *Michael H.*

47. *Nguyen,* 533 U.S. at 67.

CHAPTER THREE: WHAT THE LAW PROTECTS . . .

1. Katz, "Majoritarian Morality," 406. See also Stanley v. Illinois, 405 U.S. 645, 651 (1972).

2. Meyer v. Nebraska, 262 U.S. 390 (1923).

3. Pierce v. Society of Sisters, 268 U.S. 510 (1925).

4. *Meyer*, 262 U.S. at 626.

5. *Pierce*, 268 U.S. at 534–35.

6. *Pierce*, 268 U.S. at 534 ("No question is raised concerning the power of the state reasonably to regulate all schools, to inspect, supervise and examine them, their teachers and pupils; to require that all children of proper age attend some school, that teachers shall be of good moral character and patriotic disposition, that certain studies plainly essential to good citizenship must be taught, and that nothing be taught which is manifestly inimical to the public welfare.").

7. See Fineman and Shepherd, "Homeschooling" (arguing against homeschooling); Wisconsin v. Yoder, 406 U.S. 205 (1972) (allowing the Amish to educate their boys to be farmers and their girls to be housewives). But see Peters, "The Right to Be and Become" (arguing that homeschooling lets Black parents protect their children from racism in public schools).

8. DeShaney v. Winnebago County, 489 U.S. 189 (1989). See also Castle Rock v. Gonzales, 548 U.S. 748 (2005) (holding police had no constitutional duty to enforce a domestic-violence protection order).

9. *DeShaney*, 489 U.S. at 209 (Justice Brennan, dissenting).

10. Prince v. Massachusetts, 321 U.S. 158 (1944).

11. See generally Hill, "Whose Body? Whose Soul?" (analyzing parents' right to refuse medical care for children); Dwyer, "Children We Abandon" (arguing that allowing parents to do so violates the equal protection rights of children).

12. See Godwin, "Against Parental Rights," 74–75 (describing this view); Purvis, "Origin of Parental Rights," 653 ("For hundreds of years, children were seen as an extension of their father's body.").

13. See, for example, Locke, *Second Treatise on Government*. Compare Purvis, "Origin of Parental Rights" (arguing for a labor-based definition, where labor serves as evidence of intent to parent); Bender, "To Err Is Human" (arguing for a labor-based approach in cases of reproductive technology).

14. Blackstone, 1 *Commentaries*, 454. But see Saller, *"Pater Familias, Mater Familias,"* 185 (noting support for the "conventional modern stereotype of the tyrannical *pater familias*" but cautioning that the stereotype is based on "an extremely rare legal formula").

15. See Woodhouse, "Who Owns the Child?" 1043–44. More on this in chapter 8.

16. *Pierce*, 268 U.S. at 535.

17. See Van Schilfgaarde, "Using Peacemaking Circles," 686–89 (tracing the connections between Indian boarding schools and the modern child welfare system); Rolnick and Pearson, "Racial Anxieties in Adoption," 733 (collecting histories of Indian boarding schools in the United States).

18. See Davis, "Contested Images," 1361–71 (discussing the family law of slavery).

19. Woodhouse, "Who Owns the Child?" 1017–18.

20. *Portland Oregonian*, September 13, 1922, quoted in Holsinger, "The Oregon School Bill Controversy," 334–35 n.31, and in Woodhouse, "Who Owns the Child?" 1033.

21. As of 1992. Woodhouse, "Who Owns the Child?" 1081–82.

22. Baker, *The Justice from Beacon Hill*, 465.

23. Woodhouse, "Who Owns the Child?" 1104–05 (quoting Brief by J. P. Kavanaugh, at 93, in *Pierce*).

24. See Eichner, *Supportive State*, 138–41 (arguing that children have an interest in being raised with a coherent set of values and beliefs); Ristroph and Murray, "Disestablishing the Family" (arguing that the state shouldn't endorse a particular family structure). Compare Appell, "Virtual Mothers," 710 ("Any nondiscretionary and nondiscriminatory general rule that assigns parenthood to private citizens and minimizes state discretion in placing individual children would presumably promote the goals behind public family theories."); see also Baker, "Bionormativity," 653 ("[A] bionormative regime constructs parenthood as private, . . . exclusive, . . . and binary.").

25. The same is true for a variation on the pluralism rationale that casts the child as a creative project of the parent's, like a novel or a painting. For example, Altman, "Pursuit of Intimacy," 313–14. Contra Godwin, "Against Parental Rights," 38–39, 47–52. For a child-centered defense of something like the parent-as-artist theory, see Eichner, *Supportive State*, 138–41.

26. On this exchange-based theory of parental rights, see Appleton, "Parents by the Numbers," 36–37; Bartlett, "Re-Expressing Parenthood," 297–98; Harris et al., *Family Law*, 422.

27. Fineman, "Masking Dependency," 2187–88.

28. Huntington and Scott, "Conceptualizing Legal Childhood," 1417.

29. Britton, "America's Best Kept Secret" (describing the current state of the law on adult children's duty to support their parents); Godwin, "Against Parental Rights," 62 (contrasting the legal status of children to that of elderly and disabled adults). Compare *Guess Who's Coming to Dinner?* (Columbia Pictures, 1967) ("I owe you nothing! If you carried that bag a million miles, you did what you're supposed to do. Because you brought me into this world. And from that day you owed me everything."—Sidney Poitier as John Prentice to his father).

30. See Parham v. J.R., 442 U.S. 584, 602 (1979) (relying on parents' "natural bonds of affection" to protect adolescents from improper confinement to mental institutions). See also, for example, Byrn and Ives, "Which Came First"; Baker, "Equality and Family Autonomy."

31. *Parham*, 442 U.S. at 602.

32. See Eichner, *Supportive State*, 11–12; Buss, "Allocating Developmental Control," 31–32; Appell, "Child Question," 1181.

33. Huntington and Scott, 1421. The defense of spanking is part of an overall argument that US law is already largely organized around what's best for children.

34. Huntington and Scott, 1421 n.274.

35. Dailey and Rosenbury, "The New Parental Rights," 100.

36. Godwin, "Against Parental Rights," 19.

37. See Harris et al., *Family Law,* 422; Godwin, 22.

38. Godwin, 31.

39. Woodhouse, "Hatching the Egg," 1811 ("An enduring legacy of genetic ownership grounded in patriarchal traditions has shaped our legal definition of parenthood."); Meyer, "Constitutionality of 'Best Interests' Parentage," 857 (celebrating an "unabashedly radical" effort "to imagine a new law of parentage focused exclusively on the needs and interests of children"). But see Baker, "Property Rules Meet Feminist Needs," 1578–85 (arguing in favor of the property analogy for parental rights).

40. See Rothman, *Recreating Motherhood,* 81 ("Given our great respect for property, there are ways in which, in this society and this time, it works in the interests of children to treat them as property.").

41. See generally Pimental, "Protecting the Free-Range Kid"; Triger, "Darker Side of Overparenting."

42. Lenore Skenazy, "Why I Let My 9-Year-Old Ride the Subway Alone," *New York Sun,* April 11, 2008.

43. Colorado Office of Children, Youth and Families, Division of Child Welfare, "Frequently Asked Questions About Child Abuse and Neglect" (on file with author).

44. See Purvis, "Rules of Maternity," 435–40 (discussing enforcement disparities in the context of the free-range movement).

CHAPTER FOUR: . . . AND WHY

1. See generally, for example, Okin, *Justice, Gender, and Family;* Eichner, *Supportive State;* Mill, *Subjection of Women;* McClain, "Formative Projects, Formative Influences."

2. See, for example, Chodorow, *Reproduction of Mothering* (arguing for the effects of female child-rearing from a psychoanalytical perspective). For a critique of the cultural trend in this direction in the early 2000s, see Mezey and Pillard, "Against the New Maternalism."

3. For example, Sandberg, *Lean In;* Bachiochi, "Embodied Equality." See Williams, "Reconstructive Feminism," 81 (characterizing sameness/difference debates as debates over "tomboy" or "femme" strategies).

4. See Bartlett, "Unconstitutionally Male?" (discussing *VMI*).

5. Roe v. Wade, 410 U.S. 113 (1973), overruled by Dobbs v. Jackson Women's Health Org., 1 Gil. 3 (2022).

6. Kohlberg, "Development of Modes," 363–64. Gilligan, *In a Different Voice,* at 25, states that she used "the standard format of Kohlberg's interviewing procedure." The spelling *Heintz* is as in Kohlberg. Elsewhere I use the more customary spelling, *Heinz.*

7. Gilligan, 26.

8. Gilligan, 3, 28–29.

9. Gilligan, 100.

10. Gilligan, 28–31.

11. See generally Henrich, *WEIRDest People in the World* (pointing out that most of the criteria for a "normal" psychological profile are based on White, male, American undergraduates). "WEIRD" stands for Western, educated, industrialized, rich, and democratic. Kohlberg's scale was based on boys aged ten to sixteen.

12. Gilligan, 2.

13. I say "alleged" because their expert qualifications consisted of being college teachers or administrators rather than having conducted any research into the topic. The one who identified as feminist was Elizabeth Fox-Genovese, an antebellum historian. The district court apparently concluded that her research and publications on the history of Southern women before the Civil War qualified her to testify about her "extensive," but nowhere published, "research which shows that women reaching college generally have less confidence then men" and that the alternative women's program would "produce the same or similar outcome for women that VMI produces for men." United States v. Virginia, 852 F.Supp. 471, 476 (1994).

14. Brief Amici Curiae of Scientists, Scholars, Educators, and Professional Organizations, *United States v. Virginia* (No. 94–1941).

15. See, for example, Eisler, *Chalice and the Blade.*

16. I use the term *noble savage* to evoke its popular association with Rousseau's description of man in the state of nature, although he did not use the term. See generally D'Agostino et al., "Contemporary Approaches to the Social Contract."

17. West, *Caring for Justice,* 5.

18. See also Callahan and Roberts, "Feminist Social Justice Approach," 1205 ("Postliberal feminists tend to insist that persons 'arrive' in the world already inextricably imbedded in webs of relationships.").

19. Adams, "Re-Grasping the Opportunity Interest," convincingly argues that a terminated parent, like an unwed father, retains a protected inchoate interest that could blossom into reestablishment of parental rights.

20. Lassiter v. Department of Soc. Servs., 452 U.S. 18, 24 (1981).

21. See Sabbeth and Steinberg, "Gender of *Gideon*" (discussing the gendered allocation of the constitutional right to counsel, which includes not only *Gideon* and *Lassiter* but also the absence of a right to counsel in a wide range of civil matters, such as eviction and debt collection, which also fall heaviest on women of color).

22. Compare West, *Caring for Justice,* 20 (asserting "the genesis of the ethic [of care] in women's lives"), 118 (stating that "the mother feels the imperative of [the child's needs] as directed at her in a way the father does not"), 282 (suggesting that patriarchy pre-dates society), with *id.,* 18 (stating that there is "no ironclad correspondence" between sex/gender and the ethics of care and justice, and that whether there is "some lesser but still interesting correspondence is an exceedingly difficult empirical question on which the jury is still out"), 20 ("It is the thesis of this book that the two ethics must be regarded as necessary conditions of the other.").

23. See Tronto, "Beyond Gender Difference," 645–46 ("The equation of Gilligan's work with women's morality is a cultural phenomenon, and not of Gilligan's making.").

24. See, for example, Bradwell v. Illinois, 83 U.S. 130 (1972); Duren v. Missouri, 439 U.S. 357 (1979).

25. See generally Fine, *Delusions of Gender.*

26. Harris, "Race and Essentialism," 598. This remains the case even after decades of activism on issues of acquaintance rape. See Hendricks, "Wages of Genetic Entitlement."

27. Harris, 598.

28. MacKinnon, "Difference and Dominance," 45. See also Karlan and Ortiz, "In a Diffident Voice" (criticizing cultural feminism and Gilligan in particular).

29. See Tronto, 648–52 (reviewing literature); Donenberg and Hoffman, "Gender Differences in Moral Development," 714 (same).

30. See Tronto, 646–52.

31. Collins, *Black Feminist Thought,* 1990, 215–17 (describing an "ethic of caring" as one of four dimensions of Black feminist epistemology); Yuille, Yuille, and Yuille, "Love as Justice," 2020 (Professor Yuille, cowriting with her siblings, describing the "anti-dichotomous, syncretic relationship between love and justice for Black people"). See also Bridges, "*Windsor,* Surrogacy, and Race," 1152 ("For many African Americans, blood relationships do not necessarily create families. Much more important than genetics is love.").

32. C. West, tweet, https://twitter.com/cornelwest/status/1052585306916974592?lang = en. Compare R. West, *Caring for Justice.*

33. See Tronto, 649 ("If moral difference is a function of social position rather than gender, then the morality Gilligan has identified with women might be better identified with subordinate or minority status.").

34. W. E. Burghardt Du Bois, "The Strivings of the Negro People," *Atlantic Monthly,* August 1897, 194–97.

35. Du Bois, *Souls of Black Folk.*

36. See Olsen, "Family and the Market," 1578 ("Rather than shades of grey as an alternative to all black and all white, I envision reds and greens and blues.").

37. Becker, "Patriarchy and Inequality," 48. On the adoption of the term *relational feminism,* see Rhode, "Woman's Point of View."

38. West, "Jurisprudence and Gender," 25.

39. Fineman, "Limits of Equality," 81. See also, for example, her "Vulnerable Subject" (2008) and *Autonomy Myth.*

40. Nedelsky, *Law's Relations,* 6.

41. Fineman, "Limits of Equality," 89.

42. Harris, "Race and Essentialism," 612. See also Scales, "Emergence of Feminist Jurisprudence," 1388 ("Feminism rejects 'abstract universality' in favor of 'concrete universality.' . . . The latter . . . regards difference as emergent, as always changing.").

43. MacKinnon has made this argument in discussions of male victims of sexual harassment, something the courts continue to struggle to comprehend. See

[MacKinnon,] Brief of National Organization on Male Sexual Victimization, *Oncale v. Sundowner Offshore Servs.* (No. 96–568).

44. Obergefell v. Hodges, 576 U.S. 644, 656–57 (2016).

45. *Obergefell,* 576 U.S. at 719 n.22 (Justice Scalia, dissenting) ("The Supreme Court of the United States has descended from the disciplined legal reasoning of John Marshall and Joseph Story to the mystical aphorisms of the fortune cookie.").

46. See Lasch, *Haven in a Heartless World.*

47. Altman, "Pursuit of Intimacy," 314. At 310–12, Altman distinguishes ongoing relationships from new ones, but he appears to assume that the ongoing relationship necessarily came into existence after the birth of the child, by some affirmative reaching out across the void, rather than simultaneously.

48. Karst, "Freedom of Intimate Association," 650, 677–81. In passing, at 640, Karst treats motherhood as unproblematically chosen, "given today's facility of contraception and abortion."

49. See Appell, "Child Question," 1139 ("Indeed, childhood is the template for liberal inequality because it is the exact opposite of the reasonable man."), 1148 ("Having been reduced to a location for the reproduction of future, not current, citizens, childhood also produces a dependency in the child."). See also Godwin, "Against Parental Rights," 61 (linking the parent-child relationship to West's analysis).

50. West, "Jurisprudence and Gender," 42.

51. Becker, "Four Feminist Theoretical Approaches," 304–05.

52. Bridges, "When Pregnancy Is an Injury," 463. See also Camp, "Coercing Pregnancy."

53. Baker, "Property Rules Meet Feminist Needs," 1527.

54. This is a colloquial paraphrase of Blackstone: "By marriage, the husband and wife are one person in law: that is, the very being or legal existence of the woman is suspended during the marriage, or at least is incorporated and consolidated into that of the husband." 1 *Commentaries,* 442.

55. See generally Ansel Elkins, *Autobiography of Eve* (2015) ("Let it be known: I did not fall from grace. / I leapt / to freedom.").

CHAPTER FIVE: EXPANDING FATHERS'
RIGHTS AGAINST MOTHERS

1. See Bender, "Genes, Parents, and Assisted Reproductive Technologies," 4 (defining genetic essentialism); Roberts, "Genetic Tie," 219 (same).

2. See Strasser, "Often Illusory Protections," 59–75 (categorizing cases).

3. I first wrote about the developments and debates around the Unwed Father Cases, as discussed in chapters 5 and 6, in Hendricks, "Fathers and Feminism."

4. For a comprehensive treatment of the issues discussed in the next few pages, see Feinberg, "Parent Zero" (arguing that "the gestating parent should have a significant degree of meaningful choice in determinations of the child's second legal

parent" and that her degree of choice should not be dictated by her gender, marital status, or method of conception, or by the gender of the potential second parent).

5. Harris et al., *Family Law*, 843 ("In all states a child born to a married woman is at least rebuttably presumed to be the child of her spouse."). For example, the Uniform Parentage Act of 2017, § 204, provides that a man is presumed to be the father of a child born during or within three hundred days after his marriage to the mother.

6. Compare Pavan v. Smith, 582 U.S. _ (2017) (holding that if a state allows a husband who is not a genetic father to be listed on a birth certificate, it must allow the same for wives, but leaving open the possibility that a state could require that birth certificates list only genetic parents).

7. The exception under the Uniform Parentage Act, § 608, is that the genetic claim must be brought within the first two years after the birth and may be subject to a best interests determination if the child already has a presumed father. See Czapanskiy, "Volunteers and Draftees," 1431 (describing more lenient evidentiary standards when a man sues to "legitimate" a child than when the mother sues for child support).

8. See generally Harris, "Child Support" (arguing that the child-support enforcement system fails poor mothers); Hatcher, "Child Support Harming Children" (arguing that the reimbursement system destroys families and the social fabric).

9. See Campbell, Annotation, §§ 5, 11 (collecting cases).

10. See Brooke Adams, "Utah Dad Alleges 'Deceit,' Takes Fight for Son to Federal Court," *Salt Lake Tribune*, December 31, 2013. See also Campbell, Annotation (collecting cases).

11. Meyer, "Family Ties," 753. The cases were *In re* Kirchner, 649 N.E.2d 324 (Ill. 1995) (Richard), and *In re* B.G.C., 496 N.W.2d 239 (Ia. 1992) (Jessica).

12. Adoptive Couple v. Baby Girl, 570 U.S. 637 (2012).

13. For those who learned but have forgotten: jurisdiction *in rem*.

14. Adoptive Couple v. Baby Girl, 731 S.E.2d, 550, 553 (S.C. 2012).

15. See Berger, "In the Name of the Child," 307–8 (reporting that the trial judge initially found that Dusten had satisfied the statute by attempting to provide financial support but later reversed that finding); *Baby Girl*, 731 S.E.2d at 561 (stating that Dusten would not have had parental rights to block the adoption under state law, which required him to have contributed to child support).

16. Higdon, "Marginalized Fathers," 517; Davis, "Male Coverture"; Shultz, "Reproductive Technology and Intent-Based Parenthood," 307; Parness, "Systematically Screwing Dads." See MacKinnon, *Toward a Feminist Theory of the State*, 4 n.2 (stating that feminism analyzes the "relations . . . in which some fuck and others get fucked" and arguing that "[t]he lack of an active verb meaning 'to act sexually' that envisions a woman's action is a linguistic expression of the realities of male dominance").

17. Shirley D. Howell, "The Putative Father Registry: Behold Now the Behemoth (A Cautionary Tale)," *Alabama Lawyer* 64 (2003): 237 n.1 (quoting Job 40:15,

16, 21). Compare Totz, "What's Good for the Goose," 142 (analogizing a wife having an abortion to Lorena Bobbit cutting off her husband's penis with a kitchen knife).

18. Hochschild, *Second Shift*, 12. See Czapanskiy, "Volunteers and Draftees" (arguing that family law "actively promotes a gendered allocation of household labor"). On the relationship between these two spheres, see generally Bowman, "Socialist Feminist Legal Theory" (discussing the dual-systems theory of the family and the market); Olsen, "The Family and the Market" (discussing the dynamics of reform); Collins, *Black Feminist Thought*, 49 (suggesting the public/private split for Black women is between the Black and White communities rather than between home and work).

19. See, for example, Dowd, "Parentage at Birth," 925 (arguing that the law should assume "biological fatherhood will lead to social fatherhood and express that expectation"); Strout, "Dads and Dicta," 167 (arguing for the expressive value of acknowledging fathers' interests).

20. See generally Brito, "Fathers Behind Bars"; Patton, "Mommy's Gone, Daddy's in Prison"; Zealand, "Protecting the Ties that Bind."

21. See Lau, "Shaping Expectations," 208–14.

22. See Czapanskiy, "Volunteers and Draftees," 1442–51; Kohn, "Engaging Men," 512 n.5; Pollack and Mason, "Mandatory Visitation," 78–79.

23. Fineman, *Neutered Mother*, 82–83. See also Dinner, "Divorce Bargain" ("The bargain failed to challenge women's disproportionate responsibility for childrearing within marriage, yet enabled men to use custody rights as leverage in child support and spousal maintenance negotiations."); Law and Hennessey, "Is the Law Male," 350 ("Mothers gave up solid legal claims to marital property or child support to resist the man's 'Brer Rabbit' claim to custody."); Mayeri, "Foundling Fathers," 2332 ("By the mid- to late-1970s, some had begun to question whether feminists had put the cart before the horse."); Brinig, "Penalty Defaults," 803, 807 (describing how reforms shifted power to noncustodial parents).

24. See Dore, "'Friendly Parent' Concept," 44.

25. See, for example, Robert O. v. Russell K., 604 N.E.2d 99, 106 (N.Y. 1992) (Judge Titone, concurring). See also Higdon, "Marginalized Fathers," 539; Parness, "Systematically Screwing Dads," 658.

26. See Nevada v. Hibbs, 538 U.S. 721 (2003) (upholding the FMLA as a provision to promote sex equality pursuant to the equal protection clause). On the general question of Congress's power to protect constitutional rights more strongly than the courts do, see Katzenbach v. Morgan, 384 U.S. 641 (1966). I discussed how *Katzenbach v. Morgan* applied to the PDA in Hendricks, "Women and the Promise."

27. See generally PruneYard Shopping Ctr. v. Robins, 447 U.S. 74, 88 (1980); Milligan, "Religion and Race," 445–48.

28. Adoption of Kelsey S., 823 P.2d 1216, 1220 (Cal. 1992).

29. Troxel v. Granville, 530 U.S. 57 (2000).

30. Other people may also stand in this liminal space of being special with respect to the child and potentially eligible for full or partial parental rights. See, for example, Adams, "(Re-)Grasping the Opportunity Interest" (terminated parents).

See also Laufer-Ukeles, "Relational Rights of Children," 795–806; Bartlett, "Rethinking Parenthood as an Exclusive Status"; Boskey, "Swamps of Home"; Holmes, "Tie That Binds."

31. The principle that the child can acquire an additional constitutional parent only with the cooperation of the existing parent is well established in de facto parent doctrine, which recognizes that adding a parent necessarily compromises the rights of existing parents and therefore requires their cooperation. See generally Duncan, "Legal Fiction," 263–64; Wilson, "Limiting the Prerogatives"; Wilson, "Trusting Mothers."

32. Burbach and Lamanna, "Moral Mother," 164.

33. Burbach and Lamanna, 172 (quoting the Supreme Court of South Carolina).

34. Jo Ciavaglia, "She Gave Birth to Her Rapist's Child, Then Tried to Sever His Parental Rights in Pa. The Law Was Not on Her Side," *Bucks County Courier Times,* October 23, 2020.

35. Liz Fields, "These Women Became Pregnant from Rape, Then Fought Their Attackers for Custody," *Vice,* December 1, 2014.

36. Chris Nakamoto, Erin McWilliams, and Joe McCoy, "In Rape Paternity Dispute, Judge Awarded Child Custody to Alleged Abusive Father Despite Assault Complaints," *WBRZ.com,* June 15, 2022.

37. Rape Survivors Child Custody Act, 34 U.S.C. §§ 21301–08. I first wrote about the RSCCA issues discussed here in Hendricks, "Wages of Genetic Entitlement."

38. See Prewitt, "Giving Birth to a 'Rapist's Child,'" 853–59 (reviewing state laws).

39. Estrich, *Real Rape,* argued that this archetypal form of rape is used to trivialize and discount the experiences of marital rape, date rape, and other non-archetypal rapes.

40. 34 U.S.C. § 21302.

41. See Higdon, "Fatherhood by Conscription," 409–11.

42. See Jones, "Inequality from Gender-Neutral Laws," 435.

CHAPTER SIX: SIDELINING INCONVENIENT FATHERS

1. Gupta-Kagan, "*In re Sanders* and the Resurrection of *Stanley v. Illinois,*" 383.

2. See Matter of J.S.L., 481 P.3d 833, 843 n.4 (Mont. 2021) (collecting cases).

3. Gupta-Kagan, "The Strange Life of *Stanley v. Illinois.*"

4. U.S. Const., amend. XIV.

5. Sessions v. Morales-Santana, 528 U.S. _ (2017).

6. 8 U.S.C. §§ 1401 (1962 version) (residency periods), 1409 (formal declaration).

7. Nguyen v. INS, 533 U.S. 53 (2001).

8. See Antognini, "From Citizenship to Custody" (proposing a custodial approach to defining parenthood for purposes of citizenship).

9. See Weinrib, "Protecting Sex" (discussing this aspect of *Nguyen*).

10. George Akerlof and Janet Yellen, "An Analysis of Out-of-Wedlock Births in the United States," Brookings Institute, August 1, 1996, https://www.brookings.edu/research/papers/1996/08/childrenfamilies-akerlof; Samuels, "Surrender and Subordination," 77–78, 78 n.208.

11. For example, Bachiochi, "Embodied Equality," 927 n.142; Wardle and Robertson, "Adoption," 210. The Christian right promotes adoption as preferable not only to abortion but also to an unmarried woman keeping her child. See Joyce, "Shotgun Adoption" (describing "a pattern and history of coercing women to relinquish their children").

12. See Oren, "Unmarried Fathers and Adoption," 269–70; Strasser, "Often Illusory Protections of 'Biology Plus,'" 58–75.

13. Lehr v. Robertson, 463 U.S. 248, 264 (1983).

14. See Campbell, Annotation, §§ 5–13 (collecting cases). See also Kevin Noble Maillard, "A Father's Struggle to Stop His Daughter's Adoption," *The Atlantic*, July 7, 2015.

15. Adoptive Couple v. Baby Girl, 570 U.S. 637 (2013).

16. Indian Child Welfare Act of 1978, 25 U.S.C. §§ 1901–1963. An "Indian child" under ICWA is any child who either is a tribal member or is eligible for tribal membership and has a biological parent who is a tribal member. 25 U.S.C. § 1903. Classification as an Indian child is thus distinct from both tribal membership and Native ancestry.

17. See Roberts, *Shattered Bonds*, 234–35.

18. See also Hong, "Parens Patri[archy]," 11–31 (reviewing history of adoption). Compare Roberts, "Black Club Women" (describing the separate efforts of Black women to promote child welfare). See generally DiFonzo, "Deprived of 'Fatal Liberty'"; Platt, *The Child Savers*.

19. See Samuels, "Time to Decide?" 513.

20. See, for example, Seymore, "Adopting Civil Damages," 931 (describing the Louisiana case).

21. See Joyce, *The Child Catchers*; Joyce, "Shotgun Adoption."

22. See Seymore, "Adopting Civil Damages," 932; Joyce, "Shotgun Adoption."

23. Joyce, "Shotgun Adoption."

24. Berger, "In the Name of the Child," 345–46 (reporting on calls to reinstate *filius nullius*).

25. See Roberts, *Shattered Bonds*, especially 25–46. See also Godsoe, "Parsing Parenthood" (exploring reforms that would value parent-child relationships while addressing the socioeconomic factors underlying maltreatment of children).

26. See Joseph Malins, *The Ambulance Down in the Valley* (1895).

27. Roberts, *Shattered Bonds*, 34–35.

28. Hong, "Parens Patri[archy]," 32–33.

29. Roberts, *Shattered Bonds*, 25–46 (discussing examples).

30. Oglala Sioux Tribe v. Van Hunnik, 100 F.Supp. 3d 749 (D.S.D. 2015), vacated on grounds of *Younger* abstention, 904 F.3d 603 (8th Cir. 2018).

31. Berger, "In the Name of the Child," 302–5.

32. *Baby Girl,* 570 U.S. at 646.

33. See Berger, 327–29 (explaining rules for tribal membership); Krakoff, "Inextricably Political" (same).

34. Berger, 332.

35. But see Berger, 322–23 (discussing evidence that compliance with ICWA doesn't impede adoptions).

36. Compare Palmore v. Sidoti, 466 U.S. 429 (1984) (refusing to consider a White child's exposure to racism as a reason to deny custody to her White mother after the latter married a Black man).

37. See, for example, Higdon, "Marginalized Fathers," 549; Strasser, "Often Illusory Protections," 82–83; Megan Lestino and Erin Bayles, *NCFA's 2016 Policy Priorities and Adoption-Related Legislation,* Adoption Advocate, January 2016, at 1, 8–9, https://hopscotchadoptions.wordpress.com/2016/02/02/ncfas-2016-policy-priorities-and-adoption-related-legislation/.

38. See generally Samuels, "Time to Decide?"; Seymore, "Adopting Civil Damages."

39. *In re* B.G.C., 496 N.W.2d at 246–47.

40. When Burbach and Lamanna, "Moral Mother," 162–63, analyzed the rhetoric of unwed father decisions, they identified five of their twenty-seven cases as "Reconciliation" cases. However, their selection criteria required that the opinion include some "characterization or evaluation of the biological mother," a criterion that might be met by some types of cases more than others. A court may not necessarily mention the mother's presence in the background of the case if she had no legal standing.

CHAPTER SEVEN: LEVELING DOWN TO GENES

1. Nguyen v. INS, 533 U.S. 53, 64 (2001).

2. Stanley v. Illinois, 405 U.S. 645 (1972).

3. See *Dumbo* (Walt Disney 1941) (opening sequence, in which Mrs. Jumbo establishes her relationship with Jumbo Jr., later dubbed Dumbo, after delivery by stork; at no point does the film reference a Mr. Jumbo).

4. Lehr v. Robertson, 463 U.S. 248, 262 (1983).

5. McLaren, "Prelude to embryogenesis," 12.

6. In the Matter of Baby M, 537 A.2d 1227 (N.J. 1988).

7. Clyde Haberman, "Baby M and the Question of Surrogate Motherhood," *New York Times,* March 23, 2014 (including video).

8. Johnson v. Calvert, 851 P.2d 776 (Cal. 1993); see also Anna J. v. Mark C., 286 Cal. Rptr. 369 (Ct. App. 1991); Healy, "Beyond Surrogacy," 96.

9. Hill, "What Does It Mean to Be a 'Parent,'" 415. The court also cited Shultz, "Reproductive Technology."

10. Compare Altman, "The Pursuit of Intimacy," 313–14 (analogizing parental rights to an artist's rights in her creation).

11. But compare Appleton, "Illegitimacy and Sex" (discussing how the law of parentage regulates sex, in part by using different definitions of parenthood across the "sex/no sex" dividing line).

12. See Dawe et al., "Cell Migration from Baby to Mother," 19; Posner et al., "Neuronal Small RNAs" (finding that nematodes' nervous systems transmit information across multiple generations to control the behavior of their progeny); Wasson et al., "Neuronal Control of Maternal Provisioning" (finding that altered maternal mRNA provisioning under neuronal control prepares the next generation for environmental stresses experienced by the mother). For less technical discussions, see, for example, Centers for Disease Control and Prevention, "What Is Epigenetics?" August 15, 2022, https://www.cdc.gov/genomics/disease/epigenetics.htm; Alan Wolffe and Marjori Matzke, "Epigenetics: Regulation Through Repression," *Science*, October 15, 1999; Nancy Shute, "Beyond Birth: A Child's Cells May Help or Harm the Mother Long After Delivery," *Scientific American*, April 30, 2010. I first discussed the relationship between epigenetics and our understanding of biological parenthood in Hendricks, "Not of Woman Born," 199.

13. Roberts, "Spiritual and Menial Housework," 65–66.

14. Roberts, "Genetic Tie," 211.

15. Roberts, "Spiritual and Menial Housework," 66 (collecting examples of feminist writers with this concern).

16. Perry-Rogers v. Fasano, 715 N.Y.S.2d 19 (App. Div. 2000).

17. Rothman, *Recreating Motherhood*, 45.

18. Isaac Stanley-Becker and Michael Brice-Saddler, "They Thought Their Embryo Didn't Take. Then Their Son Was Born to a Stranger across the Country, Lawsuit Claims," *Washington Post*, July 10, 2019.

19. Bender, "Genes, Parents, and Assisted Reproductive Technologies," 32.

20. *In re* Marriage of Buzzanca, 61 Cal. App. 4th 1410 (1998).

21. Compare J.K. Rowling, *Harry Potter and the Half-Blood Prince*, 496–99 (2005) (explaining horcruxes).

CHAPTER EIGHT: HOW TO REASON FROM THE BODY

1. See, for example, Karlan and Ortiz, "In a Diffident Voice," 871 ("Our basic conclusion is that 'different voice' feminism is peculiarly ill-equipped to offer a defense of freedom of choice."). For discussion, see Hanigsberg, "Homologizing Pregnancy and Motherhood," 380, 410 ("It is indeed this dangerous and allegedly inescapable implication that I believe has kept feminist theorists, in particular, from adequately theorizing about the importance or meaning of intrauterine life."); Donley and Lens, "Abortion, Pregnancy Loss, and Subjective Fetal Personhood" ("Longstanding dogma dictates that recognizing pregnancy loss threatens abortion rights.").

2. See Burkstrand-Reid, "From Sex for Pleasure to Sex for Parenthood" (arguing that women are treated as mothers before they even have sex).

3. See Smith, "Responsibility for Life." 127 ("Women have abortions because they feel responsible for any life they bring into the world."); Hanigsberg, "Homologizing Pregnancy and Motherhood," 372 ("A strict bodily integrity framework is incomplete because it does not acknowledge intrauterine life."); Donley and Lens, "Abortion, Pregnancy Loss, and Subjective Fetal Personhood" (arguing that fetal value is "subjective and relational").

4. Dobbs v. Jackson Women's Health Org., 1 Gil. 3 (2022).

5. Siegel, "Reasoning from the Body," 275.

6. Siegel, 332.

7. Siegel, 266.

8. See Tuana, "Weaker Seed" (analyzing how gender bias affected the science of reproduction); Roe, *Matter, Life, and Generation* (analyzing the eighteenth-century debate over preformationism and competing theories).

9. Siegel, 291.

10. Lugosi, "Conforming to the Rule of Law," 123; see also Araujo, "Abortion," 1785 (asserting the status of "nascent human life" as a matter of fact).

11. Lugosi, 123–24.

12. See Maienschein, "Cloning and Stem Cell Debates," 574–75 ("Today … the preformism of genetic determinism has overbalanced our understanding of complex developmental processes."); Rothman, *Recreating Motherhood,* 36 ("When forced to acknowledge that a woman's genetic contribution is equal to a man's, Western patriarchy was in trouble. But the central concept of patriarchy, the importance of the seed, was retained by extending the concept to women." [emphasis omitted]). See also Kitchen, "Holistic Pregnancy" (describing how belief in the fetus's separate existence led to an adversarial stance toward the pregnant woman). Compare Martin, "The Egg and the Sperm" (examining how sexism and invalid theories of reproduction influence children's books about biology).

13. Planned Parenthood v. Casey, 505 U.S. 833, 856, 924 (1992).

14. See Ravid and Zanberg, "The Future of *Roe*" (finding that restrictions on abortion "strongly and consistently" correlated with a pay gap disfavoring women of childbearing age, over place and time). See also Smith, "Responsibility for Life," 138 ("[The briefs in *Casey*] reflect the view that the ultimate prize served by abortion is the freedom to be educated and work in conditions of equality, unencumbered by one's children."). I wrote about the inadequacy of this conception of equality in Hendricks, "Body and Soul."

15. *Dobbs,* 1 Gil. 3, 34 n.46 (slip op.) (quoting a government report).

16. See transcript of Oral Argument, 56–57, *Dobbs* (No. 19–1392). See also *Dobbs,* 1 Gil. 3, 34 n.45 (slip op.) (incorporating the point about safe havens). Justice Barrett's comments, unlike the opinion of the court she later signed, acknowledged that the physical impact of pregnancy remained an issue. Notably, safe haven laws have been criticized because they might conceivably impinge on the rights of genetic fathers. See Parness, "Deserting Mothers."

17. See Sisson et al., "Adoption Decision Making" ("Among women motivated to avoid parenthood, as evidenced by abortion seeking, adoption is considered or

chosen infrequently. Political promotion of adoption as an alternative to abortion is likely not grounded in the reality of women's decision making."). See also Siegel, "Reasoning from the Body," 371–72 ("Once compelled to bear a child against their wishes, most women will feel obligated to raise it.").

18. See Joyce, "Shotgun Adoption"; Berger, "In the Name of the Child," 345–46 ("Members of the Christian Right adoption movement have explicitly adopted the *filius nullius* concept, asserting that because the term 'orphan' means fatherless child in the bible, children of single mothers are by definition orphans, and therefore eligible for adoption.").

19. See, for example, Leib, "A Man's Right to Choose."

20. Dalton Conley, "A Man's Right to Choose," *New York Times*, December 1, 2005.

21. See Planned Parenthood v. Danforth, 428 U.S. 52, 67–71 (1976) (explaining why a woman's husband does not have a legal right to be involved in her decision to have an abortion); *Casey*, 505 U.S. at 887–98 (same).

22. There are also feminist proposals for something like the male right to abortion, notably Baker, "DNA Default" and Jacobs, "Parental Parity." Importantly, however, Baker's proposals for reordering parentage rules are accompanied by proposals for also reorganizing the burden of caretaking in society, and Jacobs's is designed to promote women's independence. See also Motro, "Price of Pleasure" (arguing for men to have a due-process-type right to notice and the opportunity to object to an abortion).

23. Fontana and Schoenbaum, "Unsexing Pregnancy," 336. For other explorations of the relationship between the physiological process of pregnancy and identification as a parent or parent-to-be that avoid giving men undue power over women, see, for example, Matambanadzo, "Reconstructing Pregnancy" (arguing against "biomedical essentialism" in the legal construction of pregnancy); Woodhouse, "Hatching the Egg" (arguing for a theory of "gestational fathering" that focuses on the man's relationship with the pregnant woman).

24. Fontana and Schoenbaum, 365.

25. Fontana and Schoenbaum, 354.

26. Fontana and Schoenbaum, 352.

27. *Dobbs*, 1 Gil. 3, 77–78 (slip op.) (including "the prevention of discrimination on the basis of race, sex, or disability" in an illustrative list of state interests that could justify regulating abortion).

28. Kim St. Onge, "Father Suing Mother to Be Present at Birth of Their Child," *WSMV, News4 Nashville*, July 18, 2018.

29. Plotnick v. DeLuccia, 85 A.3d 1039 (N.J. Super. Ct. 2013); Eyder Peralta, "New Jersey Judge Rules Women Can Keep Fathers Out of Delivery Room," *NPR*, March 12, 2014.

30. Fontana and Schoenbaum, 352 (emphasis in original).

31. To the extent that any pregnancy benefit could avoid "implicating" the woman's body, the *Roe/Casey* argument wouldn't be needed at all.

32. Baker, "DNA Default," 2060, argues that the potential for this sort of doctrinal innovation is a natural next step after giving fathers genetic rights to born

children. ("Many scholars have criticized the unwed father and citizenship cases as rooted in gender stereotypes and maternalism. Far fewer scholars criticize the abortion decisions on gender equality grounds; but if equality norms should be used to override women's much greater biological investment in a newborn child, then it is not altogether clear why equality norms should not be used to give genetic progenitors equal rights to a child before it is born.").

33. Compare Warren, "Moral Significance of Birth."

34. Karst, "Freedom of Intimate Association," 638.

35. See Bridges, "When Pregnancy Is an Injury," 463.

36. Frederica Mathewes-Green, "Seeking Abortion's Middle Ground: Why My Pro-Life Allies Should Revise Their Self-Defeating Rhetoric," *Washington Post*, July 28, 1996. Mathewes-Green wrote that the woman "wants an abortion like an animal, caught in a trap, wants to gnaw off its own leg." She was an anti-abortion activist and, I assume, meant to imply that abortion is a form of self-harm.

37. Harris v. McRae, 448 U.S. 297 (1980); Maher v. Roe, 432 U.S. 464 (1977). See generally Huberfeld, "Conditional Spending" (arguing that conditional funding like the Hyde Amendment is unconstitutional).

38. Hyde Amendment, Pub. L. No. 94–439, 90 Stat. 1434 (1976).

39. *Harris,* 448 U.S. at 339–40 (Justice Marshall, dissenting).

40. *Harris,* 448 U.S. at 315.

41. U.S. Const., amend. I.

42. DeShaney v. Winnebago County, 489 U.S. 189, 201 (1989).

43. *Harris,* 448 U.S. at 316.

44. Altman, "Pursuit of Intimacy," 314. Altman was speaking of parental rights as such a background institution.

45. See Ball, "The Positive in the Fundamental Right to Marry," 1204–05 (arguing that "even if the Due Process Clause primarily protects negative rights, the fundamental right to marry stands as an important exception" and contrasting the right to abortion, which, "the Court has held, is sufficiently guaranteed through the enforcement of negative rights"); Strauss, "Positive Right to Marry" (arguing for a right to be protected from domination while participating in intimate relationships).

46. See Olsen, "Family and the Market," 1522 ("The marketplace was said to be left alone by the state if courts blindly enforced contracts and refused to make any independent judgment of the equities in the existing relationship between the parties. In contrast, the family was said to be left alone by the state if courts flatly refused to enforce contracts between its members and insisted on authoritatively defining family relationships.").

47. See also Law, "Rethinking Sex and the Constitution," 957 (noting the link between sameness equality and privacy-based reproductive freedom); West, "Jurisprudence and Gender," 41 ("It is hardly surprising, then, that radical feminists borrow heavily from liberalism's protective armor of rights and distance.").

48. Obergefell v. Hodges, 578 U.S., 644, 667 (2017).

49. *DeShaney,* 489 U.S. at 212–13 (Justice Blackmun, dissenting).

50. See Foner, *Second Founding;* Black, *New Birth of Freedom.* On the Thirteenth Amendment and the right to abortion, see Koppelman, "Forced Labor"; McDonagh, "Breaking the Abortion Deadlock"; Suk, "World Without *Roe,*" 3. On the inadequacy of the first founding to protect women's interests, see Becker, "Politics of Women's Wrongs."

51. See generally Fineman, "Reasoning from the Body" ("Vulnerability theory asserts that the body as a universal concept is where theory should begin.").

CHAPTER NINE: THE BODY AND BEYOND

1. For early feminist criticism of surrogacy, see Allen, "Surrogacy, Slavery, and the Ownership of Life, 140 ("While surrogacy is certainly not the same thing as slavery, American slavery had the effect of causing black women to become surrogate mothers on behalf of slave owners."); Ikemoto, "Destabilizing Thoughts," 642 (noting that the trial court's description of Anna Johnson "echoes the mammy image"); Roberts, "Spiritual and Menial Housework," 68 ("'Surrogacy' perpetuates the racial hierarchy within the division of reproductive labor, as well as the racist valuation of genetic material.").

2. See Dworkin, *Right-Wing Women* (discussing the "brothel model").

3. See Mutcherson, "Things That Money Can Buy," 169.

4. Choudhury, "Transnational Commercial Surrogacy."

5. See Madeira, "Woman Scorned?" (criticizing legal scholars' stereotyping of "desperate women" who seek to have children through assisted reproductive technologies).

6. Bridges, "*Windsor,* Surrogacy, and Race," 1144. See also Mutcherson, "Transformative Reproduction," 217 (similar); Rao, "Assisted Reproductive Technology," 952 ("Assisted reproductive technologies possess the potential to undermine the traditional paradigm."); Appleton, "Presuming Women," 267, 283–84 (objecting to surrogacy exceptionalism that excludes gay couples from parenting, but also advocating for a functional test that defines the gestational mother as a legal parent); Appell, "Endurance of Biological Connection" (arguing for openness between biological and social parents as a challenge to the traditional nuclear family).

7. Boucai, "Is Assisted Procreation an LGBT Right?" 1070. See also Rich, "Contracting Our Way to Inequality" (describing reproduction through IVF as an unqueering strategy for a White lesbian couple who sued their fertility clinic for mistakenly giving them sperm from a Black man); Franke, "Becoming a Citizen," (chronicling the assimilating and disciplinary aspects of marriage for African Americans after the Civil War, with warnings for the prospects for same-sex marriage).

8. On the demographics of surrogacy, see Dillaway, "Mothers for Others," 312–13. See also Bridges, "*Windsor,* Surrogacy, and Race," 1139; Laufer-Ukeles, "Mothering for Money," 1234; Carbone and Madeira, "Role of Agency," 22.

9. Bridges, "*Windsor,* Surrogacy, and Race," 1127 (describing this "second-generation concern"), 1140 ("It might be that the reproductive capacities of white

women are simply more highly valued than those of women of color. It is possible that wealthy white couples that hire surrogates deem women of color untrustworthy.").

10. Laufer-Ukeles, "Collaborative Family Making," 228. Laufer-Ukeles advocates for discouraging international surrogacy because of the greater risks of exploitation, and she argues both surrogacy and adoption should be "open," meaning the surrogate/birth mother and the contracting/adopting parents know each other and stay in contact). See also Rebouché, "Contracting Pregnancy" (arguing that industry norms and mediation by parties' lawyers have more effect than law on how disputes in surrogacy contracts are resolved).

11. Ainsworth, "Bearing Children," 1094 ("Women who engage in traditional surrogacy arrangements generally report the same levels of comfort in going through with the surrogacy and relinquishing the baby to the intended parents as do gestational surrogates."), 1101 ("Women acting as surrogates indicate that they appreciate the emotional bond with the intended parents—or were unhappy if that was lacking.").

12. For example, Johnson v. Calvert, 851 P.2d at 782 ("Anna's later change of heart").

13. Hill, "What Does It Mean to Be a 'Parent,'" 397–406.

14. See Donley and Lens, "Abortion, Pregnancy Loss, and Subjective Fetal Personhood" (discussing how emotions about pregnancy are a function of expectations). Compare Purvis, "Intended Parents," 237 (citing research on surrogates finding a lack of attachment to the fetus as well as a lack of emotional volatility).

15. "Surrogate Mother Given Legal Custody of Triplets," *The Spokesman-Review*, January 8, 2005; Barbara White Stack, "Custody Battle for Triplets Becomes Class Struggle," *Pittsburgh Post-Gazette*, July 10, 2004; Moustafa Ayad, "Surrogate Mom Loses Triplets," *Pittsburgh Post-Gazette*, April 22, 2006.

16. J.F. v. D.B., 879 N.E.2d 740 (Ohio 2007).

17. P.M. v. T.B., 907 N.W.2d 522 (Iowa 2017). The facts in the text are drawn from the opinion and from Rebouché, "Contracting Pregnancy."

18. Ainsworth, "Bearing Children," 1101.

19. Shapiro, "For a Feminist Considering Surrogacy," 1366. See also Holmstrom-Smith, "Free Market Feminism"; Rebouché, "Contracting Pregnancy," 1624 (describing how surrogacy functions in practice as a relationship as much as a contract and suggesting under-enforcement is beneficial); Laufer-Ukeles, "Mothering for Money," 1228 (discussing theories of "mixed commodification"). For earlier arguments against specific enforcement of surrogacy contracts, see, for example, Allen, "Surrogacy, Slavery, and the Ownership of Life," 147; Bartlett, "Re-expressing Parenthood," 335; Brinig, "Maternalistic Approach," 2381; Callahan and Roberts, "Feminist Social Justice Approach," 1233.

20. On the benefits of having surrogacy arrangements brokered and overseen by professionals, see Carbone and Madeira, "Role of Agency."

21. Circle Surrogacy, "How to Become a Surrogate Mother and Help Others," https://www.circlesurrogacy.com/surrogates.

22. Roberts, "Spiritual and Menial Housework," 58 (quoting Macdonald, "Shadow Mothers," 250).

23. Cherry, "Nurturing in the Service of White Culture," 85 (describing her great-aunt's experience).

24. See Case, "Pets or Meat," 1134–36 (discussing the potential for exploitation).

25. Hochschield, "Love and Gold," 185–86.

26. Hochschield, "Love and Gold," 194. See also Romero, "Unraveling Privilege" (discussing the experiences of children of paid care-workers).

27. I'm greatly simplifying the options, criteria, and terminology here. For an overview of the chaotic state of the law and the accompanying terminology, especially after *Troxel*, see Higdon, "Quasi-Parent Conundrum."

28. Rothman, *Recreating Motherhood*, 209. See also Laufer-Ukeles, "Money, Caregiving, and Kinship" (arguing that categorical exclusion of paid caregivers is unjustified given the high bar that otherwise exists).

29. American Law Institute, Principles of the Law of Family Dissolution § 2.03 (2002) (comment c.ii).

CONCLUSION

1. West, *Caring for Justice*, 5.

2. See Black, "Lawfulness of the Segregation Decisions."

3. See Charlie Scudder, "'Not good enough': Uvalde victims' families react to report on police failures," *The Guardian*, July 18, 2022 (quoting the father of a murdered child who "criticized the committee for not recommending any action on gun control in the state. 'These *cabrones* can identify the height of the fence, but they never point to the militaristic weapon that killed 21 people.'").

4. See Appleton, "Reproduction and Regret"; Bridges, "When Pregnancy Is an Injury."

5. Dobbs v. Jackson Women's Health Org., 1 Gil. 3, 10–11, 17–20, 48 (2022) (slip op.).

6. See White, "One for Sorrow, Two for Joy?"

7. I discussed some of these dilemmas in advocacy for abortion rights in Hendricks, "Converging Trajectories."

8. Fineman, "Limits of Equality," 89.

9. West, "Jurisprudence and Gender," 42.

BIBLIOGRAPHY

Adams, LaShanda Taylor. "(Re-)Grasping the Opportunity Interest: *Lehr v. Robertson* and the Terminated Parent." *Kansas Journal of Law and Public Policy* 25 (2015): 31–64.

Ainsworth, Sara. "Bearing Children, Bearing Risks: Feminist Leadership for Progressive Regulation of Compensated Surrogacy in the United States." *Washington Law Review* 89 (2014): 1077–1123.

Allen, Anita. "Surrogacy, Slavery, and the Ownership of Life." *Harvard Journal of Law and Public Policy* 13 (1990): 139–49.

Altman, Scott. "The Pursuit of Intimacy and Parental Rights." In *The Routledge Companion to Philosophy of Law,* edited by Andrei Marmor, 305–14. Routledge, 2015.

Antognini, Albertina. "From Citizenship to Custody: Unwed Fathers Abroad and at Home." *Harvard Journal of Law and Gender* 36 (2013): 405–68.

Appell, Annette. "The Child Question." *Michigan State Law Review* (2013): 1137–84.

———. "The Endurance of Biological Connection: Heteronormativity, Same-Sex Parenting, and the Lessons of Adoption." *BYU Journal of Public Law* 22 (2008): 289–326.

———. "Virtual Mothers and the Meaning of Parenthood." *University of Michigan Journal of Law Reform* 34 (2001): 683–790.

Appleton, Susan Frelich. "Illegitimacy and Sex, Old and New." *American University Journal of Gender, Social Policy and the Law* 20 (2012): 347–86.

———. "Parents by the Numbers." *Hofstra Law Review* 37 (2008): 11–70.

———. "Presuming Women: Revisiting the Presumption of Legitimacy in the Same-Sex Couples Era." *Boston University Law Review* 86 (2006): 227–94.

———. "Reproduction and Regret." *Yale Journal of Law and Feminism* 23 (2011): 255–334.

Araujo, Robert. "Abortion—From Privacy to Equality: The Failure of the Justifications for Taking Human Life." *Houston Law Review* 45 (2009): 1737–1800.

Areheart, Bradley. "Disability Trouble." *Yale Law and Policy Review* 29 (2010): 347–88.

Bachiochi, Erika. "Embodied Equality: Debunking Equal Protection Arguments for Abortion Rights." *Harvard Journal of Law and Public Policy* 34 (2011): 889–950.

Bagenstos, Samuel. "*Nevada Department of Human Resources v. Hibbs:* Universalism and Reproductive Justice." In *Reproductive Rights and Justice Stories,* edited by Melissa Murray, Katherine Shaw, and Reva Siegel, 183–204. Foundation Press, 2019.

———. "Rational Discrimination, Accommodation, and the Politics of (Disability) Civil Rights." *Virginia Law Review* 89 (2003): 825–924.

Baker, Katharine. "Bionormativity and the Construction of Parenthood." *Georgia Law Review* 42 (2008): 649–716.

———. "The DNA Default and Its Discontents: Establishing Modern Parenthood." *Boston University Law Review* 96 (2016): 2037–92.

———. "Equality and Family Autonomy." *University of Pennsylvania Journal of Constitutional Law* 24 (2022): 412–79.

———. "Property Rules Meet Feminist Needs: Respecting Autonomy by Valuing Connection." *Ohio State Law Journal* 59 (1998): 1523–98.

Baker, Liva. *The Justice from Beacon Hill: The Life and Times of Oliver Wendell Holmes.* HarperCollins, 1991.

Ball, Carlos. "The Positive in the Fundamental Right to Marry: Same-Sex Marriage in the Aftermath of *Lawrence v. Texas.*" *Minnesota Law Review* 88 (2004): 1184–1232.

Bartlett, Katharine. "Re-Expressing Parenthood." *Yale Law Journal* 98 (1988): 293–340.

———. "Rethinking Parenthood as an Exclusive Status: The Need for Legal Alternatives When the Premise of the Nuclear Family Has Failed." *Virginia Law Review* 70 (1984): 879–964.

———. "Unconstitutionally Male? The Story of *United States v. Virginia.*" In *Women and the Law Stories,* edited by Elizabeth Schneider and Stephanie Wildman, 133–77. Foundation Press, 2011.

Bayefsky, Michelle. "Legal and Ethical Analysis of Advertising for Elective Egg Freezing." *Journal of Law, Medicine and Ethics* 48 (2020): 748–64.

Becker, Mary. "Care and Feminists." *Wisconsin Women's Law Journal* 17 (2002): 57–110.

———. "Caring for Children and Caretakers." *Chicago-Kent Law Review* 76 (2001): 1495–1540.

———. "Four Feminist Theoretical Approaches and the Double Bind of Surrogacy." *Chicago-Kent Law Review* 69 (1993): 303–12.

———. "Patriarchy and Inequality: Towards a Substantive Feminism." *University of Chicago Legal Forum* 1999: 21–88.

———. "The Politics of Women's Wrongs and the Bill of Rights: A Bicentennial Perspective." *University of Chicago Law Review* 59 (1992): 453–518.

Bender, Leslie. "Genes, Parents, and Assisted Reproductive Technologies: ARTs, Mistakes, Sex, Race, and Law." *Columbia Journal of Gender and Law* 12 (2003): 1–76.

———. "To Err Is Human—ART Mix-Ups: A Labor-Based, Relational Proposal." *Journal of Gender, Race, and Justice* 9 (2006): 443–508.

Berger, Bethany. "In the Name of the Child: Race, Gender, and Economics in *Adoptive Couple v. Baby Girl*." *Florida Law Review* 67 (2015): 295–362.

Black, Charles. "The Lawfulness of the Segregation Decisions." *Yale Law Journal* 69 (1960): 421–31.

———. *A New Birth of Freedom: Human Rights, Named and Unnamed.* Yale University Press, 1997.

Blackstone, William. *Commentaries on the Laws of England*, 1765.

Blecher-Prigat, Ayelet. "Conceiving Parents." *Harvard Journal of Law and Gender* 41 (2018): 119–78.

Boone, Meghan. "Lactation Law." *California Law Review* 106 (2018): 1827–84.

Boskey, James. "The Swamps of Home: A Reconstruction of the Parent-Child Relationship." *University of Toledo Law Review* 26 (1995): 805–54.

Boucai, Michael. "Is Assisted Procreation an LGBT Right?" *Wisconsin Law Review* 2016: 1065–1126.

Bowman, Cynthia Grant. "Socialist Feminist Legal Theory: A Plea." In *Research Handbook on Feminist Jurisprudence*, edited by Robin West and Cynthia Grant Bowman, 91–111. Edward Elgar, 2019.

Brake, Deborah. "On Not Having It Both Ways and Still Losing: Reflections on Fifty Years of Pregnancy Litigation under Title VII." *Boston University Law Review* 95 (2015): 995–1014.

Bridges, Khiara. "When Pregnancy Is an Injury: Rape, Law, and Culture." *Stanford Law Review* 65 (2013): 457–516.

———. "*Windsor*, Surrogacy, and Race." *Washington Law Review* 89 (2014): 1125–54.

Brinig, Margaret. "A Maternalistic Approach to Surrogacy: Comment on Richard Epstein's *Surrogacy: The Case for Full Contractual Enforcement*." *Virginia Law Review* 81 (1995): 2377–2400.

———. "Penalty Defaults in Family Law: The Case of Child Custody." *Florida State University Law Review* 33 (2006): 779–824.

Brito, Tonya. "Fathers Behind Bars: Rethinking Child Support Policy toward Low-Income Noncustodial Fathers and Their Families." *Journal of Gender, Race, and Justice* 15 (2012): 617–74.

Britton, Ann. "America's Best Kept Secret: An Adult Child's Duty to Support Aged Parents." *California Western Law Review* 26 (1990): 351–72.

Burbach, Mary, and Mary Ann Lamanna. "The Moral Mother: Motherhood Discourse in Biological Father and Third Party Cases." *Journal of Law and Family Studies* 2 (2000): 153–98.

Burkstrand-Reid, Beth. "From Sex for Pleasure to Sex for Parenthood: How the Law Manufactures Mothers." *Hastings Law Journal* 65 (2013): 211–58.

Buss, Emily. "Allocating Developmental Control among Parent, Child and the State." *University of Chicago Legal Forum* 2004: 27–56.

Byrn, Mary Patricia, and Jenni Vainik Ives. "Which Came First the Parent or the Child?" *Rutgers Law Review* 62 (2009): 305–44.

Callahan, Joan, and Dorothy Roberts. "A Feminist Social Justice Approach to Reproduction-Assisting Technologies: A Case Study on the Limits of Liberal Theory." *Kentucky Law Journal* 84 (1996): 1197–1234.

Camp, A. Rachel. "Coercing Pregnancy." *William and Mary Journal of Women and the Law* 21 (2015): 275–318.

Campbell, Ardis. "Annotation, Rights of Unwed Father to Obstruct Adoption of His Child by Withholding Consent." *American Law Reports 5th* 61 (1998): 151.

Carbone, June, and Jody Lynee Madeira. "The Role of Agency: Compensated Surrogacy and the Institutionalization of Assisted Reproduction Practices." *Washington Law Review Online* 90 (2015): 7–42.

Carbone, June, and Naomi Cahn. "The Gender/Class Divide: Reproduction, Privilege, and the Workplace." *FIU Law Review* 8 (2013): 287–316.

———. *Marriage Markets: How Inequality Is Remaking the American Family.* Oxford University Press, 2014.

———. "Parents, Babies, and More Parents." *Chicago-Kent Law Review* 92 (2017): 9–54.

———. "The Triple System of Family Law." *Michigan State Law Review* 2013: 1185–1230.

Case, Mary Anne. "How High the Apple Pie? A Few Troubling Questions about Where, Why, and How the Burden of Care for Children Should Be Shifted." *Chicago-Kent Law Review* 76 (2001): 1753–88.

———. "Pets or Meat." *Chicago-Kent Law Review* 80 (2005): 1129–50.

Cherry, April. "Nurturing in the Service of White Culture: Racial Subordination, Gestational Surrogacy, and the Ideology of Motherhood." *Texas Journal of Women and the Law* 10 (2001): 83–128.

Chodorow, Nancy. *The Reproduction of Mothering: Psychoanalysis and the Sociology of Gender.* 2nd ed. University of California Press, 1999.

Choudhury, Cyra Akila. "Transnational Commercial Surrogacy: Contracts, Conflicts, and the Prospects of International Legal Regulation." In *Oxford Handbooks Online.* Oxford University Press, 2016. https://doi.org/10.1093/oxfordhb /9780199935352.013.38.

Collins, Patricia Hill. *Black Feminist Thought: Knowledge, Consciousness, and the Politics of Empowerment.* HarperCollins Academic, 1990.

Czapanskiy, Karen. "Volunteers and Draftees: The Struggle for Parental Equality." *UCLA Law Review* 38 (1991): 1415–82.

D'Agostino, Fred, Gerald Gaus, and John Thrasher. "Contemporary Approaches to the Social Contract." In *The Stanford Encyclopedia of Philosophy,* edited by Edward Zalta, Summer 2021. https://plato.stanford.edu/archives/win2021/entries /contractarianism-contemporary/.

Dailey, Anne, and Laura Rosenbury. "The New Parental Rights." *Duke Law Journal* 71 (2021): 75–166.

Davis, Martha. "Male Coverture: Law and the Illegitimate Family." *Rutgers Law Review* 56 (2003): 73–118.

Davis, Peggy Cooper. "Contested Images of Family Values: The Role of the State." *Harvard Law Review* 107 (1994): 1348–73.

Dawe, Gavin, Xiao Wei Tan, and Zhi-Cheng Xiao. "Cell Migration from Baby to Mother." *Cell Adhesion and Migration* 1 (March 2007): 19–27.

DiFonzo, J. Herbie. "Deprived of Fatal Liberty: The Rhetoric of Child Saving and the Reality of Juvenile Incarceration." *University of Toledo Law Review* 26 (1995): 855–900.

Dillaway, Heather. "Mothers for Others: A Race, Class, and Gender Analysis of Surrogacy." *International Journal of Sociology of the Family* 34 (2008): 301–26.

Dinner, Deborah. "The Divorce Bargain: The Fathers' Rights Movement and Family Inequalities." *Virginia Law Review* 102 (2016): 79–152.

Dolgin, Janet. "Just a Gene: Judicial Assumptions about Parenthood." *UCLA Law Review* 40 (1993): 637–94.

Donenberg, Geri, and Lois Wladis Hoffman. "Gender Differences in Moral Development." *Sex Roles* 18 (1988): 701–17.

Donley, Greer, and Jill Wieber Lens. "Abortion, Pregnancy Loss, and Subjective Fetal Personhood." *Vanderbilt Law Review* 75 (2022): 1649–1727.

Dore, Margaret. "The Friendly Parent Concept: A Flawed Factor for Child Custody." *Loyola Journal of Public Interest Law* 6 (2004): 41–56.

Dowd, Nancy. "Fathers and the Supreme Court: Founding Fathers and Nurturing Fathers." *Emory Law Journal* 54 (2005): 1271–1334.

———. "Parentage at Birth: Birthfathers and Social Fatherhood." *William and Mary Bill of Rights Journal* 14 (2006): 909–42.

Du Bois, W. E. B. *The Souls of Black Folk,* 1903.

Duncan, William. "The Legal Fiction of De Facto Parenthood." *Journal of Legislation* 36 (2010): 263–71.

Dworkin, Andrea. *Right-Wing Women.* Coward-McCann, 1983.

Dwyer, James. "The Children We Abandon: Religious Exemptions to Child Welfare and Education Laws as Denials of Equal Protection to Children of Religious Objectors." *North Carolina Law Review* 74 (1996): 1321–1478.

Eichner, Maxine. *The Free-Market Family: How the Market Crushed the American Dream (and How It Can Be Restored).* Oxford University Press, 2020.

———. *The Supportive State: Family, Privacy, and Children.* Oxford University Press, 2010.

Eisler, Riane. *The Chalice and the Blade: Our History, Our Future.* HarperCollins, 1987.

Estrich, Susan. *Real Rape.* Harvard University Press, 1987.

Feinberg, Jessica. "Parent Zero." *UC Davis Law Review* 55 (2022): 2271–2336.

———. "Restructuring Rebuttal of the Marital Presumption for the Modern Era." *Minnesota Law Review* 104 (2019): 243–308.

Fine, Cordelia. *Delusions of Gender: How Our Minds, Society, and Neurosexism Create Difference.* W. W. Norton, 2010.

Fineman, Martha. *The Autonomy Myth: A Theory of Dependency.* New Press, 2004.

———. "The Limits of Equality: Vulnerability and Inevitable Inequality." In *Research Handbook on Feminist Jurisprudence*, edited by Robin West and Cynthia Grant Bowman, 73–90. Edward Elgar, 2019.

———. "Masking Dependency: The Political Role of Family Rhetoric." *Virginia Law Review* 81 (1995): 2181–2216.

———. *The Neutered Mother, The Sexual Family, and Other Twentieth Century Tragedies*. Routledge, 1995.

———. "Reasoning from the Body: Universal Vulnerability and Social Justice." In *A Jurisprudence of the Body*, edited by Chris Dietz, Mitchell Travis, and Michael Thomson, 17–34. Palgrave MacMillan, 2020.

———. "The Vulnerable Subject: Anchoring Equality in the Human Condition." *Yale Journal of Law and Feminism* 20 (2008): 1–24.

———. "The Vulnerable Subject and the Responsive State." *Emory Law Journal* 60 (2010): 251–76.

Fineman, Martha Albertson, and George Shepherd. "Homeschooling: Choosing Parental Rights over Children's Interests." *University of Baltimore Law Review* 46 (2016): 57–106.

Firestone, Shulamith. *The Dialectic of Sex: The Case for Feminist Revolution*. Morrow, 1970.

Foner, Eric. *The Second Founding: How the Civil War and Reconstruction Remade the Constitution*. W. W. Norton, 2019.

Fontana, David, and Naomi Schoenbaum. "Unsexing Pregnancy." *Columbia Law Review* 119 (2019): 309–68.

Franke, Katherine. "Becoming a Citizen: Reconstruction Era Regulation of African American Marriages." *Yale Journal of Law and the Humanities* 11 (1999): 251–310.

Franklin, Cary. "The Anti-Stereotyping Principle in Constitutional Sex Discrimination Law." *New York University Law Review* 85 (2010): 83–173.

Freedman, Ann. "Sex Equality, Sex Differences, and the Supreme Court." *Yale Law Journal* 92 (1983): 913–69.

Gilligan, Carol. *In a Different Voice: Psychological Theory and Women's Development*. Harvard University Press, 1982.

Godsoe, Cynthia. "Parsing Parenthood." *Lewis and Clark Law Review* 17 (2013): 113–70.

Godwin, Samantha. "Against Parental Rights." *Columbia Human Rights Law Review* 47 (2015): 1–83.

Grossman, Joanna. "Pregnancy, Work, and the Promise of Equal Citizenship." *Georgetown Law Journal* 98 (2009): 567–628.

Gupta-Kagan, Josh. "*In Re Sanders* and the Resurrection of *Stanley v. Illinois*." *California Law Review Circuit* 5 (2014): 383–91.

———. "*Stanley v. Illinois*'s Untold Story." *William and Mary Bill of Rights Journal* 24 (2016): 773–828.

———. "The Strange Life of *Stanley v. Illinois:* A Case Study in Parent Representation and Law Reform." *New York University Review of Law and Social Change* 41 (2017): 569–630.

Hanigsberg, Julia. "Homologizing Pregnancy and Motherhood: A Consideration of Abortion." *Michigan Law Review* 94 (1995): 371–418.

Harbach, Meredith Johnson. "Outsourcing Childcare." *Yale Journal of Law and Feminism* 24 (2012): 254–302.

Harris, Angela. "Race and Essentialism in Feminist Legal Theory." *Stanford Law Review* 42 (1990): 581–616.

Harris, Deborah. "Child Support for Welfare Families: Family Policy Trapped in Its Own Rhetoric." *New York University Review of Law and Social Change* 16 (1987–88): 619–58.

Harris, Leslie Joan, June Carbone, Lee Teitelbaum, and Rachel Rebouché. *Family Law*. 6th ed. WoltersKluwer, 2018.

Hatcher, Daniel. "Child Support Harming Children: Subordinating the Best Interests of Children to the Fiscal Interests of the State." *Wake Forest Law Review* 42 (2007): 1029–86.

Healy, Nicole Miller. "Beyond Surrogacy: Gestational Parenting Agreements under California Law." *UCLA Women's Law Journal* 1 (1991): 89–134.

Hendricks, Jennifer. "Body and Soul: Equality, Pregnancy, and the Unitary Right to Abortion." *Harvard Civil Rights–Civil Liberties Law Review* 45 (2010): 329–74.

———. "Contingent Equal Protection: Reaching for Equality after *Ricci* and *PICS*." *Michigan Journal of Gender and Law* 16 (2010): 397–452.

———. "Converging Trajectories: Interest Convergence, Justice Kennedy, and Jeannie Suk's 'The Trajectory of Trauma.'" *Columbia Law Review Sidebar* 110 (2010): 63–72.

———. "Essentially a Mother." *William and Mary Journal of Women and the Law* 13 (2007): 429–82.

———. "Fathers and Feminism: The Case against Genetic Entitlement." *Tulane Law Review* 91 (2017): 473–536.

———. "Not of Woman Born: A Scientific Fantasy." *Case Western Reserve Law Review* 62 (2012): 399–446.

———. "The Wages of Genetic Entitlement: The Good, the Bad, and the Ugly in the Rape Survivor Child Custody Act." *Northwestern University Law Review Online* 112 (2018): 75–84.

———. "Women and the Promise of Equal Citizenship." *Texas Journal of Women and the Law* 8 (1998): 51–92.

Henrich, Joseph. *The WEIRDest People in the World: How the West Became Psychologically Peculiar and Particularly Prosperous*. Farrar, Straus and Giroux, 2020.

Higdon, Michael. "Fatherhood by Conscription: Nonconsensual Insemination and the Duty of Child Support." *Georgia Law Review* 46 (2012): 407–58.

———. "Marginalized Fathers and Demonized Mothers: A Feminist Look at the Reproductive Freedom of Unmarried Men." *Alabama Law Review* 66 (2015): 507–50.

———. "The Quasi-Parent Conundrum." *University of Colorado Law Review* 90 (2019): 941–1012.

Hill, B. Jessie. "Whose Body? Whose Soul? Medical Decision-Making on Behalf of Children and the Free Exercise Clause before and after *Employment Division v. Smith*." *Cardozo Law Review* 32 (2011): 1857–78.

Hill, John Lawrence. "What Does It Mean to Be a 'Parent'? The Claims of Biology as the Basis for Parental Rights." *New York University Law Review* 66 (1991): 353–421.

Hochschild, Arlie Russel. "Love and Gold." In *The Commercialization of Intimate Life: Notes from Home and Work*, 185–97. University of California Press, 2003.

———. *The Second Shift: Working Parents and the Revolution at Home*. Viking, 1989.

Holmes, Gilbert. "The Tie That Binds: The Constitutional Right of Children to Maintain Relationships with Parent-Like Individuals." *Maryland Law Review* 53 (1994): 358–411.

Holmstrom-Smith, Alexandra. "Free Market Feminism: Re-Reconsidering Surrogacy." *University of Pennsylvania Journal of Law and Social Change* 24 (2021): 443–84.

Holsinger, M. Paul. "The Oregon School Bill Controversy 1922–1925." *Pacific History Review* 37 (1968): 327–41.

Hong, Kari. "Parens Patri[archy]: Adoption, Eugenics, and Same-Sex Couples." *California Western Law Review* 40 (2003): 1–78.

Huberfeld, Nicole. "Conditional Spending and Compulsory Maternity." *University of Illinois Law Review* 2010: 751–98.

Huntington, Clare, and Elizabeth Scott. "Conceptualizing Legal Childhood in the Twenty-First Century." *Michigan Law Review* 118 (2020): 1371–1458.

Ikemoto, Lisa. "Destabilizing Thoughts on Surrogacy Legislation." *University of San Francisco Law Review* 28 (1994): 633–46.

Jacobs, Melanie. "Parental Parity: Intentional Parenthood's Promise." *Buffalo Law Review* 64 (2016): 465–98.

Johnson, Allan. *The Gender Knot: Unraveling Our Patriarchal Legacy*. 2nd ed. Pearson Longman, 2005.

Jones, Ruth. "Inequality from Gender-Neutral Laws: Why Must Male Victims of Statutory Rape Pay Child Support for Children Resulting from Their Victimization?" *Georgia Law Review* 36 (2001): 411–64.

Joslin, Courtney. "De Facto Parentage and the Modern Family." *Family Advocate*, April 1, 2018.

Joslin, Courtney, and Douglas NeJaime. "How Parenthood Functions." *Columbia Law Review* (2023): forthcoming.

Joyce, Kathryn. *The Child Catchers: Rescue, Trafficking, and the New Gospel of Adoption*. PublicAffairs, 2013.

———. "Shotgun Adoption." *The Nation*, August 26, 2009.

Karlan, Pamela, and Daniel Ortiz. "In a Diffident Voice: Relational Feminism, Abortion Rights, and the Feminist Legal Agenda." *Northwestern University Law Review* 87 (1993): 858–96.

Karst, Kenneth. "The Freedom of Intimate Association." *Yale Law Journal* 89 (1980): 624–93.

Katz, Katheryn. "Majoritarian Morality and Parental Rights." *Albany Law Review* 52 (1988): 405–70.

Kay, Herma Hill. "Equality and Difference: The Case of Pregnancy." *Berkeley Women's Law Journal* 1 (1985): 1–38.

Kessler, Laura. "Miscarriage of Justice: Early Pregnancy Loss and the Limits of U.S. Employment Law." *Cornell Law Review* 108 (2023): forthcoming.

Kitchen, Rona Kaufman. "Holistic Pregnancy: Rejecting the Theory of the Adversarial Mother." *Hastings Women's Law Journal* 26 (2015): 207–70.

Kohlberg, Lawrence. "The Development of Modes of Moral Thinking and Choices in Years 10 to 16." PhD Diss., University of Chicago, 1958.

Kohn, Laurie. "Engaging Men as Fathers: The Courts, the Law, and Father-Absence in Low-Income Families." *Cardozo Law Review* 35 (2013): 511–66.

Koppelman, Andrew. "Forced Labor: A Thirteenth Amendment Defense of Abortion." *Northwestern University Law Review* 84 (1990): 480–535.

Krakoff, Sarah. "Inextricably Political: Race, Membership, and Tribal Sovereignty." *Washington Law Review* 87 (2012): 1041–1132.

Lasch, Christopher. *Haven in a Heartless World: The Family Besieged.* W. W. Norton, 1995.

Lau, Holning. "Shaping Expectations about Dads as Caregivers: Toward an Ecological Approach." *Hofstra Law Review* 45 (2016): 183–216.

Laufer-Ukeles, Pamela. "The Children of Nonmarriage: Towards a Child-First Family Law." *Yale Law and Policy Review* (2022): 384–464.

———. "Collaborative Family-Making: From Acquisition to Interconnection." *Villanova Law Review* 64 (2019): 223–84.

———. "Money, Caregiving, and Kinship: Should Paid Caregivers Be Allowed to Obtain De Facto Parental Status?" *Missouri Law Review* 74 (2009): 25–102.

———. "Mothering for Money: Regulating Commercial Intimacy." *Indiana Law Journal* 88 (2013): 1223–80.

———. "The Relational Rights of Children." *Connecticut Law Review* 48 (2016): 741–816.

Laufer-Ukeles, Pamela, and Arianne Renan Barzilay. "The Health/Care Divide: Breastfeeding in the New Millennium." *Columbia Journal of Gender and Law* 35 (2018): 264–337.

Law, Sylvia. "Rethinking Sex and the Constitution." *University of Pennsylvania Law Review* 132 (1984): 955–1040.

Law, Sylvia, and Patricia Hennessey. "Is the Law Male? The Case of Family Law." *Chicago-Kent Law Review* 69 (1993): 345–58.

Leib, Ethan. "A Man's Right to Choose (an Abortion?)." *Legal Times* 18 (April 4, 2005).

Locke, John. *Second Treatise on Government,* 1689.

Lugosi, Charles. "Conforming to the Rule of Law: When Person and Human Being Finally Mean the Same Thing in Fourteenth Amendment Jurisprudence." *Georgetown Journal of Law and Public Policy* 4 (2006): 361–452.

Luna, Zakiya, and Kristin Luker. "Reproductive Justice." *Annual Review of Law and Social Science* 9 (2014): 327–52.

Macdonald, Cameron Lynne. "Shadow Mothers: Nannies, Au Pairs, and Invisible Work." In *Working in the Service Society,* edited by Cameron Lynne Macdonald and Carmen Sirianni, 244–63. Temple University Press, 1996.

MacKinnon, Catharine. "Difference and Dominance: On Sex Discrimination." In *Feminism Unmodified: Discourses on Life and Law,* 32–45. Harvard University Press, 1987.

———. *Toward a Feminist Theory of the State.* Harvard University Press, 1989.

Madeira, Jody Lynee. "Woman Scorned: Resurrecting Infertile Women's Decision-Making Autonomy." *Maryland Law Review* 71 (2012): 339–410.

Maienschein, Jane. "Cloning and Stem Cell Debates in the Context of Genetic Determinism." *Yale Journal of Health Policy, Law, and Ethics* 9 (2009): 565–84.

Manian, Maya. "Comment on *Geduldig v. Aiello.*" In *Feminist Judgments: Rewritten Opinions of the United States Supreme Court,* edited by Kathryn Stanchi, Linda Berger, and Bridget Crawford. Cambridge University Press, 2016.

Martin, Emily. "The Egg and the Sperm: How Science Has Constructed a Romance Based on Stereotypical Male-Female Roles." *Signs* 16 (1991): 485–501.

Mason, Mary Ann. *From Father's Property to Children's Rights: The History of Child Custody in the United States.* Columbia University Press, 1994.

Matambanadzo, Saru. "The Fourth Trimester." *University of Michigan Journal of Law Reform* 48 (2014): 117–82.

———. "Reconstructing Pregnancy." *SMU Law Review* 69 (2016): 187–266.

Mayeri, Serena. "Foundling Fathers: (Non-)Marriage and Parental Rights in the Age of Equality." *Yale Law Journal* 125 (2016): 2292–2393.

———. "Intersectionality and the Constitution of Family Status." *Constitutional Commentary* 32 (2017): 377–412.

———. "Marital Supremacy and the Constitution of the Nonmarital Family." *California Law Review* 103 (2015): 1277–1352.

McClain, Linda. "Formative Projects, Formative Influences: Of Martha Albertson Fineman and Feminist, Liberal, and Vulnerable Subjects." *Emory Law Journal* 67 (2018): 1175–1206.

McDonagh, Eileen. *Breaking the Abortion Deadlock: From Choice to Consent.* Oxford University Press, 1996.

McGinley, Ann, and Frank Rudy Cooper. "Intersectional Cohorts, Dis/Ability, and Class Actions." *Fordham Urban Law Journal* 47 (2020): 293–342.

McLaren, Anne. "Prelude to Embryogenesis." In *Human Embryo Research: Yes or No?,* edited by Gregory Bock and Maeve O'Connor, 5–23. Tavistock Publications, 1986.

Meyer, David. "The Constitutionality of 'Best Interests' Parentage." *William and Mary Bill of Rights Journal* 14 (2006): 857–82.

———. "Family Ties: Solving the Constitutional Dilemma of the Faultless Father." *Arizona Law Review* 41 (1999): 753–846.

Mezey, Naomi, and Cornelia Pillard. "Against the New Maternalism." *Michigan Journal of Gender and Law* 18 (2012): 229–96.

Milanich, Nara. "Certain Mothers, Uncertain Fathers: Placing Assisted Reproductive Technologies in Historical Perspective." In *Reassembling Motherhood: Procreation and Care in a Globalized World,* 17–37. Columbia University Press, 2017.

Mill, John Stuart. *The Subjection of Women,* 1869.

Milligan, Joy. "Religion and Race: On Duality and Entrenchment." *New York University Law Review* 87 (2012): 393–472.

Molotch, Harvey, and Laura Norén. *Toilet: Public Restrooms and the Politics of Sharing.* New York University Press, 2010.

Morgan, Hugh, Heidi Sutherland, David Martin, and Emma Whitelaw. "Epigenetic Inheritance at the Agouti Locus in the Mouse." *Nature Genetics* 23 (November 1999): 314–18.

Motro, Shari. "The Price of Pleasure." *Northwestern University Law Review* 104 (2010): 917–78.

Mutcherson, Kimberly. "Things That Money Can Buy: Reproductive Justice and the International Market for Gestational Surrogacy." *North Carolina Journal of International Law* 43 (2018): 150–82.

———. "Transformative Reproduction." *Journal of Gender, Race, and Justice* 16 (2013): 187–234.

Nedelsky, Jennifer. *Law's Relations: A Relational Theory of Self, Autonomy, and Law.* Oxford University Press, 2011.

NeJaime, Douglas. "The Constitution of Parenthood." *Stanford Law Review* 72 (2020): 261–380.

NeJaime, Douglas, and Courtney Joslin. "Multi-Parent Families: Real and Imagined." *Fordham Law Review* 90 (2022): 2561–89.

Okin, Susan Miller. *Justice, Gender, and the Family.* Basic Books, 1989.

Olsen, Frances. "The Family and the Market: A Study of Ideology and Legal Reform." *Harvard Law Review* 96 (1983): 1497–1578.

Oren, Laura. "Unmarried Fathers and Adoption: Perfecting or Abandoning an Opportunity Interest." *Capital University Law Review* 36 (2007): 253–93.

Parness, Jeffrey. "Deserting Mothers, Abandoned Babies, Lost Fathers: Dangers in Safe Havens." *Qunnipiac Law Review* 24 (2006): 335–50.

———. "Systematically Screwing Dads: Out of Control Paternity Schemes." *Wayne Law Review* 54 (2008): 641–72.

Patton, William Wesley. "Mommy's Gone, Daddy's in Prison, Now What about Me? Family Reunification for Children of Single Custodial Fathers in Prison—Will the Sins of the Incarcerated Fathers Be Inherited by Their Children?" *North Dakota Law Review* 75 (1999): 179–204.

Peters, Najarian. "The Right to Be and Become: Black Home-Educators as Child Privacy Protectors." *Michigan Journal of Race and Law* 25 (2019): 21–60.

Pimentel, David. "Protecting the Free-Range Kid: Recalibrating Parents' Rights and the Best Interest of the Child." *Cardozo Law Review* 38 (2016): 1–58.

Platt, Anthony. *The Child Savers: The Invention of Delinquency.* University of Chicago Press, 1977.

Pollack, Daniel, and Susan Mason. "Mandatory Visitation: In the Best Interest of the Child." *Family Court Review* 42 (2004): 74–84.

Posner, Rachel, Itai Toker, Olga Antonova, Eaterina Star, Sarit Anava, Eran Azmon, Michael Hendricks, Shahar Bracha, Hila Gingold, and Oded Rechavi. "Neuronal Small RNAs Control Behavior Transgenerationally." *Cell* 177 (June 13, 2019): 1814–26.

Prewitt, Shauna. "Giving Birth to a 'Rapist's Child': A Discussion and Analysis of the Limited Legal Protections Afforded to Women Who Become Mothers through Rape." *Georgetown Law Journal* 98 (2010): 827–62.

Purvis, Dara. "Intended Parents and the Problem of Perspective." *Yale Journal of Law and Feminism* 24 (2012): 210–53.

———. "The Origin of Parental Rights: Labor, Intent, and Fathers." *Florida State University Law Review* 41 (2014): 645–96.

———. "The Rules of Maternity." *Tennessee Law Review* 84 (2017): 367–446.

Quinn, Mae. "Fallen Woman (Re)Framed: Judge Jean Hortense Norris, New York City—1912–1955." *University of Kansas Law Review* 67 (2019): 451–512.

Rao, Radhika. "Assisted Reproductive Technology and the Threat to the Traditional Family." *Hastings Law Journal* 47 (1996): 951–66.

Ravid, Itay, and Jonathan Zandberg. "The Future of *Roe* and the Gender Pay Gap: An Empirical Assessment." *Indiana Law Journal* 98 (2023): forthcoming.

Rebouché, Rachel. "Contracting Pregnancy." *Iowa Law Review* 105 (2020): 1591–1642.

Rhode, Deborah. "The 'Woman's Point of View.'" *Journal of Legal Education* 38 (1988): 39–46.

Rich, Camille Gear. "Contracting Our Way to Inequality: Race, Reproductive Freedom, and the Quest for the Perfect Child." *Minnesota Law Review* 104 (2020): 2375–2470.

Rimalt, Noya. "The Maternal Dilemma." *Cornell Law Review* 103 (2018): 977–1048.

Ristroph, Alice, and Melissa Murray. "Disestablishing the Family." *Yale Law Journal* 119 (2010): 1236–79.

Roberts, Dorothy. "Black Club Women and Child Welfare: Lessons for Modern Reform." *Florida State University Law Review* 32 (2005): 957–72.

———. "The Genetic Tie." *University of Chicago Law Review* 62 (1995): 209–74.

———. *Killing the Black Body: Race, Reproduction, and the Meaning of Liberty.* 2d ed. Penguin Random House, 2017.

———. *Shattered Bonds: The Color of Child Welfare.* Basic Books, 2002.

———. "Spiritual and Menial Housework." *Yale Journal of Law and Feminism* 9 (1997): 51–80.

Roe, Shirley. *Matter, Life, and Generation: Eighteenth-Century Embryology and the Haller-Wolff Debate.* Cambridge University Press, 2003.

Rolnick, Addie, and Kim Pearson. "Racial Anxieties in Adoption: Reflections on *Adoptive Couple,* White Parenthood, and Constitutional Challenges to the ICWA." *Michigan State Law Review* 2017: 727–54.

Romero, Mary. "Unraveling Privilege: Workers' Children and the Hidden Cost of Paid Childcare." *Chicago-Kent Law Review* 76 (2001): 1651–72.

Rothman, Barbara Katz. *Recreating Motherhood: Ideology and Technology in a Patriarchal Society.* W. W. Norton, 1989.

Sabbeth, Kathryn, and Jessica Steinberg. "The Gender of *Gideon.*" *UCLA Law Review* 69 (2022): forthcoming.

Saller, Richard. "*Pater Familias, Mater Familias,* and the Gendered Semantics of the Roman Household." *Classical Philology* 94 (1999): 182–97.

Samuels, Elizabeth. "Surrender and Subordination: Birth Mothers and Adoption Law Reform." *Michigan Journal of Gender and Law* 20 (2013): 33–82.

———. "Time to Decide? The Laws Governing Mothers' Consents to the Adoption of Their Newborn Infants." *Tennessee Law Review* 72 (2005): 509–72.

Sandberg, Sheryl. *Lean In: Women, Work, and the Will to Lead.* Knopf Doubleday, 2013.

Scales, Ann. "The Emergence of Feminist Jurisprudence." *Yale Law Journal* 95 (1986): 1373–1404.

Schlackman, Elise. "Unwed Fathers' Rights in New York: How Far Does the Protection Extend?" *Cardozo Women's Law Journal* 1 (1993): 199–220.

Schultz, Vicki. "Taking Sex Discrimination Seriously." *Denver University Law Review* 91 (2015): 995–1120.

Seymore, Malinda. "Adopting Civil Damages: Wrongful Family Separation in Adoption." *Washington and Lee Law Review* 76 (2019): 895–962.

Shanley, Mary. "Unwed Fathers' Rights, Adoption, and Sex Equality: Gender-Neutrality and the Perpetuation of Patriarchy." *Columbia Law Review* 95 (1995): 60–103.

Shapiro, Julie. "For a Feminist Considering Surrogacy, Is Compensation Really the Key Question?" *Washington Law Review* 89 (2014): 1345–74.

Shultz, Marjorie Maguire. "Reproductive Technology and Intent-Based Parenthood: An Opportunity for Gender Neutrality." *Wisconsin Law Review* 1990: 297–398.

Siegel, Reva. "Reasoning from the Body: A Historical Perspective on Abortion Regulation and Questions of Equal Protection." *Stanford Law Review* 44 (1992): 261–382.

———. "You've Come a Long Way, Baby: Rehnquist's New Approach to Pregnancy Discrimination in *Hibbs.*" *Stanford Law Review* 58 (2006): 1871–98.

Sisson, Gretchen, Lauren Ralph, Heather Gould, and Diana Greene Foster. "Adoption Decision-Making among Women Seeking Abortion." *Women's Health Issues* 27 (2017): 136–44.

Smith, Priscilla. "Responsibility for Life: How Abortion Serves Women's Interests in Motherhood." *Journal of Law and Policy* 17 (2009): 97–160.

Spitko, E. Gary. "The Constitutional Function of Biological Paternity: Evidence of the Biological Mother's Consent to the Biological Father's Co-Parenting of Her Child." *Arizona Law Review* 48 (2006): 97–148.

Stevens, Emily, Thelma Patrick, and Rita Pickler. "A History of Infant Feeding." *Journal of Perinatal Education* 18 (2009): 32–39.

Strasser, Mark. "The Often Illusory Protections of Biology Plus: On the Supreme Court's Parental Rights Jurisprudence." *Texas Journal on Civil Liberties and Civil Rights* 13 (2007): 31–84.

Strauss, Gregg. "The Positive Right to Marry." *Virginia Law Review* 102 (2016): 1691–1766.

Strebeigh, Fred. *Equal: Women Reshape American Law.* W. W. Norton, 2009.

Strout, Jean. "Dads and Dicta: The Values of Acknowledging Fathers' Interests." *Cardozo Journal of Law and Gender* 21 (2014): 135–68.

Suk, Julie. "Gender Equality and the Protection of Motherhood in Global Constitutionalism." *Law and Ethics of Human Rights* 12 (2018): 151–80.

———. "A World Without *Roe:* The Constitutional Future of Unwanted Pregnancy." *William and Mary Law Review* 65 (2022): forthcoming.

Totz, Mary. "What's Good for the Goose Is Good for the Gander: Toward Recognition of Men's Reproductive Rights." *Northern Illinois University Law Review* 15 (1994): 141–236.

Triger, Zvi. "The Darker Side of Overparenting." *Utah Law Review OnLaw* 2013: 284–89.

Tronto, Joan. "Beyond Gender Difference to a Theory of Care." *Signs* 12 (1987): 644–63.

Tuana, Nancy. "The Weaker Seed: The Sexist Bias of Reproductive Theory." *Hypatia* 3 (1988): 35–59.

Van Schilfgaarde, Lauren, and Brett Lee Shelton. "Using Peacemaking Circles to Indigenize Tribal Child Welfare." *Columbia Journal of Race and Law* 11 (2021): 681–710.

Waldman, Emily Gold. "Compared to What? Menstruation, Pregnancy, and the Complexities of Comparison." *Columbia Journal of Gender and Law* 41 (2021): 218–27.

Wardle, Lynn, and Travis Robertson. "Adoption: Upside Down and Sideways; Some Causes of and Remedies for Declining Domestic and International Adoptions." *Regent University Law Review* 26 (2013): 209–70.

Warren, Mary Anne. "The Moral Significance of Birth." *Hypatia* 4 (1989): 46–65.

Wasson, Jadiel, Gareth Harris, Sabine Keppler-Ross, Trisha Brock, Abdul Dar, Rebecca Butcher, Sylvia Fischer et al. "Neuronal Control of Maternal Provisioning in Response to Social Cues." *Science Advances* 7 (August 20, 2021).

Weinrib, Laura. "Protecting Sex: Sexual Disincentives and Sex-Based Discrimination in *Nguyen v. INS.*" *Columbia Journal of Gender and Law* 12 (2003): 222–74.

West, Robin. *Caring for Justice.* New York University Press, 1997.

———. "Jurisprudence and Gender." *University of Chicago Law Review* 55 (1988): 1–72.

West, Sonja, and Dahlia Lithwick. "The Paradox of Justice John Paul Stevens." *Northwestern University Law Review* 114 (2020): 1849–58.

White, Pamela. "'One for Sorrow, Two for Joy?': American Embryo Transfer Guideline Recommendations, Practices, and Outcomes for Gestational Surrogate Patients." *Journal of Assisted Reproduction and Genetics* 34 (2017): 431–43.

Widiss, Deborah. "Equalizing Parental Leave." *Minnesota Law Review* 105 (2021): 2175–2258.

———. "Shadow Precedents and the Separation of Powers: Statutory Interpretation of Congressional Overrides." *Notre Dame Law Review* 84 (2009): 511–84.

Williams, Joan. "Deconstructing Gender." *Michigan Law Review* 87 (1989): 797–845.

———. "Reconstructive Feminism: Changing the Way We Talk about Gender and Work Thirty Years after the PDA." *Yale Journal of Law and Feminism* 21 (2009): 79–118.

Williams, Wendy. "Equality's Riddle: Pregnancy and the Equal Treatment/Special Treatment Debate." *New York University Review of Law and Social Change* 13 (1984–85): 325–80.

Wilson, Robin Fretwell. "Limiting the Prerogatives of Legal Parents: Judicial Skepticism of the American Law Institute's Treatment of De Facto Parents." *Journal of the American Academy of Matrimonial Lawyers* 25 (2012): 477–532.

———. "Trusting Mothers: A Critique of the American Law Institute's Treatment of De Facto Parents." *Hofstra Law Review* 38 (2010): 1103–90.

Woodhouse, Barbara Bennett. "Hatching the Egg: A Child-Centered Perspective on Parents' Rights." *Cardozo Law Review* 14 (1993): 1747–1866.

———. "'Who Owns the Child?': *Meyer* and *Pierce* and the Child as Property." *William and Mary Law Review* 33 (1992): 995–1122.

Yuille, Lua Kamál, Ruhiyyih Nikole Yuille, and Justin Yuille. "Love as Justice." *Langston Hughes Review* 26 (2020): 49–77.

Zealand, Elise. "Protecting the Ties That Bind from Behind Bars: A Call for Equal Opportunities for Incarcerated Fathers and Their Children to Maintain the Parent-Child Relationship." *Columbia Journal of Law and Social Problems* 31 (1998): 247–82.

Zinman, Daniel. "Father Knows Best: The Unwed Father's Right to Raise His Infant Surrendered for Adoption." *Fordham Law Review* 60 (1992): 971–1002.

Bender, Leslie, 144
Berger, Bethany, 125
best-for-the-child rationale for parental
rights, 54, 61–64, 66, 106, 134, 183–84.
See also parental rights
best interests of the child, legal standard,
41, 98, 105–06, 134
bigotry, 57–58. *See also* racism
Bill of Rights, 31–32, 152, 169. *See also* U.S.
Constitution
biological fatherhood and the law, 34–36,
103–7, 118–26, 190–91. *See also* fatherhood; genetics and parental rights
biology-plus-relationship test: application
of, 65–66, 137–38, 146–47; biology
component of, 35, 39, 91; *Caban* and,
33–34, 38–39; *Michael H. v. Gerald D.*
and, 46; origin of, 29, 203n2; purpose
of, 47–48, 127–28. *See also* caretaking;
parental rights; Unwed Father Cases
birth control, 24, 118, 125. *See also*
pregnancy
birth mothers: adoption and rights of,
37–38, 41, 94–99, 104–5, 121–22, 125–
26, 157; proposed increase in rights for,
190–92; as term, 4. *See also* motherhood; pregnancy
Black Americans: child welfare system and,
48; cultural feminism and, 77, 78;
enslaved women and parental rights,
29–30; paternity rights and, 35, 44;
racial justice for, 14; as unmarried
mothers, 118. *See also* racism
Blackmun, Harry, 168–69, 170
Blackstone, William, 55, 211n54
blood testing, 34, 35. *See also* genetics and
parental rights
boarding schools, 56, 120
Boucai, Michael, 172–73
Boulais, Joseph, 115–16, 117, 188
breastfeeding, 21, 22, 23–24, 25, 26, 193
Brennan, William, 44–45, 46, 48
Breyer, Stephen, 24
Bridges, Khiara, 85
Brown, Dusten, 97–98, 119, 120–21, 124,
191
Brown v. Board of Education, 8
Burbach, Mary, 107

Burger, Warren, 45
Buzzanca, John and Luanne, 145

Caban, Abdiel, 33, 36, 42, 81
Caban v. Mohammed, 33, 36, 37, 44, *196*
CalFed v. Guerra, 12–13, 15, 17–18, *196,*
200n12
California: disability cases in, 9–11; paternity rights cases in, 46, 104, 136–38;
pregnancy accommodations in, 12–14,
15, 104; surrogacy cases in, 134–35, 139,
145, 174, 176
California Federal Savings & Loan Association, 12
Calvert, Crispina, 134–36, 145, 178
Calvert, Mark, 134, 135, 136
Canada, 21–22
caretaking: beyond the body, 181–85; functions of, as defined in divorce, 63; laws
on paternal rights and, 36–38, 112; by
nannies, 181–83; parental rights and, 1,
3, 33–34, 49, 59–60, 183–85; pregnancy
as, 20–27, 181–85. *See also* biology-plus-
relationship test; childcare; emotional
attachment; feminine *vs.* masculine
values; relationships; Unwed Father
Cases
caring for justice, 76, 78–79
Caring for Justice (West), 76
cave-diving, 18–19, 24
Cawman, Jordan, 161
Cherokee Nation, 120, 124
childcare, 181–83. *See also* caretaking
children: abuse of, 52–53, 74–75, 166;
best-for-the-child rationale, 54, 61–64,
66, 106, 183–84; best interests of the
child, legal standard, 41, 98, 105–06,
134; childcare for, 181–83; education of,
51–52, 55–57; free-range movement for,
64–65; gun violence against, 188–89;
labor by, 53; neglect *vs.* abuse of, 122–24,
203n7; –parent contract, 54, 58–61; as
property, 50, 53–54; religion and, 53,
120; spanking of, 62–63. *See also* parental rights
child-welfare system, 48, 122–23. *See also*
foster care
choice and insurance, 19

feminist arguments: for abortion access, 162–65; on autonomy *vs.* relationships, 67, 80–82; cultural (and liberal), 67–75, 187; difference feminism, as term, 68; dominance feminism, 84; parental rights and, 1, 3; on pregnancy and disability cases, 11–12, 67–68; on privatization of dependency, 59; reasoning badly from the body, 152–55; reasoning better from the body, 162–65; reasoning without the body, 155–62; on redefining pregnancy as term, 158–59; relational, 80–82, 87, 111, 148, 151, 188, 194; reproductive justice movement and, 14–15; on stronger paternal rights, 101–2; on surrogacy, 140, 146, 172–73, 178; on Unwed Father Cases, 41–43, 86–88; on workplace discrimination and pregnancy, 13–14, 16–17

filius nullius rule, 29, 35

Fineman, Martha, 59, 80, 81, 193

Firestone, Shulamith, 26

Fontana, David, 158, 160

forced pregnancy, 151, 155, 157, 162. *See also* abortion; pregnancy

forced removal of American Indian children, 56, 119–20. *See also* American Indians

foreign language teaching to children, 51, 55, 56

formula *vs.* breastfeeding, 22, 25, 26

forum shopping, 119

foster care, 62, 113. *See also* child-welfare system

Fourteenth Amendment, U.S. Constitution, 8, 31–32, 50, 56, 165. *See also* equal protection clause; liberty clause; U.S. Constitution

Fox-Genovese, Elizabeth, 209n13

freedom of speech, 165, 187

free-range–kids movement, 64, 123

Fugitive Slave Act, 168, 169

full surrogacy, 132–34, 174, 191. *See also* surrogacy

Garland, Lillian, 12, 14, 17–18

gay couples. *See* same-sex couples

Geduldig, Dwight, 9, 10

Geduldig v. Aiello, 9–11, 13, 15, 18–19, 23, 28, 41–42, 100, 156, 189, *196*, 200n8

gender identity and terminology, 4

gender stereotyping, 3, 13–14, 18–19, 41–42, 69, 72, 128–29, 155, 179–80. *See also* inherent differences

genetic essentialism, as term and concept, 92, 142, 154

genetics and parental rights, 1, 3, 91–103; blood testing on, 34, 35; defining genetic essentialism, 92, 131–32; of mothers, 127–31, 137; ownership of genes, 145–46. *See also* biological fatherhood and the law; parental rights

German immigrant communities, 56, 57

gestation. *See* pregnancy

gestation-only surrogacy, 134–39, 191. *See also* surrogacy

Gideon, Clarence Earl, 74–75, 166

Gideon v. Wainwright, 74–75, 166

Gilligan, Carol, 69, 70–72, 76–77

Ginsburg, Ruth Bader, 7, 68

Godwin, Samantha, 63, 64

Gorsuch, Neil, 13, 16

grandparent visitation, 105–6, 183, 185, 205n46

Granville, Tommie, 105–6

Guerra, Mark, 12

gun violence, 188–89

Gupta-Kagan, Josh, 44, 112–13

Hale, Matthew, 189

The Handmaid's Tale (Atwood), 132, 171

harm, definition of, 62–63. *See also* abuse; best-for-the-child rationale for parental rights

Harris, Angela, 77

Harris v. McRae, 164

Heinz dilemma, 69–71, 78–79

Hibbs v. Nevada, 200n8

Higdon, Michael, 100

Hill, John Lawrence, 135, 138, 174–75

Hochschild, Arlie, 182

homeschooling, 52. *See also* education of children

Huntington, Clare, 59, 62

Hyde Amendment (1976), 164–65

ideal worker, as category, 11, 13, 15, 194
Illinois, 30, 44, 50, 95–96
immigrant communities, 56, 57, 121
Immigration and Naturalization Service, 115–17
In a Different Voice (Gilligan), 69, 71–72, 78
India, 171, 172, 173
Indian Child Welfare Act (ICWA; 1978), 119–21, 123, 124–25, *196*, 215n16
infantile dependency, 74
inherent differences, 7–8, 75–80. *See also* difference approach to sex-equality law; gender stereotyping; masculine *vs.* feminine values
In re Marriage of Buzzanca, 145
insurance, 18–19, 164. *See also* disability cases
intent rule, 135, 136, 138, 142, 145
international surrogacy, 171–72. *See also* surrogacy
intersectionality, 77–78
In the Matter of Baby M, 132–34, 176, 177, *196*
involuntary surrogacy, 141–44. *See also* surrogacy
Iowa, 126, 177–78
IVF (in vitro fertilization), 1, 92, 141, 147, 191–92. *See also* surrogacy

Jaramillo, Jackie, 10–13, 19, 23, 85
Jehovah's Witness, 53, 57
Johnson, Anna, 134–39, 145, 147, 176
Johnson v. Calvert, 134–39, 145, 176, *196*
judicial bias, 57
"Jurisprudence and Gender" (West), 73, 82, 84

Karst, Kenneth, 83, 84, 117, 162
Kennedy, Anthony, 82–83, 168
Kim, Mina, 1, 3, 143–44, 148, 188
Krill, Kara, 22, 48
Ku Klux Klan, 57

lactation. *See* breastfeeding
Lamanna, Mary Ann, 107
Lassiter, Abby Gail, 74–75, 81, 83, 166

Lassiter v. Department of Social Services, 74–75, 113, 166, *196*
Laufer-Ukeles, Pamela, 173, 222n10
Lawyer Moms of America (organization), 68
Lehr, Jonathan, 38–42, 51, 98, 119
Lehr v. Robertson, 38–42, 47, 92, 98, 119, *196*, 204n29
lesbian parents. *See* same-sex couples
liberal and cultural feminism, 67–75, 187. *See also* feminist arguments
liberalism, as concept, 68
liberty clause, 31–32, 34, 50, 52, 57, 152. *See also* Fourteenth Amendment, U.S. Constitution
Louisiana, 108, 121–22

MacKinnon, Catharine, 77–78, 84, 210n43
Maher v. Roe, 164, *196*
Maldonado, Christina, 97–98, 191
male-right-to-abortion argument, 158
marriage: common-law, 30–31; law on parental rights and, 29–30; legal support of institution of, 167–68; marital supremacy in parental rights decisions, 35, 41–46; in *Obergefell*, 82–83; Unwed Father Cases and, 86–88. *See also* divorce
Marshall, Thurgood, 44–45, 46, 48, 164
masculine *vs.* feminine values, 166–67, 169–70, 187–88, 192–94. *See also* autonomous man; relationships
Massachusetts, 53, 57, 107
maternity leave, 2, 12–16, 20–22, 67. *See also* pregnancy; workplace discrimination
Mathewes-Green, Frederica, 163
Mayeri, Serena, 42, 45
McReynolds, James, 57
Medicaid, 164, 167, 168, 193
menial *vs.* spiritual motherhood, 25, 140–41. *See also* motherhood
Meyer, David, 95–96
Meyer v. Nebraska, 51, 55, *196*
Michael H. v. Gerald D., 46, 93, 99, *196*

Michigan, 113, 139
Middleton, Kate, 20
Mill, John Stuart, 73
Miller, Christine and Peter, 1, 177–78
miscarriages, 135, 175, 176
misogyny, 157–58
Mohammed, Maria, 33
Moms Demand Action (organization), 68
Morales, José, 114
Morales-Santana, Luis, 114–15
morality, 68, 69–71, 74, 78, 210n31
mother, as term, 4, 151
motherhood: genetic essentialism on,
    127–31, 137, 147; menial *vs.* spiritual, 25,
    140–41; mother, as term, 4, 151. *See also*
    birth mothers; parental rights;
    pregnancy

nannies, 181–82, 185. *See also* caretaking
National Organization for Women
    (NOW), 13
Native Americans. *See* American Indians
natural bonds of affection, 61
natural *vs.* artificial constraints, 7–8, 11, 17,
    156
Nebraska, 51, 55, 56
Nedelsky, Jennifer, 80–81
negative and positive rights, 165–70
neglect *vs.* abuse, 122–24, 203n7
nesting-doll theory, 153–54
New Jersey, 133, 176
New York, 22, 33, 142, 143, 145
Nguyen, Tuan Anh, 115–16, 188
*Nguyen v. Immigration & Naturalization
    Service*, 115–18, 127, 147, 190–91, *196*
normalcy, discourse on, 24–26
normative judgements, 153
nuclear family structure, 42, 44–45, 46.
    See also marriage; patriarchal family
    structure

Obergefell v. Hodges, 82–83
Ohio, 177
One-Parent Doctrine, 112–13, 117, 125, 147,
    190
one-year residency rule, 114. *See also*
    citizenship
On the Origin of Species (Darwin), 153

opposites, 72, 82. *See also* gender
    stereotyping
Oregon, 51, 57

parent, legal definition of, 30, 47–48,
    50–53, 137, 147, 189–90
"parental functions," 63
parental rights: best-for-the-child rationale
    for, 54, 61–64, 66, 106, 183–84; caretak-
    ing and, 1, 3, 33–34, 49, 59–60, 183–85;
    contract rationale for, 54, 58–61, 138–39;
    of enslaved women, 29–30; genetics and,
    1, 2, 3, 91–103; legal cases on, 1–3, 28;
    legal definition of parent, 30, 47–48,
    50–53, 137; marital supremacy in,
    41–46; *Michael H. v. Gerald D.* on, 46;
    One-Parent Doctrine, 112–13, 117, 125,
    147; over children, 52–64; pluralism
    rationale for, 54, 55–58, 207n25; prop-
    erty rationale for, 53, 54–55, 64, 146;
    Quilloin on, 33; rape and, 1, 3, 77, 91,
    107–11, 189; of same-sex parents, 35, 36;
    Stanley on, 30–33; in surrogacy, 132–44;
    timeline of cases on, *196*. *See also* chil-
    dren; fatherhood; genetics and parental
    rights; motherhood
parent-child contract, 54, 58–61
Parent Zero, 40, 211n4
Parness, Jeffrey, 100
paternity leave, 21–23
paternity rights, 1; adoption and, 94–95,
    98–99, 103–7, 118–21, 124–26; caretak-
    ing and laws on, 36–38, 112; citizenship
    law on, 114–18; One-Parent Doctrine
    on, 112–13, 117; putative-father registry
    and, 39–40, 41, 100–101, 118, 159;
    Stanley on, 30; Unwed Father Cases on,
    2–3, 30–34. *See also* fatherhood
patriarchal family structure, 42, 44–45,
    107, 205n42. *See also* fatherhood;
    nuclear family structure
Pavan v. Smith, 212n6
Pennsylvania, 107
Perry-Rogers, Deborah, 141–44, 145, 147,
    148
Perry-Rogers v. Fasano, 141–44, 145, 146,
    147, 154, *196*
physical abuse. *See* abuse

physiological reasoning: badly from the body, 152–55; better methods for, 162–65; without the body, 155–62

Pierce, Walter, 57

Pierce v. Society of Sisters, 51, 57, 58, *196*

Planned Parenthood v. Casey, 156, 193, *196*

pluralism rationale for parental rights, 54, 55–58, 207n25. *See also* parental rights

political revolution, 193–94

positive and negative rights, 165–70

potential life of a fetus or embryo, 152–55, 160, 161. *See also* abortion

poverty, 119–24, 125

power, 78–80. *See also* classism; Heinz dilemma; racism

precedent, 45–46

pregnancy: 18th and 19th c. theories on, 153–54; author's experience with, 175–76; birth control and, 24, 118, 125; *CalFed* on, 12–14, 15, 17–18; caretaking and, 20–27, 181–85; as dis/advantage, 2, 3, 9, 28; feminist arguments on, 11–12, 67–68; forced, 151, 155, 157, 162; *Geduldig* on, 9–11, 13, 15, 18–19, 23, 28, 41–42, 100, 156, 189; Hill on, 174–75; law of equality and, 8–18; miscarriages of, 135, 175, 176; proposed redefinition of, 158–59, 162, 189–90; stereotyping and, 18–19; timeline of cases on, *196*. *See also* abortion; birth mothers; maternity leave; workplace discrimination

Pregnancy Discrimination Act ("PDA;" 1978), 12, 13, 14, 23–24, 193, *196*, 200n8

pregnant person, as term, 199n3

prime mover argument, 135, 138–39

Prince, Sarah, 53

Prince v. Massachusetts, 53, 57, *196*

private schooling, 55–57. *See also* education of children

privatization of dependency, 59

property rationale for parental rights, 50, 53, 54–55, 64, 146. *See also* parental rights

public schooling, 51, 57, 206n7. *See also* education of children

Puente, Josephine, 23, 24

Puente v. Ridge, 23, 24, *196*

pursuit of intimacy, 83–84. *See also* marriage

putative-father registry, 39–40, 41, 100–101, 118, 159. *See also* paternity rights

"The Putative Father Registry: Behold Now the Behemoth" (Howell), 100–101

quasi-parent, 173, 183–85. *See also* de facto parents, parental rights

Quilloin, Leon, 36–37, 51

Quilloin v. Wolcott, 33, 36–37, 190–91, 203n13

"Race and Essentialism in Feminist Legal Theory" (Harris), 77

racial justice, 14. *See also* Black Americans

racism: adoption and, 120–21, 124–25, 126; anti-abortion reasoning and, 153; care work and, 182; in child welfare system, 48; against families, 56, 65, 120; by McReynolds, 57–58; neglect *vs.* abuse and, 122–23; parental rights and, 29–30, 35; in research studies, 77; surrogacy and, 1, 140–41, 173, 177–78. *See also* American Indians; Black Americans; classism; power

rape, 1, 3, 77, 91, 107–11, 189, 214n39. *See also* sexual abuse

Rape Survivor Child Custody Act (RSCCA; 2015), 108–10, 147, 193, *196*

"Reasoning from the Body" (Siegel), 152–53, 163

Rehnquist, William, 45

relational feminism, 80–82, 87, 111, 148, 151, 162–65, 188, 194. *See also* cultural feminism; feminist arguments

relationships: of gestation and surrogacy, 137–38; payment and, 181, 182–84; protecting existing *vs.* enabling new, 146–48. *See also* biology-plus-relationship test; caretaking; feminine *vs.* masculine values; marriage

religion: child's welfare and, 53, 120; CPCs and, 122; pluralism rationale for parental rights, 55, 57

reproductive justice movement, 14–15, 118, 125. *See also* abortion

revolution, 193–94

Roberts, Dorothy, 25, 140
Robertson, Lorraine, 38–42
Roe v. Wade, 69, 118, 152–53, 155, 168, 189,
    193, *196*
Rogers, Robert, 141–44, 145
Rosenbury, Laura, 63
Rothman, Barbara Katz, 184
royal princess job description, 20

safe haven laws, 157
sameness approach to sex-equality law, 1, 3,
    8–9, 13–15, 17, 18, 22, 26–27, 31–32,
    155–56, 200n8. *See also* sex-equality law
same-sex couples, 35, 36, 82–83, 172–73
Sarkeesian, Anita, 45
Scalia, Antonin, 46, 82–83
Schoenbaum, Naomi, 158, 160
Scott, Elizabeth, 59, 62
Session v. Morales-Santana, 114–15
sex-equality law: abortion and, 155–57;
    artificial *vs.* natural constraints, 7–8;
    cases of, 1–3, 200n8; difference
    approach to, 2, 8, 9, 11, 15, 18, 26, 44–45;
    genetic essentialism *vs.*, 99–103; preg-
    nancy and, 2, 3, 8–18; sameness
    approach to, 1, 3, 8–9, 13–15, 17, 18, 22,
    26–27, 31–32, 155–56, 200n8
sexism, 15, 19, 58, 76–77, 99–103, 136, 152–
    55, 179–80
sexual abuse, 1, 52, 203n7. *See also* rape
Shapiro, Julie, 179
Shultz, Marjorie Maguire, 100
Siegel, Reva, 152–53, 156, 168
single mothers, loss of rights of, 103–7
Skenazy, Lenore, 64, 65
slavery, 29–30, 56, 168–69. *See also* racism
Smith, Adam, 73
spanking, 62, 207n33
spiritual *vs.* menial motherhood, 25, 140–
    41. *See also* motherhood
Spitko, Gary, 35
Stanley, Peter, 30–33, 42, 48, 81
Stanley v. Illinois, 30–33, 36, 92, 113, 190, *196*
state power: to allow/restrict abortion, 152,
    164–65; on potential life of fetus or
    embryo, 152, 155, 160, 161
Stern, Elizabeth and William, 132–34,
    176–77

Stevens, John Paul, 45, 46
Stewart, Potter, 45
surrogacy, 1; as contract for family, 25,
    48–49, 174–81; contracts in, 1, 3; full,
    132–34, 174, 191; gestation-only, 134–39,
    191; in *The Handmaid's Tale*, 132, 171;
    improved laws on, 191; international,
    171–72; involuntary, 141–44; as job
    description, 20; parental conflicts and,
    173–74; race and, 140–41, 173. *See also*
    IVF (in vitro fertilization)
"Systematically Screwing Dads" (Parness),
    100

ten-year residency rule, 114. *See also*
    citizenship
Texas, 165
Thailand, 171
Thirteenth Amendment, 169
Thornton, Haley, 1
timeline of cases, *196*
Tomasson, Patti, 21, 22, 48
traditional surrogacy, 132–34. *See also*
    surrogacy
transgender parents and parental rights, 47
tribal membership, 124–25, 215n16
Troxel, Brad, 105–6
Troxel v. Granville, 105–7, 183, 185, 190, *196*

Uniform Parentage Act (2017), 212n5,
    212n7
United States v. Virginia ("VMI"), 7, 8, 11,
    68–69, 72–73, 209n13
universal health, 8, 194. *See also* Medicaid
universal public schooling, 51, 57, 206n7
"Unsexing Pregnancy" (Fontana and
    Schoenbaum), 158, 159–60, 161
Unwed Father Cases, 30–35, 40–49, 81,
    86–88, 92–93, *196*, 216n40. *See also*
    biology-plus-relationship test; father-
    hood; *names of specific cases;* paternity
    rights
UPS (United Parcel Service), 24
U.S. Constitution: equal protection clause,
    8, 9, 31, 34, 50, 155–56; Fourteenth
    Amendment, 8, 31–32, 50, 56, 165;
    liberty clause, 152; Thirteenth Amend-
    ment, 169

Utah, 95
Uvalde, Texas, 188–89

vaccines, 65
VAP (voluntary acknowledgement of
    parentage), 38, 93–94
Virginia, 7. See also *United States v. Vir-
    ginia* ("VMI")
Virginia Military Institute, 7. See
    also *United States v. Virginia*
    ("VMI")
visitation orders, 46, 105–6, 141, 183,
    205n46
VMI case. See *United States v. Virginia*
    ("VMI")
vulnerability theory, 80

Warburton, Richard, 95–96
Washington (state), 105
West, Cornel, 78–79
West, Robin, 73, 78–79, 80, 82, 84, 187, 194
Whitehead, Mary Beth, 132–34, 176
Whitehead, Richard, 132–33, 134
white supremacy, 56. *See also* racism
Williams, Joan, 11
Woodhouse, Barbara Bennett, 57
workplace discrimination, 2, 3, 11–15,
    200n8. *See also* disability cases; mater-
    nity leave; pregnancy

Young, Peggy, 24
Young v. UPS, 24, 28, *196*, 202n42
Yuille, Lua Kamál, 78